DRIVE FOR FIVE

DRIVE FOR FIVE

THE REMARKABLE RUN
OF THE 2016 PATRIOTS

CHRISTOPHER PRICE

ST. MARTIN'S PRESS ❦ NEW YORK

www.stmartins.com

Designed by Steven Seighman

The Library of Congress Cataloging-in-Publication Data is available upon request.

ISBN 978-1-250-16705-7 (hardcover)
ISBN 978-1-250-16706-4 (ebook)

Our books may be purchased in bulk for promotional, educational, or business use. Please contact your local bookseller or the Macmillan Corporate and Premium Sales Department at 1-800-221-7945, extension 5442, or by email at MacmillanSpecial Markets@macmillan.com.

First Edition: September 2017

10 9 8 7 6 5 4 3 2 1

For Noah, better known to readers as The Kid. In a lifetime spent covering sports, he's my favorite athlete of all time.

CONTENTS

FOREWORD: "THIS IS NOT ANY OTHER PATRIOT TEAM"

IF YOU WANT TO UNDERSTAND the 2016 season, it began with the heartache that came at the end of the 2015 season.

Every year, we talk about forgetting what happened the year before. When you win a Super Bowl and the next year lose by 2 points in the AFC championship, you can't help but question what went wrong. And so, I won't bore you with the beginning of 2016; Tom was suspended, Gronk was hurt, and our best defensive player—Jamie Collins—was traded to Cleveland.

But one of the biggest turning points in the season happened mid-December, a stretch where we started to realize just how special this team could be. Our schedule was going to get a lot tougher with Baltimore coming to Foxboro on a Monday night followed by a trip to Denver on a short week. *Thank you, NFL.* Playing Monday night then having to fly to Denver looks bad on paper. But it changed our season.

The Baltimore week, all we heard was how the Ravens were

the one team that never has a problem coming to Foxboro and not only playing us tough, but beating us at home. I can still remember hearing Bill's voice in the morning meetings reading the actual record of the two teams over the last couple of games. Then he kept reminding us this was not the same team that had to play Baltimore in years past.

That Monday night was electric; the stadium was rocking, and we battled Baltimore for four quarters making plays on offense and defense. Then we took control when were able to kill the clock in the fourth quarter with the running game. But afterward, you could sense in the locker room that win wasn't enough for this team. After the game, everyone was already talking about being prepared to go play on a short week in Denver.

The next week started with a similar message from coach: this wasn't the same team that had a losing record in Denver. I truly think those words encouraged us to ignore all the noise and just go play our game. As we got to the end of the week, you could feel the emotion building, and as a player, you couldn't help but feel like we had been in this situation before. It was that time of year where every game was a must-win. We competed with a tough Denver team all game in below-freezing temperatures and came out with a victory in a gutsy, ugly type of contest. The locker room in Denver told the story of the season: we captured the AFC East, and from that moment, I believe everyone on the team knew we what it took to go out and win it all. In true Belichick fashion, he came in repeating what he said all week: "THIS IS NOT ANY OTHER PATRIOT TEAM." He reminded us that even though every article all week was about our struggles in the past in Denver, *no one knew the 2016 Patriots.*

Jump ahead, and when it came to preparing for the Super Bowl, it felt like the team understood how we needed to practice and execute to be successful in the game. We had some hard, intense practices in Foxboro and in Houston. We felt ready. I still remember what I told all the defensive backs in pregame: *This game isn't about anyone who has ever doubted you. It's about the people that love and believe in you.*

Little did I know, the game would come down to belief in each other's will to play for sixty minutes. Even though we prepared well, we found ourselves down 28–3 in the third quarter. Every doubter believed we had no chance to win, but those who believed in us still had faith. Once again, all I could hear was "This isn't any other Patriot team." Bill was right; this team was filled with great men who believed in themselves and every other man in that locker room. That comeback will be talked about for years.

The 2016 team was filled with men of faith. Our team chaplain, Jack Easterby, would always talk about how God was doing something special on our team, and he was right. It took a full season, but we got to celebrate that special team the right way: with confetti falling on us.

—DEVIN MCCOURTY

DRIVE FOR FIVE

INTRODUCTION: THE GREATEST

TOM BRADY WAS CRYING.

The Patriots quarterback has always been able to harness his emotions and put them to good use. A hype video his social media team released before the start of the 2016 postseason included an interview from Bruce Lee where Lee extolled the virtues of utilizing your feelings to your advantage: *Empty your mind. Be formless, shapeless, like water. Now, you put water into a cup, it becomes the cup. You put water into a bottle, it becomes the bottle. You put it in a teapot, it becomes the teapot. Now, water can flow or it can crash. Be water, my friend.*

That approach had always benefited him. When he needed to unleash his emotions in hopes of playing better, he could. When he needed to tamp down those feelings and slow everything down around him, he could. He was in control. He could turn it on and off. He could flow and he could crash. He was water. Always.

But now, standing on the floor of NRG Stadium in Houston,

the emotions were coming faster than he had anticipated. The Patriots had just pulled off a 34–28 overtime win over the Falcons in Super Bowl LI where the two teams had combined to tie or break 31 Super Bowl records. That included a 25-point comeback engineered by Brady, one that ended with the first overtime finish in Super Bowl history. Given the circumstances and the magnitude of the event, it was the finest hour of his career, at the end of his most remarkable year in the NFL.

And so, as the madhouse swirled around him and confetti flew and music played at the end of the most amazing Super Bowl of all time, he was crying. While his teammates raced around the field and piled on each other and the crowd went nuts around him, Brady wept. There might not be crying in baseball. But football? No problem.

Why the tears? He didn't sob with joy after the previous four Super Bowl wins. After those games, there were smiles and hugs and celebrations. And after Super Bowl losses in 2008 and 2012, there was no crying; instead, his face was a stoic mask on both occasions when he and his teammates came up short. What made the win over the Falcons more important, more special, and more emotional than the 200-plus others he had enjoyed as a starting quarterback in the NFL?

In the end, there was a simple explanation: because it was so very *personal*. He wanted this one more than just about any of the others because of what was at stake at the end of an already emotional season.

It was personal because of his ghastly battle against the commissioner for last two years. He had ground through a lengthy war with Roger Goodell over Deflategate, a fight that had ravaged his reputation while costing the NFL millions of dollars.

It left him sidelined for the first four games of the 2016 season, forced into exile by a commissioner who appeared to disregard scientific evidence and good judgment in the name of bringing down the hammer and exercising his own personal brand of justice.

It was personal for him because he wanted desperately to come through for a locker room and coaching staff that had stood by him so devoutly. While many players around the league now questioned Brady's truthfulness, the rest of the New England locker room stood shoulder to shoulder with their teammate. On so many occasions, Brady had carried the franchise through adversity. In return, his teammates defended his name, backing him to the last. The quarterback wanted to repay them with another wake-up-the-echoes performance that would reward that unshakeable faith.

It was personal for him because—as he said on several occasions over the last year-plus—he's now fully cognizant of his football mortality. The quarterback wants to play into his mid-forties, but with his fortieth birthday staring him in the face, at this stage of his life, each trip to the Super Bowl is a truly special occasion. (The list of quarterbacks age forty or more to win a playoff game is a short one: Brett Favre. The list of quarterbacks age forty or more to win a *Super Bowl* is even shorter: none.) One day, sooner rather than later, you'll be forced from the game, and all you'll have left are your memories.

"You can't be around this long and not realize that the world will keep spinning and the sun will come up tomorrow without you," Brady said early in the 2016 season, striking a rare note of melancholy when asked about the fleeting nature of life in professional football. "That's just the way it goes. I think you enjoy just the experiences that you have, and then also understand that [the game] just keeps going on."

It was personal for him because of the health struggles that his mother had been facing. He wanted to win for *her*. His mother Galynn had been diagnosed with cancer roughly two years before, and because of health issues, she hadn't been to one of her son's games all year. (But she received the OK to travel to Super Bowl LI.) The quarterback has always leaned on his family, but the emotion wore on Brady in the week leading up to the Super Bowl; he got teary at a press conference when he talked about his dad being his hero.

"He was just a great example for me, and he was always someone who supported me in everything I did, to come home at night and bring me out, hit me ground balls and fly balls," Brady said of his father. "I loved baseball growing up. And to have a chance to go to 49ers games on the weekend with him and my mom and throw the ball in the parking lot before the games; those are memories that I'll have forever."

And so, with the season on the line and a fifth Super Bowl ring in his sights, on a brilliant afternoon in February, Brady and the Patriots took the field against the Falcons. Atlanta featured an impressive offense and sturdy defense, but the oddsmakers—and most of the analysts—believed that the Falcons' quest for the first Super Bowl in franchise history would come to an end at the hands of Brady and the Patriots. Atlanta certainly had something to offer, but the afternoon would be little more than a coronation of Brady. The Falcons were merely set pieces in a much larger drama.

Only problem was that over the course of the first two quarters, someone rewrote the script. For Brady and New England, the first half was pretty much a nightmare. Stacked against his six other Super Bowl appearances, it was the two worst quarters of his Super Bowl career. The numbers didn't look overly *awful*—16-for-26 for 184 yards, 2 sacks, 1 interception, and 0 touchdown passes—but he was sluggish and out of sorts in the early going. He overthrew receivers, missed some targets, and appeared to be unnerved by the Atlanta pass rush.

The low point was the pick-six he tossed to Falcons cornerback Robert Alford, and not just because it gave Atlanta a 21–0 lead in the second quarter. The last guy to have a shot at Alford was Brady, but the cornerback was just out of reach. The sight of the lunging Brady swinging and missing while trying to get to Alford appeared to be more than just a missed tackle. It was a metaphor that showed the young and speedy Falcons racing past the old and tired Patriots. *Things were different. Tonight would be different. Brady's time was through.* Like the noise in the Superdome fifteen years before when Ty Law picked off Kurt Warner and took it all the way back for a shocking score, there was a sense that something bigger was happening. An upset was brewing.

It all left the Patriots in a 21–3 hole, one that turned into a 28–3 deficit early in the third quarter. Inside NRG Stadium, the video board was showing celebrity Falcons' fans partying, eagerly anticipating the celebration that was sure to come.

But the Patriots' offense started to find some vulnerabilities, the defense made the necessary adjustments, and the special teamers made the plays, winning the battle of field position. While they had their lunch handed to them in the first half, things started to turn midway.through the third quarter. While the New England offense hadn't finished a drive with a touchdown, they had been on the field for an extended stretch. And so, as the fourth quarter started, it wasn't a complete surprise that the Atlanta defense started to tire.

Brady locked in on a handful of receivers, including James White, who was the best and most consistent offensive-skill position player all night on the New England roster. He found the wildly underrated Danny Amendola for a couple of big catches. There was Chris Hogan and Martellus Bennett, as well as the youngster Malcolm Mitchell. Things went from 28–3 to 28–9 late in the third when Brady connected with White on a 5-yard touchdown pass. After a missed extra point, the Patriots added a 33-yard field goal from Stephen Gostkowski to make it 28–12 with just under ten minutes to go. There was suddenly life. The margin for error for the Patriots had slipped to zero, but there was life.

After a few big defensive stops, New England cut it to 28–20. Then, it was Julian Edelman who delivered one of the signature moments of the season. No one was closer with the quarterback than his fellow Northern California native. And late in the fourth quarter, with the Patriots down by a score and needing to keep the chains moving, he made the catch of the season, wedging his way in between three Atlanta defenders to come away with a reception that was inches away from hitting the ground. It turned out to be one of the most memorable grabs in Super Bowl history. *Sports Illustrated* would cement the legacy of the reception by putting it on the cover the following week with the headline "MIRACLE."

It all culminated on a touchdown drive that saw White plunging over from the 1-yard line, and Brady connecting with Amendola on a 2-point conversion. At the start of the fourth quarter, it was 28–9. Now, it was 28–28, and New England was a runaway train with a legendary quarterback at the controls. The Falcons? They were simply the unlucky ones standing on the track when the train rolled through the station.

"We stay back and [defensive coordinator Matt Patricia is] going over defense and we're like, 'Matty P, we're not going out there. There's no way we're going out there. Tom Brady's in the groove. He's doing everything we need him to do to win this game,'" recalled defensive back Duron Harmon when asked about what was going on on the New England sidelines late in the game. "And that's what happened. He led that team down that whole fourth quarter.

"That's Tom Brady's quarter. That's what we're going to call it from now on."

If the Patriots had managed to wring all the momentum from the Falcons in the fourth quarter, overtime was simply more of the same. By this point, things had gotten completely turned around in the Patriots favor, and there was nothing the gassed Atlanta defense could do about it. In the extra session, New England's drive started on its own 25-yard line. It ended in football nirvana: an 8-play, 75-yard sequence that took 3:58 and ended with White scoring from the 2-yard line.

"He was the same as he always is; cool, calm and collected," Amendola said after the game when asked about Brady. "He's the leader. The general. The best ever. And that's the end of the story."

Of course, it wasn't just a win for Brady. This was a victory for the franchise; validation that their team-building approach wasn't perfect, but still good enough to capture another Super Bowl, the fifth in franchise history.

It was more vindication for Bill Belichick, who steered the team through a turbulent season that included wave after wave of distraction, some of which was his own doing.

It was a victory for the coaching staff and front office, which had hit the reset button in the middle of a season that presented them with multiple challenges, including the trade of Jamie Collins and finding a way to succeed without Rob Gronkowski.

It was a sweet victory for the likes of franchise foundations like Edelman, Malcolm Butler, LeGarrette Blount, and Matthew Slater, all of whom were overlooked prospects coming out of college but would become absolutely vital to the success of a Super Bowl champion.

It was a testament to the hard work and dedication of professionals like Devin McCourty, Dont'a Hightower, and Nate Solder, who added a second ring to their résumés while fortifying their credentials as some of the best in the game at their position.

And it was a hard-won triumph for the new veterans like Bennett, Hogan, and Chris Long, who got to experience their first Super Bowl win after years of wandering the NFL wilderness with other teams.

The greatness of Belichick and Brady aside, the truth is that this New England team was a wholly unique group that managed to do things that few other teams had ever managed to do: They were the first team since the 1987 Redskins to win a title in a season where they had three different quarterbacks pass for 400 yards or more. They were only one of a handful of teams in the history of the league to win eight regular-season road games in one year. They were only one of a few Super Bowl champions that would rely on a feature running back who was thirty or older in Blount.

But ultimately, their identity didn't come from one thing or one individual statistical trend. Instead, they were a team full of grinders who remained disarmingly practical when obstacles were placed in their path: Lose Brady for the first four games? *We've got two other quarterbacks on the roster.* Lose backup Jimmy Garop-polo the second game of the year? *We have faith in Jacoby.* Lose Gronkowski? *Let's figure out how to make it work without him.* Win three games in twelve days under impossibly difficult circum-stances? *No big deal.* Figure out a way to slow one of the great offenses in the recent history of the game in the Super Bowl? *We got this.*

At the heart of it all was Brady.

After the quarterback had come up for air at the end of the game, he saw Blount.

"You're the greatest. *You're the fucking greatest, bro,*" Blount said as the running back pointed at Brady's chest.

The greatest. Brady had secured his legacy with the win over the Seahawks in Super Bowl XLIX, becoming the only quarterback in the salary cap era to win four rings. Despite that victory, there was—remarkably—still some debate about who exactly was the greatest quarterback of all time. Critics argued that because Brady *lost* two Super Bowls, he still came up lacking when stacked against his childhood idol Joe Montana, who was a perfect 4-0 in Super Bowls. A popular meme that circulated had a picture of Montana mocking Brady for a litany of things, including the fact that Brady needed a kicker to "win [his] Super Bowls. I did it my-self." (The idea of using the fact that Brady reached more Super Bowls than Montana in the cap era against him was a mostly moot point to those critics, who thought the way they wanted to think about Brady because of Deflategate, regardless of what some sci-entific evidence might suggest.)

But the win over the Falcons gave him five rings, more than any quarterback in the history of the game. It allowed him to start to gain some separation on the rest of the field. He was now one ring ahead of Montana, the only other quarterback who was even in the conversation before that night in Houston. It also allowed him to end, once and for all, every stupid sports-talk radio debate about who is the best quarterback of all time. They won after Spygate. They won after Deflategate. There were no more questions. To paraphrase another New England hero: *Do you like apples? I've got five Super Bowl rings. How do you like them apples?*

Ultimately, what happened that Sunday night in Houston was more than just a game. It was the culmination of one of the more remarkable seasons in recent league history, the final chapter in a daily drama that stretched out over six months. It began with Brady in exile. It ended with him crying while kneeling on the floor of NRG Stadium in Houston.

"There was a lot of shit that happened tonight," Brady sighed to a handful of reporters after the game.

The truth is that if you *really* want to unpack all of the shit that happened, it's best to go back to the beginning.

1. AN OFF-SEASON OF UNCERTAINTY

It has been a challenging 18 months and I have made the difficult decision to no longer proceed with the legal process.
—Tom Brady on Facebook, July 15, 2016

Loneliness is the penalty of leadership, but the man who has to make the decisions is assisted greatly if he feels that there is no uncertainty in the minds of those who follow him, and that his orders will be carried out confidently and in the expectation of success.

—Ernest Shackleton

Tom Brady was running out of time.

No time to operate. No time to drop back in the pocket, assess the field, and find a receiver. No time to look left, look right, consider the options and make the throw. Where's Rob Gronkowski? Where's Julian Edelman? No time for that. Snap, step, throw, and hope you get lucky and find a target. And do it *now*, before you get crunched again.

Read the field? Hell, the way the Denver pass rush was coming against the New England offensive line, there wasn't even any time to *breathe*. On the afternoon of the 2015 AFC title game, Von Miller, Malik Jackson, DeMarcus Ware, and Derek Wolfe made it their mission to ensure the Patriots quarterback was going to be profoundly uncomfortable. And as the game continued, it was clear they were succeeding. The Broncos team defense was overwhelming; the secondary slowed the Patriots receivers and disrupted the timing routes. That extra moment or two forced Brady to hold on to the ball as the pass catchers tried to get separation. That led to the Broncos' pass rush getting to Brady and doing all sorts of horrible things to him, much to the delight of the sold-out Denver crowd.

I'd say they were like sharks smelling blood, but sharks have a more pleasant disposition.

"I want to eat your children," Wolfe growled at Brady at one point.

With right tackle Sebastian Vollmer on the left side because of an injury to Nate Solder, it left backup tackle Marcus Cannon against Miller, a matchup Denver was able to exploit. Compounding issues was the fact that the New England ground game was down to veteran Steven Jackson, a very nice guy who was pulled out of retirement in December by the Patriots shortly after their *entire starting backfield* went down for the season. For New England, facing the Broncos without LeGarrette Blount and/or Dion Lewis and a hobbled offensive line was like walking into the ring against Mike Tyson with one arm tied behind your back. (Jackson had 4 carries for 8 yards on the day. It would be the last contest of his professional career.) The leading rusher for the Patriots that afternoon was Brady, with a scant 13 yards. And most of that yardage came as a result of the quarterback running for his life.

The Broncos hit Brady 20 times on 56 dropbacks, eventually sacking him four times. The only reason they didn't have more sacks? Brady had a handful of pass attempts that were simply balls flung wildly downfield when he was already in the grips of a Broncos pass rusher.

"It's our job to hit the quarterback," Wolfe said after the game, "and we did our job well tonight."

All that being said, the last few minutes of regulation were among the finest of Brady's and Gronkowski's careers, as they managed to almost single-handedly keep the Patriots in the game. Down 20–12 with just under five minutes left, a fourth-down heave for Gronkowski in the end zone was off the mark. That looked like it might have been the end of it, but New England managed to get the ball back, and drove down the field again with less than two minutes to go.

A fourth-down reception that kept the chains moving late in regulation and an against-all-odds touchdown catch with 12 seconds left—both from Brady to Gronkowski—were amazing plays. The fourth-down catch was down the seam where Gronkowski split a pair of defenders and went tumbling forward after the reception, holding onto the ball. Then, there was the late touchdown, where the big tight end maneuvered between two Denver defenders to make a terrific catch to draw the Patriots to within two, 20–18, with 12 seconds left. (Kicker Stephen Gostkowski missed an extra point earlier in the game, which forced New England to have to go for two late.) But the 2-point conversion was off the mark, as the pass for Edelman was tipped away and eventually picked off by Denver defensive back Bradley Roby.

(The thing that creased some New England fans? A rewatch of the 2-point conversion appeared to show Gronkowski open on the play.)

And so, it was over. The Patriots went into the off-season, while the Broncos went to San Francisco, beat the Panthers, and got to carry off the Super Bowl 50 trophy. Much to the consternation of New England fans everywhere, that also meant that Peyton Manning got the fairy-tale ending he was hoping for: a Super Bowl victory and send-off smooch from his buddy Papa John before he rode off into the sunset.

As for Brady, he went home. Fully aware of the fact that he was about to turn thirty-nine in August, he reset the countdown clock on his own gym for Super Bowl LI, a year away in Houston. Now, both literally and metaphorically, the veteran was well aware the clock was ticking. Super Bowl trips, especially at this stage of a quarterback's career, were precious. Brady and Manning were part of a short list of quarterbacks who had won Super Bowls after their thirty-fifth birthday. (Johnny Unitas, Jim Plunkett, Roger Staubach, and John Elway were the others.) He was going to do all he could to make sure he would get a crack at another one.

But the off-season was not going to be so easy. Brady had gotten his Deflategate punishment pushed back when Judge Richard Berman cleared the way for him to play in 2015, but in the spring of 2016, a three-judge panel of the U.S. Court of Appeals for the Second Circuit in Manhattan ruled 2–1 he must serve a four-game suspension to start the upcoming regular season. That left him looking for one last legal Hail Mary: Was he going to try and take it to the Supreme Court? Would he accept the ruling? Spring stretched into summer, and while the Patriots went through their off-season program, it remained unclear what was going to happen.

Ultimately, the answer popped up in everyone's Facebook feed on the morning of July 15, 2016. He was giving up the fight. Roughly two weeks before the start of training camp, for the quarterback and the team, there was finally clarity and closure. With Brady's announcement, it appeared the black cloud that had thrown so much of the Patriots' game planning and approach to the 2015 season into chaos had been lifted. He would sit. No matter how rock-headed the decision was on the part of the commissioner, Brady acceded to the demands of Roger Goodell and agreed to give up his legal battle against the NFL. Finally, there was a road map for the quarterback and the team. He was gone for the first four games, and the Patriots would have to move on. It wasn't exactly *palatable*, but it was finally done.

It was another setback for the Patriots in their battle against the league. The first came at the owners meetings in May 2015, when owner Robert Kraft said he was going to accept the punishment that was handed down by the commissioner. While making it clear he wasn't thrilled with the decision—he called the ban and loss of draft picks "way over the top" and "unreasonable and unprecedented"—he said he was going to go along with Goodell.

"I don't want to continue the rhetoric that's gone on for the last four months," he said. "I'm going to accept, reluctantly, what he has given to us, and not continue this dialogue and rhetoric, and we won't appeal."

He added: "Now, I know that a lot of Patriots fans are going to be disappointed in that decision, but I hope they trust my judgment and know that I really feel at this point in time that taking this off the agenda, this is the best thing for the New England

Patriots, our fans, and the NFL, and I hope you all can respect that. You know, I would normally take questions, but my desire is truly not to continue the rhetoric, and so I'm going to leave this discussion exactly here. Thank you very much."

Of course, this being Deflategate, nothing was what it seemed. Following an appeal from Brady, the league upheld the ruling late that summer. That sparked a fiery statement from Kraft at the start of training camp where he reversed field *again,* lashing into the league and Goodell by saying "the decision handed down by the league yesterday is unfathomable to me. It is routine for discipline in the NFL to be reduced upon appeal." While Berman backed Brady prior to the 2015 season, allowing him to play, the back-and-forth over Brady in 2016 added another layer of intrigue to the relationship between Kraft and Goodell. The two were once thought to be close, and while both are pragmatic businessmen, it was evident to many league insiders the events around Deflategate had dented a once positive relationship.

Brady's decision also ended what was something of a dicey issue for the team and quarterback, particularly as it related to his fight involving the National Football League Players Association. While the team had given up the battle, and Kraft had said they were willing to accept Goodell's decision, there was no such feeling from the NFLPA. Brady was a member of the Patriots, and the team needed to assemble a contingency plan if their quarterback wasn't going to play. But Brady was also a high-profile NFL player involved in what some considered to be a landmark legal battle with the league over Goodell's disciplinary policy. The longer the fight was extended, the more the sense of uncertainty surrounding the Patriots and what might happen in 2016. If he did get some sort of legal stay and then lost again down the road, the possibility existed of him missing games in the middle of the year or even (gasp) the postseason.

But now, the battle was done.

"There's definition to it now," Belichick said of Brady's situation in July 2016. "We'll move forward based on that definition."

Ultimately, the Brady decision put the capper on an off-season of uncertainty for the Patriots:

They didn't have a first-round pick, so the margin for error when it came to the draft—as well as the trade market and free agency—would be slimmer than usual.

They weren't going to have their starting quarterback for the first quarter of the season, so they'd presumably be counting on backup Jimmy Garoppolo to take over for Brady for the first four games.

Their No. 1 receiver, who had a history of foot issues and was coming off a broken bone in his foot that dogged him late into the 2015 season, spent a sizable portion of the off-season in a walking boot.

The bulk of their backfield was unable to finish the 2015 season because of various injuries, which cast doubt on their collective ability to perform in 2016.

While they had a bunch of new faces—both rookies and free agents—they had no idea how their new acquisitions would do when it came to getting up to speed within the framework of the team. And many of *those* new offensive faces would have to spend their time trying to establish chemistry with two different quarterbacks.

They just released 2014 first-round pick Dominique Easley, a defensive lineman who was thought to be a foundational element for the next decade.

And the offensive line that had proved to be the fatal flaw of the 2015 team—a group that was drowned by wave after wave of Denver's pass rushers—didn't look much better going into 2016.

Other than that, no worries. *Right?*

Brady or no Brady, no one was shedding any tears over the Patriots and their plight, and frankly, the team was OK with that. When you win as much and as consistently as they have over the last decade-plus, that's just what happens. (You're going to get opposing defensive linemen saying they want to eat your quarterback's kids.) And the simple fact was that spring, regardless of all the drama, they were still part of that short list of teams who were considered to be genuine Super Bowl contenders because they were still expected to have Brady for twelve regular-season games and into the postseason. There was Gronkowski and Edelman and Hightower and Collins and Butler. These were the sorts of first-world NFL problems that they would have killed for in Jacksonville or San Francisco. Even without Brady, you could put them down for—at a minimum—twelve wins and a spot in the NFL's Final Four.

But as history had shown, the margin for error at the top of the mountain was ridiculously thin. The team-building process for elite-level franchises was an incredibly delicate procedure. One ill-timed injury or suspension could cause the whole house of cards to come crashing down. A financial miss in free agency could upset the structure of the locker room, and wreak havoc with a carefully crafted salary cap scenario. With AFC rivals like Denver, Baltimore, and Pittsburgh poised to take advantage, New England couldn't afford to be less than perfect if it wanted a chance at a fifth Super Bowl title. And so, as the new league year dawned that March, it was a pivotal time for the franchise. If they wanted to get back to where they wanted to be, they not only needed to augment their roster with the right free agents, they also had to make sure they hit on the draft that spring as well.

New England's approach to team building, particularly free agency, has traditionally been slow and steady. The philosophy is best embodied in a phrase from John Wooden: *Don't mistake activity for achievement.* With precious few exceptions, unless they identified what they thought would be an absolutely perfect fit, Belichick and New England did not engage in the high-stakes world that accompanies the first few days of the NFL's feeding frenzy. (They swung for the fences on occasion. They just didn't do it as often as their counterparts.) While it's different from year to year, that was one of the reasons why the Patriots didn't make a mad dash into free agency that spring. Instead, they operated cautiously, identifying a handful of veterans and leaving no doubt about their intentions. It was a group that included defensive linemen Chris Long and Terrance Knighton and wide receiver Chris Hogan.

In particular, Long and Knighton were part of a very specific type of player the Patriots had targeted in recent years. In what seemed to be an annual tradition, New England almost always went after at least one veteran defensive lineman near the end of his career, a guy who usually caught the eye of Belichick and the Patriots for a few reasons, including the fact that he was still *effective* on the field and *cost-effective* away from the field. It was a tradition that went all the way back to Anthony Pleasant, and included Keith Traylor, Ted Washington, Tommy Kelly, Albert Haynesworth, Shaun Ellis, Andre Carter, and Alan Branch. (Let's be honest: sometimes it worked, sometimes it didn't. In the case of Haynesworth, it was more the latter than the former.) Usually, these guys were smart veterans who had missed out on a ring to that point in their careers, but were willing to play for something below market value in hopes of landing a title. Knighton and Long were quickly identified as this year's model.

Long, who was the second overall pick of the Rams in 2008 but had never played in the postseason, was a well-liked vet who had been dogged by injury issues the previous few years. A guy who had made his bones as a pass rusher, the son of Hall of Famer Howie Long had managed to carve out an impressive career of his own with 54.5 sacks in eight years. Released by the Rams that spring, he received a vote of confidence from Al Groh, a former defensive coordinator for the Patriots who also served as a colleague of Belichick's. Groh coached Long at the University of Virginia, and knew the type of guy the Patriots were hoping to land.

"Bill has certainly gotten outstanding production from these types of players over the years, a group like Andre Carter, Corey Dillon, Rodney Harrison, Roman Phifer," Groh said. "Chris falls into that category of guys who have done a lot of things in their careers; they've achieved success on the field, financial reward. But the one thing they all hunger for at the end is to win. That's important for him. That's what he's in it for—that's what he's always been in it for."

As for Knighton, in addition to being the type of veteran capable of contributing late in his career, he had three things in his favor when it came to making a case with the area fan base: one, he grew up in New England (specifically, Hartford). He knew what it meant to live and die with the Patriots. Two, he was a colossal Celtics fan, going so far as to actively attempt to get free agent Kevin Durant to sign with Boston via social media. (Brady would join in the recruitment pitch when he flew to the Hamptons to talk to Durant about playing in New England.) Knighton was no casual fan; he knew the game, and was serious in helping the Celtics pursue Durant. And three, he had a track record of success against the Patriots, as he mauled former New England offensive lineman Logan Mankins in the 2013 AFC title game when he was with the Broncos.

"I just felt like it was a once in a lifetime opportunity to play for a team that obviously I loved to watch playing growing up," Knighton said shortly after signing with the Patriots.

"It got kind of hard in our house for a while, with him being a Bronco and then a Redskin," said his mom, Rochelle. "My youngest is a diehard Patriots fan, and he wore his stuff all the time. Terrance used to give him such a hard time. 'Really?' But our family is so happy now, especially my youngest—who can wear his Patriots stuff again without being made fun of."

But the biggest off-season move, at least from a personnel perspective, came on St. Patrick's Day when they traded for tight end Martellus Bennett. The Patriots acquired Bennett, brother of Seattle defensive lineman Michael Bennett, and a sixth-round selection from the Bears for a fourth-round pick. Bennett, nicknamed "The Black Unicorn," was an undeniable talent—he averaged 66 catches a year from 2012 through 2015, including 90 in 2014 with the Bears. So why was he available? The underachieving Bears were in the midst of a rebuild, and Bennett's occasionally quirky nature clashed with some coaches and teammates.

Quickly, it was pretty clear Bennett was going to be a different sort of Patriot; in his introductory conference call with the media, when he was asked about his reaction to the trade, he compared himself to a dandelion, saying, "Just like any other thing in life, you just prepare to make sure you flow where the wind goes." And later that spring, when he was asked about fitting in with the culture in New England, he was the first player in franchise history to reference Oscar Wilde and Dr. Seuss in the same interview.

"Dr. Seuss said, 'No one can be you-er than you.' Oscar Wilde said, 'Be yourself, because everyone else is taken.' I can only be one person," Bennett said during a break in the spring practice sessions. "I just try and continue to be who I am and don't change that. I'm a little chameleon. I just try and fit in wherever I am. When you're authentic, people appreciate that."

The funny stuff was one thing. But Bennett's previous body of work and his overall skill set sparked some conversation about the ceiling for the Patriots passing game, particularly at tight end. With Gronkowski and Bennett, New England was capable of having the most production at the tight end position in one season in the history of the game. Of course, a lot of that would depend on whether Gronkowski could stay healthy—given his injury history, that was a sizable risk. But it certainly seemed reasonable to assume they could challenge the mark set by the 2011 Patriots, which got 169 catches for 2,237 yards and 24 touchdowns from the tight end position that year.

A week after Bennett signed, the prospect of finding a way to defend New England's tight ends in the passing game was already causing ice-cream headaches among AFC East coaches, including Buffalo's Rex Ryan.

"I have no idea," Ryan said. "I just think it's unusual to have two guys that are like 6-[foot]-7 and can run, catch, block. So, yeah, it's going to be a major challenge. There's no doubt about that. It's scary when you look at them. Those are two huge guys. How we're going to defend them, I don't know."

For what it's worth, Bennett showed that he would fit in immediately, joining in on the emerging social media scene in the Patriots' locker room. He posted a picture to Instagram of himself shaking hands with Brady when Chicago and New England met in 2014. He included the caption: "Hi Tom. I'm Marty. Let's do this." And in one Facebook post from Brady, the quarterback was seen blowing into a conch shell, ostensibly putting out a call to his receivers, Ron Burgundy–style. Edelman, Amendola, and Gronkowski all replied with responsive posts of their own. Meanwhile, Bennett also joined in, posting an Instagram video with him saying, "I don't always answer bird calls, but when I do, they're from Tom Brady and Gronk."

Draft weekend was the first of what promised to be several reminders that the Patriots were going to be haunted by Deflategate for months to come. Thanks to You Know What, they were without a first-round pick, and so Goodell's opening night party, live from Chicago, went on without them. The good news for New England was that it was one of the least eventful first rounds in recent NFL history, one that was underscored by almost constant booing of the commissioner every time he approached the podium.

As the weekend went on, Goodell appeared to smarten up. Close to midway through the night, while fans were going hoarse, he brought out the Payton family as part of the Walter Payton Man of the Year Award. Big cheers. Then he brought out a youth football team from Chicago. More cheers. And he had a Make-A-Wish youngster come out with him to make Denver's draft pick. Another big round of cheers. With each in a series of human shields that accompanied him to the stage, the booing lessened slightly. In hindsight, it was easy to think of Goodell and his crew rummaging around backstage for more sympathetic props. *Anyone have any puppies? I could carry out a puppy. There would be no way they'd boo a puppy, right? Any more cute kids hanging around back here?*

(To Goodell's credit, he appeared to manage some self-actualization as the draft wore on. When the boos began at the start of the third day, he managed a smile and appeared to acknowledge the vitriol by saying, "Bring it on." *Do your worst, you savages. The thirty-two owners are making more money than they know what to do with. I'm not going anywhere.*)

Despite the fact the Patriots didn't have a first-rounder, they were still able to land a handful of rookies that weekend who would become key contributors in their first year in the NFL. With the sixtieth overall pick—their first of the draft—they took Cyrus Jones out of Alabama, a highly regarded corner from the national champions who also had serious special teams value as a returner. A pair of North Carolina State products were taken in the third round in quarterback Jacoby Brissett and offensive lineman Joe Thuney, and they went after Georgia wide receiver Malcolm Mitchell in the fourth round. They rounded things out with the selection of defensive lineman Vincent Valentine, linebackers Kamu Grugier-Hill and Elandon Roberts, offensive lineman Ted Karras, and wide receiver Devin Lucien.

Brissett was an interesting pick on a few levels. He was a protégé of Bill Parcells, and had roots with some extended members of the Patriots' family, including former New England offensive coordinator Charlie Weis, who initially recruited him to Florida.

Brissett came out of Dwyer High School in Palm Beach Gardens, Florida, and Parcells spends the winters in nearby Jupiter. The pro at Parcells's golf club is the father-in-law of Dwyer's football coach, Jack Daniels, and Parcells was drawn to Brissett, later telling MMQB.com Brissett was "tremendously dedicated, tremendously committed and he is smart."

Brissett ended up transferring to North Carolina State, and while he didn't have the collegiate pedigree of some other quarterbacks in the draft that spring, he had many of the elements that the Patriots look for when they go get a signal-caller, including an impressive ability to take care of the football. He took over the starting job at North Carolina State in 2014, and threw 187 straight passes without an interception that year, the seventh longest streak in ACC history. In his two years as the starter for the Wolfpack, he completed 60 percent of his passes— traditionally, one of the benchmarks in trying to figure out if a college quarterback will have success at the next level—and had a 4-to-1 touchdown-to-interception ratio.

Ultimately, Parcells became an unofficial advisor to Brissett before the draft, occasionally meeting him for lunch and talking about the schedule of team visits. Before Brissett's pre-draft visit with New England, Daniels remembers Parcells telling him he better be ready to be drilled on every little thing about his college film.

"He's a good player, a good kid," Belichick said after Brissett was added. "We'll see how it goes."

Of course, the Patriots can't simply just *draft a quarterback.* Each time a signal-caller is taken, some believe it serves as a referendum when it comes to just how long Brady is going to play. But considering the fact that current backup Garoppolo would be going into the last year of his rookie contract, combined with the uncertainty about Brady's status in regard to Deflategate, it made you wonder about the context to go after Brissett.

"There's always an element of team planning, especially at that position," Belichick said. "If you can you try to look ahead a little bit. If you can't, then take it as it comes. Things change, but there's an element of planning at all positions on your team, certainly that one."

In all, there was a lot to unpack when it came to the weekend, but the other real notable pick of the group was Mitchell, an overachieving pass catcher out of Georgia with a Hollywood-style life story that read like something out of *The Blind Side*. Coming from a background where he struggled, he taught himself to read at a young age, eventually joined a book club, and later authored a children's book while in college. (It was believed that between Mitchell, Bennett, and Edelman, the 2016 Patriots had the only roster in the history of the league to feature three players who had written children's books.)

"Solid kid," Belichick said of Mitchell. "He's got a good story. [He] works hard, and [he's] versatile. He's a good player."

The draft class was nice, but the Patriot who made the biggest splash that weekend was former New England running back Kevin Faulk. Part of a group of ex-players who were taking part in the draft by announcing picks, when it was his turn to announce one of the third-round selections, he strolled out on stage in a suit jacket. He was set to reveal the selection of Thuney, and he opened his jacket, showing a Brady jersey underneath. It was a surprise move on the part of Faulk, who was one of Brady's closest teammates.

"There was a process where you got on the green room, and the woman from the NFL comes to get you to bring you to the stage," Faulk said, explaining how he made it to the stage wearing Brady's gear. "The person who came to get me, she was a huge Patriots fan. She said, 'Oh, I love it.' I got out there, and I heard some cheers and some boos. There will always be some negatives and some positives, but it was mostly positive."

"That's why Kevin Faulk is a potential member of the Patriots Hall of Fame," Patriots director of player personnel Nick Caserio said with a smile after Day Two of the draft when asked about Faulk's move earlier that night. "We all love Kevin Faulk."

Caserio added: "Kevin Faulk's one of the best Patriots on a multitude of levels, and I think he certainly showed that tonight."

"Love Kevin," Belichick said with a grin. "He always makes good decisions. Looked sharp out there."

By the spring of 2016, even the hard-core Goodell backers had to admit that Deflategate was an embarrassment for all involved. *Brady's balls* was a go-to pop culture punch line soon after Deflategate broke, and Goodell's ineffectiveness on everything from his dealings with the Patriots to putting together a sound domestic violence policy to concussion protocol and research was also comedic fodder. But *South Park* distinguished itself with its razor-sharp attacks on Goodell and the NFL, offering up a sharp send-up: in the midst of a dream, Cartman imagines Brady, Belichick, and Goodell all cursing each other out over Deflategate. "Fuck you, you broke the rules." "I can do whatever I want. I'm breaking the rules." (This was on the heels of a memorable episode where Goodell was pictured as a robot, offering up clichés and sound bites in a discussion with cartoon Daniel Snyder.)

But while there were moments of surreal comedy throughout the whole process, if you were to put the time stamp on when it went from a $20 million clown show to full-on Theater of the Absurd, it was probably May 2016. That's when comedian Jim Breuer was injected into the proceedings.

The former *Saturday Night Live* star told *Sports Illustrated* he ran into John Jastremski, the equipment guy who was at the center of the saga, at a resort in Cancún the previous November. According to Breuer, Jastremski approached him in the gym while the comedian was watching Deflategate coverage on TV. Breuer says Jastremski introduced himself as the "Deflategate guy" and told him he and his family were on vacation "to get away because they were being so harassed in the Massachusetts area." Jastremski then reportedly went on to rip the Patriots for how he'd been treated in the wake of what happened, saying the team was "holding him down" and wouldn't let him speak to the press.

As for whether the footballs were deflated in the AFC Championship Game against the Colts?

"He wouldn't answer the question," Breuer told SI. "But he just kept saying, 'Tom's my guy. Tom takes care of me.'"

While people around the league spent the off-season pointing to New England's potentially game-changing acquisitions like Bennett, Knighton, Long, and Jones as evidence the Patriots were going to turn things around in 2016, locally, the pickup that ended up meaning the most to the long-term success of that team was a sixty-eight-year-old ex-Marine.

Dante Scarnecchia, who bore a slight resemblance to famed test pilot Chuck Yeager—right down to the occasionally plain-spoken approach—had been asked to return and deliver a quick fix to the New England offensive line. He had been gone for two years, having decided to retire following the 2013 season. Dave DeGuglielmo replaced him, and while DeGuglielmo was pretty much accepted as one of the funniest and most open guys on the coaching staff with the media—a Massachusetts native, "Googs" was a self-confessed "smart aleck" who quoted *GoodFellas* and famously referred to Brady as "The Ninja"—because of what happened in Denver, a move needed to be made.

"Your quarterback gets hit twenty times in a game, someone has to be the fall guy," said NFL Network analyst Brian Baldinger, referencing the bloodbath. "I've never seen a quarterback hit twenty times in a game before."

It was unfair to blame *everything* that happened in Denver on DeGuglielmo, but someone had to take the fall. Under the auspices of not renewing his contract, he was shown the door, and it was back to Scarnecchia. The former sergeant, who had made his bones as one of the best offensive line coaches in the league over a twenty-year span, had managed to continue to work part-time for the franchise while he was away. He would pop up every so often at a random Pro Day, as well as the Senior Bowl and the combine. An unofficial member of Belichick's kitchen cabinet while he was "retired," he would consult and watch film, all while being mindful not to step on DeGuglielmo's toes.

But after the Denver debacle, the franchise had to make a change. A few days after the loss, Belichick called Scarnecchia, who was on a trip with his wife, to see if he'd be interested in a full-time return. Scarnecchia had thought briefly about getting back into the game in some form or fashion, but at that stage of his life, it had to be the right gig. And he wouldn't take another job in a different location.

After taking a few days to talk it over with his family, he decided to get back into the mix in Foxboro. Full-time retirement would have to be put on hold.

"You become very used to a very nice lifestyle," Scarnecchia said earlier that spring, shortly after he returned. "We talked about it, my wife and I, and we decided this would be a good thing on a lot of different levels. And I like coaching football. I love coaching football. I didn't retire because I didn't like coaching football. I retired because I got tired of the lifestyle. Two years off? I'm OK."

In his thirty-one previous seasons in New England, he had guided his fair share of Pro Bowl offensive linemen, including Logan Mankins and Matt Light. And those high-level players will tell you that Scarnecchia's influence helped craft them into some of the best in the league at their positions. But in the big picture, the genius of Scarnecchia wasn't so much in his ability to take standout prospects and make them better (although he did that on a routine basis). He had a unique gift—the ability to take an overlooked JAG (in the parlance of NFL personnel men, Just Another Guy) and turn him into a key part of a championship offensive line. Through the previous decade-plus, he had managed to take an untold number of undrafted free agents and mold them into winners: guys who were relatively anonymous when they arrived in New England became key cogs in the machine. He took guys like Stephen Neal, Russ Hochstein, and Dan Connolly and made them champions.

Scarnecchia's other trait was one that was shared across the board by New England: he could identify a scheme-fit for his system better than most. This is especially important when it comes to assessing offensive line play; five linemen are all separate working parts, but all must work together. You'd like to find the five best offensive linemen but it's more important to find the five offensive linemen *that comprise the best unit.* For years, the Patriots had utilized the first few games of the season to figure out the best offensive line combination. (By way of example, because of ineffectiveness, rotation, and injury, New England had an NFL-high 39 different offensive line combinations in 2015.) Provided everyone stayed healthy, that would change in 2016.

But at the start of camp, Scarnecchia indicated that the emphasis in the early going was going to be more about finding the five best and sticking with them as long as possible.

"I think that we're going to try to keep the guys—whoever's the first five—we're going try to keep those guys together as much as we can," Scarnecchia said. "It's not always practical to do that, and there's competition at multiple positions so there may be some in and out that way.

"But the thing is, if we can keep the left tackle playing the left tackle, the right tackle [playing right tackle], and try to keep the guards playing on the same side as much as we can, that'll really help everybody. There's got to be some guys that swing around in there, because we only end up with eight or nine linemen. [But] I think it'll be fine. I really do."

In training camp that summer, in the far corner of the field, there was some shuffling. But it soon became evident that the fatal flaw of the 2015 team—the offensive line—wasn't going to be an issue this time around. The occasionally salty Scarnecchia was back, and while the guidance was more R-rated than anything, it was clear that the first step in the remaking of the New England offense was under way.

"Dante is like family, man," said running backs coach Ivan Fears. "I've been with him for so long. I don't notice any difference. It's like he took a day off and we're back going."

"[There's] a total calming effect with Dante being here. [He's] just a great coach, a great guy and even better man," said defensive coordinator Matt Patricia.

One of the best things about interviewing Scarnecchia was the fact that he had exactly zero fucks to give when it came to the game of football. He was free to speak his mind as he saw fit. Belichick's assistant coaches were shielded from the media—they spoke with reporters only a handful of times over the course of the season—but when they did talk, you always learned something from Scarnecchia, either about the game of football or offensive line play in particular. Smart and insightful, he was as good an interview as you were going to get. He didn't seek out the spotlight—on Super Bowl media day a few years prior, one reporter found him hiding from reporters behind Belichick's podium. And when it came to game planning and personnel and technique, he wasn't giving away state secrets. But the fact that he didn't necessarily *need* the job at this stage of his life, combined with a peerless résumé, allowed him more leeway in dealing with the media as opposed to some of his other coaching colleagues. That's why it was no surprise to hear him downplay his return with a mixture of saltiness and self-deprecation when he met reporters before the start of training camp.

"Look, we ain't *building rockets*. Really, it's the truth," he said with a small smile when asked about how his coaching technique might differ or improve the state of the offensive line. "Step with this foot, get this shoulder in there. It's really that. That's the approach we're going to take. We're really going to be very precise in what we do and the way we do it. We're going to try and play as hard as we can. If we can do that, we have a chance."

The last stages of Deflategate and the return of Scarnecchia were just two of the biggest off-season events faced by the franchise. There was also the matter of figuring out what to make of the fact that Gronkowski and Dion Lewis saw only limited action over the course of the spring. If they were healthy, they were two of the most dynamic offensive options on the New England roster, and allowed the Patriots to take things to a whole different level. If Garoppolo had a healthy Gronkowski and Lewis riding shotgun for the first four games of the season, it would certainly make life easier for the young quarterback.

But they weren't on the field for a sizable chunk of the spring workouts; they were present at the T-shirt and shorts practice sessions at the end of the spring, but that was about it. And given their histories, it was reasonable to speculate about their immediate future, at least as it related to the start of the 2016 season.

There was the matter of replacing defensive end Chandler Jones (traded) and linebacker Jerod Mayo (retired), two parts of the defense who had been vital to the success of the franchise over the previous five years or so. Jones's production had been sporadic over the previous two seasons, but two things ultimately did him in when it came to the Patriots: one, he was going into the last year of his rookie deal, and was one of a handful of players who would be an unrestricted free agent at the end of the 2016 season. Given the market for even middle-of-the-road pass rushers, New England wanted to get something for him in return.

And two, there was his bizarre involvement in a case involving synthetic marijuana late in the 2015 season that reflected poorly on him and the franchise as a whole. In the post–Aaron Hernandez world, the incident (combined with his occasionally inconsistent level of play) made him expendable. So he was shipped to the desert for offensive lineman Jonathan Cooper and a second-round pick. (Through a series of trades, the Patriots acquired another two draft picks that would go on to net them Thuney and Mitchell.)

As for Mayo, he was a foundational element for several seasons after he arrived in 2008, but age and injury the previous few years had slowed him. His presence as a leader, however, couldn't be discounted for a few reasons, not the least of which was the fact that he had THE LOCKER. It was prime real estate in the New England locker room, the spot nearest to the players' exit, a location not given out to just anyone. When Gillette first opened in 2002, it belonged to Willie McGinest, who used the spot to keep a close eye on everyone who was coming and going. You had to pass by McGinest's locker if you were leaving, and if he was still there, *that* was no easy feat. ("*I* was scared of Willie," Brady said a while back when talking about having to pass that corner.) That spot was later taken by Mayo, who had the same level of cachet with his teammates from 2008 until his retirement after the 2015 season. That locker meant more than being a captain, or wearing the green dot on the back of the helmet (the latter of which was given to the type of leader capable of manning the coach-to-player communication system in his helmet). That real estate meant you were a leader, the type of person the team would aim to build around.

The simple truth was the fact that Mayo was a classic bridge guy; other than Brady, he was the only guy who could connect the last vestiges of the 2008–09 era Patriots to the modern roster. He played with Junior Seau and Collins, Mike Vrabel and Hightower. With Mayo gone, it would leave a leadership void that would be difficult to replace.

Now, it belonged to Hightower, a quiet guy who delivered crushing hits on a regular basis. The linebacker had an impressive pedigree when he came into the league in 2012, arriving after helping Alabama win a pair of national championships. However, he struggled for a sizable portion of his rookie year, so much so that some critics called him a bust. In a memorable locker room Q&A near the end of his first year in the league, he displayed a keen level of self-awareness, acknowledging his problems because, in his words, he had tried to do too much, and had gotten away from what he was good at.

But Hightower had made massive gains at the end of his first season, and by 2013, was already being looked to as one of the next great linebackers in the New England scheme. He truly arrived at the end of the 2014 season, when he took complete command of the linebacking corps following a season-ending injury to Mayo. Hightower was now considered one of the best in the league at his position and a pillar of the Patriots' defense; Pro Football Focus named him a first-team All-Pro, as he finished the season with 6 sacks, many of them the result of his skillful ability to execute the A-gap blitz as a surprise rusher.

That postseason, he delivered his signature moment. It was the sort of play that elevated him from quality starter to defensive centerpiece. From regular-season stud to postseason legend. Late in the fourth quarter of Super Bowl XLIX against Seattle, he was playing with a shoulder issue that would require surgery at the end of the season. But when the Seahawks tried to bang it in with Marshawn Lynch on the goal line, Hightower met him with an awesome shoulder tackle, stopping his progress and keeping Seattle out of the end zone—all while being hammered by Seattle offensive lineman Russell Okung. That set the stage for Malcolm

Butler's memorable interception to help save the season. While Butler's play is remembered as one of the great Super Bowl plays of all time, Hightower's stop might be one of the most underrated.

In the *Do Your Job* documentary about the 2015 team, then–linebackers coach Patrick Graham recalled the play—specifically, how quickly Hightower closed the hole that had been opened for Lynch by the Seattle offensive line.

"From up in the [coaches'] box, it looks wide open. I mean, [the hole] was *wide open*. I remember texting him two days later, I said, 'Have you seen this play?' I said, 'How in the world did you do this?'

"He bench-presses Okung off of him and he tackles Lynch with his shoulder."

In 2015, Hightower occasionally struggled with injury, but with Vince Wilfork gone and Mayo with one foot out the door, the defense belonged to him. It wasn't completely due to his presence, but it wasn't completely coincidental that when he was on the field and when he was off, the yards per play allowed splits that were dramatic. Never was that more the case than in that year's regular-season game against the Broncos in Denver—in that one, the Broncos averaged 2.9 yards per carry before Hightower left. After he departed because of a knee injury, they averaged 8.0 yards per carry and scored 3 rushing touchdowns, including C. J. Anderson's 48-yard game-winner in overtime.

He had the green dot on his helmet. He had the primo locker space. He was about to be named a captain for the first time in his professional career. Now, he was about head into a contract year knowing that a large part of the success or failure of the New England defense that season would rest on his broad shoulders.

While the Patriots felt good about Hightower, Jamie Collins, and their linebacking corps, there were other questions facing the 2016 team: Would they suffer any hangover from their loss in the AFC title game? (And could they recover from seeing the hated Broncos lift the Lombardi Trophy? More than one Patriots fan confessed to throwing up in their mouth a bit when Peyton walked away with the title.) Would the team follow Garoppolo like they would Brady? And could the rest of the team collectively raise its game to a point where it could paper over any deficiencies that arose in the wake of them having to go to Garoppolo in place of their veteran superstar?

"We're at the bottom like everybody else in the league is, starting all over again. We've got a long way to go. We've got a lot of work to do, but it's exciting to start on that trip," Belichick said as camp opened. "I think the players are, hopefully, ready to handle the challenges of training camp; working in different spots, doing the things that we did in the spring but doing them at a more competitive level, eventually in pads, eventually against good competition on the practice field and in preseason games. Like I said, we'll just go day-by-day here."

2. THE SUMMER OF JIMMY

Reporter: What happens if Jimmy plays better?
Belichick: Look, I told you what's going to happen.
Reporter: There's no chance?
Belichick: Jesus Christ.
—EXCHANGE BETWEEN BELICHICK AND A REPORTER WHEN
HE WAS ASKED IF THERE WAS A CHANCE BRADY COULD LOSE
HIS JOB TO GAROPPOLO IF THE YOUNGSTER PERFORMED
WELL OVER THE FIRST FOUR GAMES OF THE SEASON

I've dated two girls at the same time before.
—MARTELLUS BENNETT, WHEN ASKED IF HE WOULD
HAVE ANY PROBLEM GETTING USED TO WORKING WITH
TWO DIFFERENT QUARTERBACKS DURING TRAINING CAMP

TO KNOW THE STORY OF the 2016 Patriots, you have to know the story of The Hill.

Also known as *That Fucking Hill* to some. Or Mount Belichick to others.

There would be a lot of places where that team would author memorable, season-defining moments. On the practice field. Within the confines of Gillette Stadium. And in faraway places like Denver and Houston and Cleveland.

But it all started on The Hill.

The story of the 2016 team, the Super Bowl champions, began on The Hill. Just about every practice that summer culminated with a series of sprints up and down The Hill, located over a ridge deep in the back corner of the practice fields, with the team running until there was puke and sweat. While fans would wait for post-practice autographs and the media would wait for availability, in the heat of July and August, the team came together, building up a level of cardio and forging a bond that would allow them to start fast and finish strong.

There are actually two parts to The Hill. One is long and sloping, the other is quick and steep, and both have yard markers to make sure everyone knows just how much distance they have left before they can stop, bend over, and start retching and puking.

After a ninety-minute padded practice, it's not easy work. But then again, it wasn't easy building a champion, either.

"It definitely teaches you how to become comfortable with being uncomfortable," receiver Danny Amendola told Phil Perry of Comcast SportsNet. "It's a beast."

"That hill's great," director of player personnel Nick Caserio told SiriusXM Radio. "That hill gets them in shape pretty quickly. Those guys don't like it, but they'll probably—in the fourth quarter—realize it's worthwhile."

(The Hill also offered a pair of bonuses: one, it provided a quick escape route for a player and staff member out of sight of the media if there was an injury. If you weren't paying attention and suddenly a player went missing, it was usually because he had suffered some sort of health issue and the team had slipped him off the field, down The Hill and to the locker room, out of sight of reporters. *Hey, wasn't so-and-so just out here? What happened?* And two, that summer, it provided Brady with a quick exit. Instead of walking past reporters after practice, he could sneak down The Hill and out of sight, heading off to the locker room without being dogged by the media.)

When it came to The Hill, there were no exceptions. *Everyone* would take part. That included some of the coaches, as well as the quarterbacks. Despite the fact that he was now set to miss the first four games of the regular season, Brady ran that summer as part of the group.

The work in the spring sessions and off-season conditioning programs was important. And the individual off-season workout sessions in far-flung places like Phoenix and South Florida were vital for building toward success. But the push toward Super Bowl LI as a team? It began on The Hill.

For the Patriots, the first practice of the summer came on July 28, and the running started shortly after that. The only ones who were excused were those who opened camp on the physically-unable-to-perform list, as well as the few who were absent for one reason or another. That group included special teams ace Nate Ebner, who had received permission from the franchise to pursue his Olympic dream in rugby. A former teenage rugby star, he had made the United States' rugby sevens team, and was set to compete at the Olympics in Rio. The first day of camp, teammate and fellow special teams star Matthew Slater wore Ebner's No. 43 as a way to honor his buddy. (Over the course of the first couple of weeks of camp, the team would gather to watch Ebner's matches on TV, while coaches would don Ebner's rugby number, 12, during one of the joint workouts with the Saints.)

"I've talked to Nate several times. [I] wish him well in his endeavor," Belichick said. "It's a great opportunity for him to follow his passion, participate in the Olympic Games. We're pulling for him to bring back something around his neck."

Ebner fell short of his ultimate goal—the U.S. team was eventually eliminated by Fiji and failed to medal—and he returned to the team in mid-August. (It wasn't the only reason, but it probably wasn't coincidental that the Patriots coverage units were pretty bad in the preseason opener against the Saints, allowing punt returns of 48 yards and 19 yards, and a kick return of 30 yards.)

The rest of the roster? They spent that time doing a lot of running. That group included the quarterback, even though he wasn't supposed to take a significant snap until October. Not only was he running The Hill with the rest of his teammates, but there were multiple occasions where Brady was on the field for an hour after practice had ended, working in the far corner of the field with a resistance band and a staffer, doing sprints, and mixing in some drop-back work.

The events of the previous year-plus had undoubtedly stoked Brady's competitive fire. It wouldn't be a surprise if he considered walking away from his post-practice routine, then thought of the prospect of a cackling Goodell and then decided to return for one or two more reps with the resistance band. But in a post-Deflategate world—and facing a four-game ban to start the 2016 regular-season—his work on The Hill and his attention to the post-practice portion of his schedule were another sign that when it came to the veteran quarterback, the training camp focus was still where it needed to be: in the corner of the practice field, working on resistance-band drills and putting down that investment he hoped would pay off in January and February.

"I try to approach it the same way [and] I think that's been successful for me," Brady said before one August practice that summer. "I don't try to change a whole bunch of things up. I try to work hard every day, and I try to do what I need to do on the practice field to prepare myself. That's just kind of what the routine is. . . . In the meantime, I'm just trying to prepare this week like I would have last year and the year before, and just try to prepare the best I can so I can be the best quarterback that I can for this team."

"Whatever circumstance you put Tom in, he's never going to change," said Gronkowski, who had returned to the field that summer to start workouts. "If he's suspended, if he's not suspended, if he's playing, if he's not playing—no matter what the circumstances are, I've never seen Tom Brady come out and not give it all in practice. There's never any change in him."

Despite the insistence he was trying to make it seem as normal as possible, it was a strange summer for the veteran. There were some unexplained absences. The preseason schedule was all out of whack. The simple fact was that no matter how well he did or how much film he watched, he was still going to have to sit. For a guy who approached every practice like he was playing for his job—even at the age of thirty-nine—there was a sense of injustice.

But there were two things to remember when it came to why he was going so hard that summer: First, he was a starting quarterback on one of the best teams in the NFL. Going hard went with the territory. Second, Brady is not wired like your average individual. He's completely aware of how he got his shot as a starting quarterback. He worked and worked and worked some more in 2000 and the days leading up to the 2001 season, and when his opportunity arose to unseat an entrenched starting quarterback, he made the most of it. That's not to try and draw a direct line between Brady and Drew Bledsoe. And it's not to say he didn't get along with Garoppolo or any of the other backups he encountered along the way. It's just that he's possessive about his job, and he's obsessive in his quest to keep it. And he knows that it only takes a little slippage for an entrenched starter to be yesterday's news in the NFL. That nature is one thing that kept him so great for such an extended period of time.

"I'm just taking the advice of Coach Belichick, and whatever he wants to do, I'm going to do everything I can to be ready to go when I'm called upon," Brady said. "That's what my responsibility is, so that's what I'm preparing to do."

When he was on the field, there was a familiar consistency. In a summer of uncertainty, the practice field was where he found refuge from the madness that had swirled around him for the previous year-plus. The quarterback reveled in the drudgery of those workouts, but where he really lit up was in the side sessions with the pass catchers who had been welcomed into his circle of trust. The sessions, which usually took place during special teams drills, were held in a far corner of the field, away from the rest of the team and occasionally under the watchful eye of one or two coaches. These were high-level periods where the quarterback demanded nothing short of excellence. In previous years, it had included Randy Moss and Wes Welker, and occasionally included one or two defensive backs as well. (The one-on-one sessions between

Darrelle Revis and Gronkowski in the summer of 2014—with Brady throwing to the tight end while Revis tried to shut him down—were amazing to watch.) In those moments, Brady was not taking an interest in those guys because he liked them. The goal was to help craft the foundation for offensive success down the road, working on a series of routes and combinations that would ensure everyone was on the same page. A quick nod or hand gesture communicated from quarterback to target on a quiet practice field in May, June, or July can be the difference in a game that's won or lost in November.

In the summer of 2016, those sessions included Bennett, Edelman, and Gronkowski, as well as cameo appearances from others like fullback James Develin and wide receiver Aaron Dobson. In those gatherings, the work was crisp and the direction was clear. The goal on each play? Perfection. And while they didn't hit the mark dead-center on every occasion, there was enough good there to see that a completely healthy New England offense was going to be a bear to try and deal with.

Once practice was complete, there were many aspects to Brady's post-practice workout regimen. The biggest thing, however, was not necessarily building speed or cardio. Brady was never going to be mistaken for Michael Vick; Edelman had referred to him on occasion as "The Clydesdale," although he would occasionally show an ability to take off and run in 2016—even missing the first four games of the season, he broke 60 yards rushing for the year for the first time since 2011. Instead, it was the ability to remain as flexible and as pliable as possible. Early in his career, it was clear that when Brady was sacked, he showed an ability to minimize damage on his body by focusing on remaining limber. While other quarterbacks would go down awkwardly, Brady seemed to use a

Gumby-like flexibility to find a way to absorb the hit that would allow him to get back up and continue playing. (Other than the hit he took from Bernard Pollard at the start of the 2008 season, of course.) Part of that was due in part to his diet; he no longer consumed dairy, white sugar, or white flour, which helped with flexibility. But the truth of the matter was that one of the things that continued to define him as a player and as an athlete was the fact that he relied more on flexibility than on pure strength.

Above all else, Brady could still compartmentalize. Despite all the nonsense, he could keep his focus on what was important. That's because when it came to ignoring the noise, over the course of the summer, it was clear Brady's headphones worked better than anyone else's around the league.

"I always try to do the best that I can to prepare and be ready to go," Brady said. "That's the kind of mode that I've got to get into, and that's what I've been trying to do. We try to do that in the spring and try to do that during training camp and deal with the situation as it comes. That's just where the focus has been. . . . I've obviously got work to do, and that's where my focus is."

While his media sessions were few and far between at the start of training camp, he did surprise folks when he showed up unannounced for Faulk's induction ceremony into the Patriots Hall of Fame on August 1 . . . wearing a Faulk jersey. It was a nice little way to return the favor for Faulk wearing the Brady jersey during the draft. Onstage with his former teammate sporting Faulk's old No. 33, Brady said he felt "a lot faster in this jersey already."

"Faster, more elusive, better hands," he said. "A lot tougher."

The quarterback also praised Faulk's contributions to the team as "exceptional," and noted that he was there to help induct someone who was less than a year older than he was.

"It's such a special night," he said. "What's not very special about tonight is when the guys that are going into the Hall of Fame are your age."

Brady was smiling when he said it, but he raised an interesting point. The age disparity between veterans and rookies was one thing. There were generational differences that arose in every locker room between the twentysomethings and thirtysomethings. But at the age of thirty-nine, the difference between Brady and some of his teammates was more like a chasm. By way of example, rookie linebacker Elandon Roberts was seven years old when Brady and the 2001 Patriots won Super Bowl XXXVI. Being able to connect with teammates almost half his age was an ongoing challenge he spoke about later in the season.

"I'm a hell of a lot older than most guys in the league now . . . I think that's part of the fun part for me. Your role always changes, and still as a leader and a veteran, I still can express things to my younger teammates and things they're going through and try to help them through those things, because I've been through those things," he said. "I have a lot of experiences where Tedy [Bruschi] helped me and Rodney [Harrison] helped me and Willie [Mc-Ginest] helped me. . . .

"It may not be like we're going out together on Friday nights, but it might mean more than that. I might be able to share things that might be able to help them in their career or help them with their family just because of the experiences that I've had . . . I love that. I try to embrace that . . . and that's a great responsibility. . . ."

Alongside teammates who were in grade school when he won his first Super Bowl, Brady continued to prep with the feverish intensity of a man who was going to play all sixteen games. But the spotlight shifted more and more to Garoppolo. The young signal-caller with the movie-star looks—as a rookie, his team-mates compared him to the animated Prince Aladdin from the Disney movie—he hadn't taken a single significant snap in his two seasons in New England. But now, the second-round pick out of Eastern Illinois was being trusted to hold the fort in the wake of Brady's ban. It was an occasionally dicey situation, one fraught with the possibility of disaster: Was the youngster gunning to un-seat the veteran superstar? Was there the possibility of anger and enmity between the two? And what might happen if the kid was snapped in half by a rogue defensive lineman?

But Garoppolo had prepped for this opportunity longer than many had realized. In high school, when he was being tutored by throwing coach Jeff Christensen, he was put through the same series of drills that Brady endured at the hands of his late quarter-backing guru, Tom Martinez. (Martinez, who was a touchstone for Brady from high school through college and into the NFL, passed away in 2012.) It makes sense that a young quarterback would try and take whatever he could from the likes of Brady. But Christensen said with Garoppolo, it went beyond the usual.

"This is so surreal to me, it's almost frightening," Christensen said after the Patriots took Garoppolo in 2014. "EVERYTHING we did was off Tom Brady. Brady set the standard for perfect technique, and so it just made sense for us to follow everything that Tom Martinez did with Brady."

He added: "I don't know if I brainwashed him, but he's been raised on Tom Brady's technique ever since he was in high school. Literally, it was all Brady, all the time."

In college, Garoppolo started all forty-five games that he ap-peared in for EIU and completed 623 percent of his passes for 13,151 yards to go along with 118 touchdowns and 51 interceptions.

When he was drafted in 2014, he didn't have the national rep of some of the other quarterbacks taken that year, but his foundation with Christensen and the Martinez method helped make things a little easier in the New England system.

Garoppolo wasn't Brady. Not by a long shot. But that summer, he stepped adroitly into the spotlight, holding his own in the face of what was a suddenly national media crush. If there was any doubt he had learned from Brady on multiple levels, that was dismissed pretty quickly. Garoppolo managed to distinguish himself as a leader from the first time he arrived at Gillette Stadium; in his first spring as a rookie, he would walk up to fellow first-year players and give them a play, and those youngsters had to respond with what their responsibility was on that play. It was a small sample size, but it certainly reminded some of the way Brady went about his business as a first-year player. As a rookie in 2000, he commanded the scout team offense in a way that caught the attention of the rest of the roster, and ultimately paved the way for his ascension.

But that was a tough line to walk; Garoppolo had to exhibit leadership characteristics and distinguish himself because he was a quarterback. He had to command the huddle. But he also had to be mindful of his place in the overall pecking order. On the sidelines, that played out in stark terms. When the starting offense would come off the field, Brady would come off the field and sit on one end of the bench next to offensive coordinator Josh McDaniels. The backup would have to stand off to the side, or find a cooler to sit on while listening in. The bottom line was that he could exert leadership skills in certain situations, but also had to have the level of self-awareness to be deferential at other times. For any competitor, it's tough to do.

That summer, Garoppolo wasn't walking up to Edelman or Gronkowski in the cafeteria and quizzing them about play calls. But there was an air of assuredness when it came to him that came through with both his teammates (in the locker room and on the practice field) and the media in his weekly press availability. With reporters, the youngster was pleasant and answered every question, but also proved to be a quick study when it came to the art of speaking nicely but saying nothing: "Your guess is as good as mine," was a favorite fallback phrase for him when he was asked about what might happen in the future.

There were rumors that he and Brady didn't get along. But over the previous couple of seasons, a level of comfort and familiarity developed between them to the point where, according to one longtime observer of the team, Garoppolo had become Brady's second-favorite younger backup behind Brian Hoyer, an immensely popular signal-caller who had bounced around the league for a few seasons after being released by New England after the 2011 season.

It's important to note that Brady and Garoppolo weren't best pals for a few reasons, including the fact that there was a massive age difference between the two. Garoppolo was ten years old and in grade school when Brady and the Patriots won Super Bowl XXXVI. Garoppolo was a single guy on his rookie contract; Brady was wealthy beyond his wildest dreams, married to the world's most famous supermodel, and had multiple children. Even if they were particularly close, those sorts of differences would create a gulf between two people that would be difficult to bridge. Instead, what you had with the two of them at that point in their careers was a positive working relationship that was more productive than either of the two most successful quarterback succession plans that had played out in previous years in Brett Favre/Aaron Rodgers and Joe Montana/Steve Young.

"I love being with Jimmy," Brady said when he was asked what it would be like to see Garoppolo under center for the first four games of the season. "I wish him the very best, obviously, for our team, for him personally. When you see people who it means a lot to, you always want them to succeed, as well. It will be tough to watch, but I will be excited to watch and excited to learn. And hopefully when I come back in October, I'll be a better player than I am today."

In a perfect world for the Patriots, despite the age difference, the relationship between the two would run along the same path as the one enjoyed by Brady and Drew Bledsoe (as well as veterans like Damon Huard and John Friesz) in 2000 and 2001.

"I think you're learning a lot from those guys. At least I was," Brady said of the other QBs through the years. "I was trying to learn a lot from Drew Bledsoe, and I learned a lot from Drew because he was such a phenomenal player and leader. He was tough, disciplined. It meant so much to him. I think I learned a lot from him, I learned a lot from Damon, I learned a lot from John Friesz when I was first here. I think I used all those people as great examples because they were already pros. I had a lot to learn. I just came in, tried to do the best I could do with the experiences that I already had and then tried to transition those to a different level, a different caliber of playing, and just do the best I could do. It's easy to do when you love what you do."

This wasn't just lip service. The quarterback room turned out to be a very positive place in 2016. The three signal-callers— Brady, Garoppolo, and Brissett—would eventually start to call themselves "The Wolfpack," a reference to Zach Galifianakis's speech from *The Hangover*. (Brady would take that public by posting part of Galifianakis's speech on his Instagram page, and Brissett would wear a "Wolfpack" shirt with a picture of all three quarterbacks on it the day of the Super Bowl.) No one was quite sure which quarterback was Alan, Stu, Phil, or Doug, but it was a group that managed to form the same sort of unique connection.

"The group is awesome together," Brissett said. "Just helping each other out, and learning from each other, going out there and competing against each other, even when we're in the classroom. I feel like it's a healthy relationship."

But there were still questions to be answered about how the reps were going to be divided up and how the summer workload would be distributed. So it was no surprise that 16 of the 22 questions in Belichick's first press conference of camp had to do with Brady, Garoppolo, or the quarterback situation in general, including one hypothetical that included the possibility of Brady sitting when he came back because of an otherworldly performance from Garoppolo for the first four games.

Belichick wanted to make it clear: Brady was not about to get Wally Pipp-ed by Garoppolo, at least not this time around. It was going to be Brady's job when he returned.

"Tom will return as the starting quarterback when he comes back," Belichick said. "But in the meantime, we have to prioritize the first part of our schedule, and that'll be to get Jimmy ready to go."

For Belichick, the challenge was unlike anything he had faced over the course of his coaching career. The head coach, who turned sixty-four that off-season, first went to training camp as a special assistant with the Baltimore Colts in 1975 at the age of twenty-three, and he'd been working in the league ever since. That July marked the start of his 42nd consecutive season in the National Football League, the last 17 of which had come as head coach of the Patriots. Belichick was the longest-tenured head coach in the league with his current team (the closest was Cincy's Marvin Lewis, who took over the Bengals in 2003), marking an impressive run for any coach in the NFL.

Since 2001, he had been gifted with a remarkable run of stability at the quarterback position. But now, the coach had to change things up a bit if he wanted to make sure his team was ready for the 2016 season. When it came to coaching, there was always some carryover in preparation, but in his experience, his approach over the previous 41 seasons was to take each one as its own animal. And no matter who was under center for the first four games of the season, 2016 would be no different in that regard. Change would dictate the need to remain as flexible as possible.

"Fundamentally, I think a lot of things are the same; things you have to do in camp in order to prepare for a season," Belichick said at the dawn of the new season. "But each year is different. Players are different, teams we play are different, things change in the league, there are some rule modifications, or whatever. Things like that. So, every year is different and the chemistry—each team is different. Even with some of the same players there's still always a little bit of a different mix."

Of course, the challenge of getting two different quarterbacks ready could be tough; you needed to make sure that the signal-callers both got up to speed, and that the new guys got their chance to build chemistry with each quarterback. It was something that the Patriots had never had to worry about in the Brady/ Belichick Era. No matter how unsettled the rest of the depth chart was, you knew what was going to happen at the quarterback position. It was going to be Brady, and then everyone else.

But the reps were split fairly evenly over the course of the summer, as the two appeared to evenly divvy up the workload. While it was occasionally tough to figure out personnel schemes, both quarterbacks got plenty of chances with the starters, as well as the backups.

The biggest difference? That came in the preseason games. Brady usually ramped up his in-game workload over the course of the summer, peaking in the third game, where he played most or all of the first three-plus quarters. Now, there was some sense of mystery to the whole thing. Brady missed the preseason opener with what was later described as a mysterious "personal issue." He missed the second one of the summer because he apparently cut his finger while getting something off his cleats. He played in the third and fourth preseason games, even while some were wondering: *If he's not playing in the first four regular season games, what's the point in risking him in* any *preseason games? Get the kid ready!*

Part of the whole preseason "Who was going to start at quarterback?" drama appealed to Belichick's coaching nature. The coach often used the preseason games to throw curveballs at his team to see how they might respond to an unforeseen set of circumstances. He would routinely yank a guy from a preseason contest—sometimes, trying to mimic an injury situation—just to gauge the response of the coaches and the rest of the players on the roster. (In one preseason game against the Giants, he had wide receiver Troy Brown take a few snaps under center.) Was the backup ready to go? How did the teammates alongside him respond? Was there any slippage in play? Anything to try and get a read on how a scenario might play out for real. Their reaction could often provide some insight into whether or not they'd be ready to go when the regular season rolled around. And the uncertainty at the quarterback situation that summer allowed him to get a read on just how prepared his offense was when it came to game action. After all, it just takes one injury to change everything. Would they be ready?

Garoppolo did get more game reps than usual over the first two preseason contests because Brady wasn't there, and there were some uneven performances in the early going from the youngster. His training camp performances were up and down; after a good start—including a razor-sharp 10-for-10 on 11-on-11 drills with the No. 2 offense in one session at the end of the first week—there were struggles in the second week of camp. Despite having the opportunity to work with the ones, a group that included Gronkowski and Bennett, he had issues moving the ball. It wasn't all his fault obviously, but the occasional ineffectiveness was striking, especially in comparison with Brady, who looked like he was having a very good summer.

Garoppolo had his good points: there was an 8-for-11 stretch late in his start against the Saints where he looked sharp, a series that was capped off by a 56-yard pass play to White where the back scooted impressively through traffic. But there were shaky parts as well, including the start of that same game where he was 3-for-7 for 33 yards and a pair of sacks. It was those sorts of outings that caused even the most optimistic Patriots fan to walk back from the idea of a 4-0 or 3-1 start.

One other thing that gave New Englanders some pause was the fact that Garoppolo still had issues when it came to scrambling. Against the Saints, he was able to pick up a first down on a rushing attempt, but the fact that he didn't slide upset some of the coaches. The quarterback chalked that up to eagerness, adding that was when being a football player just kicked in. In a round-about way, it would be a lesson he'd learn the hard way sooner rather than later.

The Brady-Garoppolo reps breakdown was just one of several dozen things that stood out over the course of the summer. When the Bears came to town for joint practices in mid-August, the intensity was cranked up a bit for two reasons: one, it's always good to spend a few days measuring yourself against another team for once instead of your own. And two, Chicago came to town with a rep as, in the words of their own quarterback, Jay Cutler, a "dumb" team. In the heat of the summer, that can result in the occasional scrap. And while there were no such throwdowns when the Saints came calling earlier in the month, things got a little heated when the Bears showed up.

First, it has to be acknowledged that football fights are stupid, pointless exercises that involve guys swinging on each other while wearing helmets. Of course, if you've been banging on an opponent for the better part of two hours in 90 degree heat, you're *probably* not thinking straight anyway, and so it's reasonable to think that's what happened when the Patriots and Bears met under the hot sun on August 15. Near the end of the fully padded practice, things boiled over. The main event was a showdown between Malcolm Butler and Chicago receiver Alshon Jeffery that featured more than a dozen participants from each side. Butler got tossed, while Jeffery was allowed to watch the rest of practice from the sideline.

Brady finally saw his first game action of the summer in Week Three of the preseason in Carolina against the Panthers. That night, after Garoppolo started, Brady came off the bench, his first relief role since September 23, 2001, when Mo Lewis knocked Bledsoe sideways. The place lit up, and the reigning MVP Cam Newton wasn't even the most relevant quarterback in his own building. Coming off the bench late in the first quarter, Brady delivered an instant jolt of electricity to an otherwise sleepy preseason affair. *It's him! He's playing! Brady's playing!* His first pass attempt of the night was a 37-yarder to Dobson, which set up a field goal. Good, but the real payoff came on the next drive, where he dropped a perfectly placed pass right into Hogan's arms as the new receiver was flying down the right sideline, a 33-yard touchdown reception that was as good as you were going to get when it came to preseason football. In the end, the numbers weren't terribly impressive for either quarterback—Brady finished 3-for-9 for 76 yards with 1 touchdown, while Garoppolo was 9-for-15 for 57 yards—but the eye test certainly revealed that Brady was ready to roll.

Brady didn't talk after the game, but Belichick offered a fairly standard assessment of where they were at that point in the summer: good, but there was still work that needed to be done.

"We've moved ahead in a lot of areas, but we're certainly not where we need to be," Belichick said after the 19–17 preseason win. "I don't think any player is, any coach is. I'm sure no team is at this point. We're all making progress, which is good. We've just got to keep our foot on the gas."

And keeping in line with the Patriots' nontraditional summer, Brady played the following week as well, marking the first time he started a final preseason game in five years. Playing every snap in the first half, he went 16-for-26 for 166 yards and 1 touchdown (a 7-yard pass play to Keshawn Martin late in the first quarter), and one interception. Brady also connected with Dobson a few times, including a 38-yarder.

"I was happy I was able to play as much as I did," Brady said. "It was a good opportunity to get out there and play. We did a decent job of moving the ball, but we turned it over too many times."

His last play before he started his four-game exile? A kneel down at the end of the first half in a 17–9 preseason loss to the Giants.

"I haven't thought about it much," Brady said after the game when asked about his looming ban. "I always take it as it comes and do the best that I could do."

The summer culminated with a series of final cuts. In a mild surprise, Knighton was let go, as well as running back Donald Brown. The most notable cut was probably Dobson, the second-round pick who finally ran out of chances in New England after three occasionally tantalizing but mostly fruitless seasons. Also out the door was offensive lineman Bryan Stork, an ornery and occasionally brilliant performer who was absolutely stellar as a rookie in 2014, but whose performance slipped dramatically over the 2015 season, partly because of head and neck issues.

(The Stork situation was an odd one. Reports initially surfaced that he was released. Then, there was a story that he had been traded to the Redskins. Then, a failed physical nullified the deal. Eventually, the Patriots cut Stork loose, and after no one picked him up, he decided to retire following the 2016 season.)

They also went out of their way to acquire underperforming linebacker Barkevious Mingo from the Browns for a fifth-round pick in 2017. The crazy-lean Mingo, who once flirted with a 5,000-calorie-a-day diet in hopes of maintaining his playing weight, was another classic case of a high draft pick not working out with another team and the Patriots taking him on, hoping to find him a role.

The conventional wisdom was that Mingo would be able to find a spot as a backup linebacker, but as the year went on, it was clear New England had other ideas in mind. Mingo and fellow linebacker Shea McClellin (another former first-round pick who was acquired by the Patriots that off-season) would help form part of an impressive special teams nucleus. Mingo would end up playing a whopping 72 percent of the special teams snaps in 2016, serving as a long-limbed disruptor who was a handful to deal with. McClellin worked into the defensive rotation as needed, but also developed a rep as a core special teamer.

Turns out New England would need defensive depth, especially in the early going. Days before the start of the regular season, there was a lightning bolt of an announcement: Rob Ninkovich was hit with a four-game suspension to start the season after testing positive for a banned substance. The veteran was expected to be out for the first month with a triceps injury, but for a guy who had a spotless reputation, it was a shocking turn of events. He owned it, and expressed culpability over what happened.

"Any supplement I've ever used was bought at a store. I was unaware something I bought had a substance in it that would give me a positive test because it wasn't listed [as an ingredient]," Ninkovich told Mike Reiss of ESPN. "One thing I have learned is that if a supplement is not NSF certified, there are no regulations that ensure that what is on the label is 100 percent accurate. That is a hard lesson for me to learn at this stage in my career, but I take responsibility for it. It's a mistake I made and it hurts that I won't be there for my teammates."

In the post-2007 era, Ninkovich was one of New England's greatest success stories. He was a primary example of the Patriots' ability to identify someone wasting away in another system and make him a key component in their own program. An available body who was signed in August 2009 after stops in New Orleans and Miami, he was thought to be the type of player who could add some depth on special teams and (maybe) defense. But in short order, he had managed to become an absolutely vital part of the New England defense for a few reasons, not the least of which was his ability to play defensive end, as well as both outside and inside linebacker. In many ways, he was a Vrabel-esque presence who had a knack for versatility and durability; in addition to being able to line up and play at multiple spots, he boasted the third-longest streak of consecutive games played (102) among NFL defensive ends at the end of the 2015 season. Adding to his résumé was the fact that he almost always came up big against the Jets. On several occasions, he managed to stick a dagger in New York with a game-changing play, either a forced fumble, fumble recovery, or interception. Ninkovich did it all.

While Belichick isn't the type who dips into hyperbole, he was almost always willing to talk about Ninkovich, who was one of just three guys in the NFL who had at least 18 sacks, 4 interceptions, and 8 passes defensed between 2010 and 2012. (Clay Matthews and LaMarr Woodley were the other two.)

"Rob's got a great feel for the game," Belichick said of Ninkovich in 2016. "First of all, he's got great physical skills. He can run, he's athletic, he's strong, so he can hang in there against the big guys but is athletic [enough] to play in space. Whether that be in the kicking game or as an off-the-line linebacker; you can drop him into coverage from the line of scrimmage.

"Mentally, he sees the game as well. He can move around, do different things. He doesn't get bogged down. He has the ability to play in coverage, which means you have to see the game a little bit behind you in pass coverage. It's not all in front of you, especially in zone defense. There are plays behind you. You have to have an awareness for where receivers are, where people are on the field.

"Mike [Vrabel] was able to do that. Junior [Seau] was able to do that, although Junior primarily played inside linebacker, but he played on the line quite a bit, rushed quite a bit. Tedy [Bruschi] certainly did that over the course of his career even though the majority of his college career was down and the majority of his pro career was up, but he showed the ability to do both of those things at a very high level . . . Lawrence [Taylor] did that, Carl [Banks] did that, Pepper [Johnson] did that in New York."

The loss of Ninkovich presented a new series of challenges for New England. He led New England's front seven in snaps in 2015 while notching 6.5 sacks and a career-high 7 pass deflections. The bottom line was that between the trade of Jones and loss of Ninkovich, the Patriots would be losing 19 of their 49 sacks from 2015 in the first four games of 2016. Defensive end Jabaal Sheard was a pleasant surprise with 8 sacks the previous season, but while he was set to return, someone else would have to assert himself as a consistent and steady presence when it came to New England's pass rush. While it was a possibility that Mingo and McClellin could also chip in as needed, the early money was on youngster Trey Flowers, a country-strong lineman who flashed positively at times during training camp after a solid 2015 season. Flowers, who once said his football inspiration was Bobby Boucher—Adam Sandler's character in *The Waterboy*—would take on greater importance in 2016 than he had in his first two seasons in the league.

As the regular season loomed without Brady, Ninkovich, right tackle Sebastian Vollmer, and Lewis (who was still rehabbing a knee injury he had suffered the previous season), there was talk of the Patriots being vulnerable over the first four games. The Broncos, Ravens, Steelers, Chiefs, Colts, Bills, and Dolphins were all poised as potential challengers to New England for AFC supremacy. But as the season dawned, the one team above all others who might have the best chance of taking advantage of Brady's absence was Baltimore. Gifted with a relatively easy schedule to open the year—they faced the Bills, Browns, Jaguars, Raiders, and Redskins right out of the gate, teams that went a combined 32–48 in 2015—the Ravens were the one AFC team that could conceivably start fast and boast of a track record of mental toughness and an ability to hold up down the stretch.

But Brady or no Brady, no teams were taking New England lightly, at least publicly.

"(Jimmy) Garoppolo can play," Jets coach Todd Bowles told the New York *Daily News* as New York opened camp. "They don't worry about who they have. They just have a system in place and they go play football. I think people underestimate that. You still have to knock off the champs. It's theirs until somebody takes it from them.

"They've got a good team," Bowles added. "They're a tough team. They're a tough out. They've had a coach and a quarterback and a system in place for a long time. There's a bunch of ways to skin a cat. They've found pretty good ways to skin it. They do what they have to."

And more than a few players were a little put out about the fact Brady wouldn't be out there for a quarter of the season. They followed the philosophy of Ric Flair: To be the best, you have to beat the best. And if Brady was going to be out, a win over the Patriots didn't mean as much as it would have if the two-time MVP was under center.

"I don't like playing the Patriots when [Brady is] not on the field," Jets defensive lineman Sheldon Richardson told reporters. "I like knocking the top dogs off their chair. Personally, I like the challenge. I like going against the best. [Brady is] one of the best. Probably the best to ever play."

"I am glad they [have] problems. I don't care," Pittsburgh running back D'Angelo Williams told reporters who asked about what it meant to play the Patriots without Brady. "Everybody has their problems, and I am glad they have theirs. . . . I don't know why everybody thinks that affects us. We don't care. You think [Steelers quarterback Ben Roethlisberger] wants to beat a Brady-less team? That proves nothing to him."

Of course, Brady was gone, but there were reminders of his presence everywhere. Just prior to the start of his suspension, the Patriots hung a giant banner of their quarterback along the length of the lighthouse at Gillette Stadium. The sentiment behind the banner was the same as when the team changed its Twitter avatar on the night of the draft to a shot of a Brady jersey. Brady was gone, but he certainly wasn't going to be forgotten.

It was also fairly reminiscent of what the Saints did the year that coach Sean Payton was suspended a full season because of Bountygate. That year, New Orleans hung a giant banner of the coach inside the practice facility with the message "Do Your Job." With that in mind, it was no surprise that the Saints coach retweeted a picture of the Brady banner off the Patriots' account.

"There aren't a lot of people that can understand what Tom's going through," Payton said when quizzed by ESPN about tweeting a shot of the banner. "Certainly, I'm one of them."

(Then there was what the Saints did when the two teams got together for joint practices in 2015. That week, their Twitter feed posted a shot of a New England fan and a Saints fan next to each other and a message that included the hashtag #defendthewall, a popular phrase among the Patriots' fan base when it came to the ongoing battle with Goodell.)

While Payton may not have come from the Belichick coaching tree, he managed to build a close relationship with the Patriots' coach over the years, one that was deepened in the wake of their franchises' shared experiences with the commissioner. That much was clear after Belichick was asked about Payton's decision to Tweet the picture of the banner.

"I have a good friendship with Sean," Belichick noted. "We go back quite a ways. We've had a great working relationship, great professional relationship and a good personal relationship, so, I've always appreciated his support. He's had ours. We've had his. You can't say that about everybody, but certainly he's been a good friend and good supporter."

"It's nice," Garoppolo told WEEI when asked about the Brady banner. "It overlooks the whole stadium. It's a nice little reminder of what's going on. It's good to have it there."

Belichick appreciated the support from Payton. But the banner itself? Not so much.

"Yeah, really focused on Arizona right now," Belichick said. "That's who we play this week. All the other decorative and marketing things and so forth are not really part of the team's preparation. We're focused on Arizona."

That focus took a hit, however, as the Friday before the game, the team announced that Gronkowski, Solder, and guard Jonathan Cooper would be downgraded to out, and wouldn't accompany the team to Arizona for the opener.

The Summer of Jimmy was complete. The Patriots had done their due diligence, prepared two different quarterbacks, gotten the new faces as acclimated as possible to their system, and were set to jump into the Great Wide Open that was the 2016 regular-season schedule. But with no Brady and no Gronkowski on the road against a team that reached the conference finals the year before, the first challenge of the year wasn't going to be easy.

3. WAKE ME UP WHEN SEPTEMBER ENDS

Licking my chops. You get a rookie quarterback, pretty much, it's always exciting when you get a guy like that for his first game because he's going to be nervous. He's probably going to be sitting there holding the ball a little longer or trying to get rid of it quick, throwing bad balls. As a vet, we definitely pride ourselves on welcoming [quarterbacks] the right way.
—Arizona defensive lineman Calais Campbell in July 2016 on CBS Sports Radio's *Tiki and Tierney,* when asked about playing Jimmy Garoppolo in the opener

I saw a guy who played with great poise. He wasn't rattled by the pressure. [He was] a guy that was an accurate passer, who had some mobility to escape the rush. I saw a guy playing way beyond his years. I was impressed by him.
—Dolphins defensive coordinator Vance Joseph on Garoppolo

You guys might not know this, but I consider myself a bit of a loner. I tend to think of myself as a one-man wolf pack. But when my sister brought Doug home, I knew he was one of my own. And my wolf pack, it grew by one. So there . . . there were two of us in the wolf pack. I was alone first in the pack and then Doug joined in later. And six months ago, when Doug introduced me to you guys, I thought, "Wait a second, could it be?" And now I know for sure: I just added two more guys to my wolf pack.

—Alan Garner, *The Hangover*

Since the whole sordid mess started, Deflategate had become a litmus test for how New England fans viewed the opposition. Some opponents (including coaches and owners) were given more leeway because they came across as more understanding or sympathetic to Brady's cause. Among those who came out OK were those like Aaron Rodgers, who was on record as liking his footballs a little overinflated. In the 2015 preseason, the Green Bay quarterback was conciliatory when asked about Brady and the Patriots, saying that Brady "was a friend," and he could sympathize with what he was going through. Other quarterbacks chimed in with their own support like Roethlisberger ("Tom's the greatest in the world, and I mean that," he said that September), Cutler, and Drew Brees. Most quarterbacks closed ranks around Brady for a few reasons, not the least of which was the fact that they were completely cognizant of what all of this might mean for their own careers.

Of course, there were other teams and other players who felt differently. Owners like Houston's Bob McNair tsk-tsked Brady and the Patriots in the summer of 2015, saying that his guy J. J.

Watt would have handled things differently if he had to turn over his cell phone to the league: "What escalated the whole thing is that Brady and the Patriots were going to cooperate fully, and then when it came down to it, they didn't. If it was J. J. Watt, I think he would have been cooperative, and it wouldn't be a question," McNair told Houston's Sportsradio 610. "*I don't think J.J. would destroy his cell phone.*" (For the record, Brady has denied destroying his phone in reaction to the investigation.)

And as the 2016 regular season loomed, Brady's critics apparently included Arizona quarterback Carson Palmer, the rare example of a veteran signal-caller who didn't necessarily see eye-to-eye with Brady and the way he went about his business.

"I tried not to follow [Deflategate] just because it was everywhere for so long, but I go back and . . . you follow what the rulebook says and go about your business and your work, and if they tell you not to do it and you get busted and what happens, happens, then you suffer the consequences," Palmer said in the days prior to the opener. "Whatever the league comes down upon and whatever ruling they make is what they make. You don't have much of a decision after that and you can fight it for a little bit. But after awhile, you've just got to abide by what they say."

That pretty much ended any sort of good feeling that Patriots fans might have had toward Palmer. From that point on, he was consigned to New England's enemies list, a group that would include former players turned analysts Bart Scott, Marshall Faulk, and others as the season continued.

But the simple fact was that Brady was now gonzo. Out for the first four games of the regular season. He was seen here and there over the month. He was in Michigan at a Wolverines game where he played catch with his son and hung out with Wolverines head coach Jim Harbaugh. He went to Italy with his wife, where he was spotted sunbathing in the nude by paparazzi. He started his own "newspaper," the *TB Times*, via social media. (It would publish a mock front page following every Patriots game that would pop up on Facebook as soon as the game was done.) He filmed a bunch of commercials and hype videos (including one for Team USA's appearance in the Ryder Cup), and served as a pro- motional pitchman for his TB12 brand—he gave interviews and did his part to help move merchandise. (In one interview, he con- fessed to never having eaten a strawberry.)

And he discovered the Red Zone Channel. Sounding like a suburban dad who stumbled across the programming by hap- penstance one weekend when he was sitting on the couch, he marveled at what it offered.

"I watched that one channel—that Red Zone Channel that captures everything, which is pretty amazing," Brady told Jim Gray of Westwood One as part of his weekly interview series. "It's a great way to kind of watch how a lot of the flows of the games are going. You see a lot of situations. There's a lot to learn every week in the NFL."

During his time away, Brady did engage in a little rest and re- laxation. But there was also throwing to be done, and while his wife, supermodel Gisele Bundchen, jokingly posted a picture of the two of them tossing a football back and forth at one point that month, there was also some more serious work going on. He spent some quality time with old friend Wes Welker, as well as Ryan McManus, a former Dartmouth receiver who had worked out for the Patriots the previous spring. Those sessions were about as high-intensity as he could get for those four weeks.

But there was no football for him in Foxboro. Not only was he not allowed to be on the premises at Gillette Stadium, he wasn't allowed to practice with his teammates. While he got into the Red Zone Channel, he couldn't watch game film. He had to fundamentally remove a piece of his brain that had been in place since he was a teenager.

Back in southeastern Massachusetts, it was a strange and surreal thing for the quarterback to be missing from the facility. The rest of the roster had to go on without Brady, the only player around the team since 2001 (other than the 2008 season). And the idea of heading into the regular season opener on the road against the Cardinals, a team that some had picked as a Super Bowl favorite? It was a sizable challenge for any franchise, much less one that would be operating without its starting quarterback.

For Julian Edelman, it went above and beyond. The receiver with the most experience in the New England system, he had gone from being a seventh-round afterthought in 2009 to Brady's favorite target—from 2013 to 2015, he had 258 catches. (Only four other guys—Antonio Brown, Demaryius Thomas, Julio Jones, and Brandon Marshall—had more receptions in that same span.) You toss in his postseason heroics, which included 9 catches for 109 yards and a touchdown in Super Bowl XLIX, and you could make a case he had grown into one of the most important offensive players in the league. And a large part of that was because of his deep and abiding relationship with the quarterback.

There was a long-running debate as to the most vital presence in the Patriots' offense, but there was no doubt about Edelman's bona fides when it came to his chemistry with Brady. The two California natives had found a second home in New England, and spent a considerable amount of time together off the field. The truth was that Edelman was simply following a long tradition of undersized overachievers bonding with Brady: it started with Troy Brown, and included Faulk, Deion Branch, and Welker. Brady welcomed the big-play targets over the years like Gronkowski and Randy Moss. But the little guys with the make-you-miss ability and knowledge of how to get to the sticks on a third-down pass play had always been his offensive bread and butter.

Ultimately, Edelman came in for plenty of ribbing when it came to his relationship with Brady, but the bromance between the two was very real. That's why Edelman sounded pretty melancholy when he was asked about not having Brady around as the regular season loomed.

"I'm not going to lie; it's like one of your buddies going to jail," Edelman said of the situation in early September. "It's one of those types of things. The whole situation is unfortunate, but it's happened and we've got to move on. We love him to death—on the field, off the field, he's been a great help in my life. But we've got to deal with the situation. And right now, the situation is thinking about the Arizona Cardinals and who's going to be out there to play against these guys."

Edelman had a few questions of his own heading into the 2016 season, particularly when it came to his health. The receiver had blown out his left foot at the end of the 2015 regular season, and spent six-plus games on the sideline before returning for the playoffs. But he was also in a walking boot for a sizable portion of the off-season, and when he went down with what appeared to be a foot issue in one of the joint practices against the Saints in early August, all of New England held its breath. It turned out to be a minor thing, but it simply underscored the delicate nature of life at the top of the food chain in the NFL: one false step, and it can all come crumbling down in a blink.

While Edelman had limited reps in the preseason, he appeared to be in fine form as the opener approached. But at the same time, his situation had some similarities to just about everyone else in the league at the start of the regular season. Because of limits on practice time and padded practices that were instituted as part of the previous Collective Bargaining Agreement, teams were more uncertain than ever when it came to an overall state of readiness heading into the regular season. Sure, you can do your due diligence when it comes to conditioning and practice and game planning, but the reality of the situation is that when all 32 teams step off the cliff and into Week One of the regular season, there is no guarantee their parachutes will open . . . or if they will plummet to earth at 900 mph, Wile E. Coyote–style.

The Patriots had questions at quarterback; that much couldn't be denied. But there were ways they could maximize their strengths and minimize any perceived weaknesses. Belichick was able to do it in 2008 when Brady went down with a knee injury in the regular-season opener and they leaned on backup Matt Cassel that year. While Cassel was able to play relatively well and ultimately parlay that season into a sizable new deal and a starting job with the Chiefs, it was the support system around him that year that really allowed him to thrive. In 2007, the Patriots were one of the best passing teams in the history of the league, but in 2008, without Brady, they became one of the best and most effective rushing teams in the NFL that year. They also ramped things up on defense, with more responsibility on the shoulders of a group of veterans who were able to keep them in just about every game.

In hindsight, the 2008 Patriots benefited from an easy schedule, but they also provided enough multiple looks on offense to keep teams on their toes. *If Belichick could do it with Cassel over a full season,* went the thought process in New England, *he could do it with Garoppolo for four games.*

Of course, it's easier said than done. Without Brady, the two things the Patriots knew they needed to get from their offense over the first four weeks of the season were clear: a steady and consistent performance out of the offensive line and a similar effort out of the ground game. The line had settled into place nicely that summer, and despite the fact that Vollmer had been placed on PUP (Physically Unable to Perform) to start the season, there was a sense of optimism there. As Scarnecchia intimated, the juggling that took place in previous years never really materialized. Thuney emerged as a consistently dependable presence at left guard, while the rest of the group—including veteran left tackle Nate Solder, back after almost a year on the shelf because of an injury—stabilized nicely.

As for the running back position, there were some early questions. Over the previous fifteen years, running backs had been viewed as mostly fungible assets in New England. The Patriots had rotated a series of backs through their system in the last dozen-plus years; while they had occasionally utilized relatively early key draft choices on guys like Laurence Maroney, Stevan Ridley, and Shane Vereen, most of the time, they were happy to find plug-and-play guys. That meant there were some surprises along the way in Antowain Smith and BenJarvus Green-Ellis, both of whom surprised by rushing for 1,000-plus yards in the New England system. They did go after a talented back on occasion—Corey Dillon set numerous franchise records when he was with the Patriots. But for the most part, that was a position where they were content to ID some under-the-radar types who might be able to flourish in their system and get coached up by Fears. Because of this approach, it was no surprise that New England had little continuity at running back; dating to his days as head coach of the Browns in the early 1990s, no running back had ever rushed for 1,000 yards in back-to-back seasons under Belichick.

The one thing you pretty much knew? If they were healthy, Blount was going to be the primary between-the-tackles guy, while James White and Dion Lewis would be the best pass-catching options out of the backfield. White was a unique breed in that he almost *never* actually carried the ball in his first two years. To be fair, he was a backup for a sizable portion of that stretch, but the truth was that when he was on the field in 2014 and 2015, the Patriots threw the ball on almost every snap. There weren't a lot of "tells" in the New England offense through that period, but White's presence on the field was one of them. If he was out there, the Patriots were almost certainly going to throw the ball.

With a stabilized offensive line and a cautiously optimistic feeling about the running game, Garoppolo threw himself into the start of the regular season. Publicly, his only misstep came in his first press conference of the regular season when he was asked if he was excited to be the only player teammates were looking to as the leader of the offense. It was an innocuous answer to a fairly routine question.

"Yeah, it's a smoother operation, I'll say that," Garoppolo said of the fact that it was just him and Brissett in the meeting room and at practice. "It's just me and Jacoby [Brissett], all the reps are just between the two of us now, and we kind of know where we sit on that. It's different without Tom [Brady], no question about it. But it is what it is at this point."

Again, a fairly straightforward answer, at least to those who were present for the exchange. But those who didn't see the press conference or those looking to generate more clicks boiled it down to four words—*smoother operation* without Brady—and assumed it was a shot at the old man. It generated conversation for a day or so, but that was pretty much the end of that.

The message to Garoppolo was simple: The Patriots weren't going to radically overhaul their offense because they had to go to a backup quarterback. The only thing he had to do was try not to be Brady. *Be your own man out there.*

"You have to make your own [way]," Garoppolo said in early September. "Me and Tom are two different people, obviously. You kind of just have to go out there and play your game. You don't know who you're going to have out there with you, who's not going to be out there. You just have to go out there and do your thing."

"We don't need anybody to be somebody else," Josh McDaniels said of the quarterbacking situation. "We certainly don't need our guys to be thinking about trying to do anything that's really not something they're comfortable doing. Jimmy is going to work hard this week to do what we're asking Jimmy to do, and we're not going to ask any more than that."

The truth was that New England had been prepping for this sort of doomsday scenario. One of the things that differentiated the Patriots from the rest of the league when it came to team building was the inherent belief you shouldn't neglect the backup quarterback position. Despite the fact that they were as stable as anyone in the league over the previous decade-plus when it came to the quarterback spot, New England always managed to go out and find a quarterback every spring. Regardless if it was a draft pick, an undrafted free agent, or a camp signee designed to take some of the workload off the shoulders of Brady or the rest of the backups, the message was always clear: every spring, get a quarterback. The Patriots drafted nine quarterbacks between 2000 and 2016. Only four teams—the Jets, Niners, Broncos, and Washington—have gone to the well for a college signal-caller more often in that time than New England. (That didn't include undrafted and rookie free agents, as well as random acquisitions like Andrew Walter and Tim Tebow.)

The franchise has used the Colts' 2011 season as a cautionary tale. The "Suck for Luck" campaign yielded a franchise quarterback, but it also necessitated a slide all the way back to the bottom of the league and a 2-14 record. In 2014, shortly after the Patriots selected Garoppolo in the second round, Belichick dropped a not-so-subtle hint that they were not about to go through the same freefall that happened in Indy after the Colts lost Manning. The truth of the matter is that Indy fundamentally neglected the backup quarterback spot for the better part of a decade with Jim Sorgi and Curtis Painter until the team was finally forced to deal with the situation.

"In our organization I don't think we would put together a team the way Indianapolis did it when they lost Manning and they go 0-16, 1-15 or whatever it was," Belichick said soon after the Garoppolo pick was made. "I don't think that's really what we're looking for.

"When we lost Tom in 2008—we had a player that could step in and we won eleven games. We want to be competitive even if something happens to a player at any position.

"I think depth is always important. You never know when you're going to need it. But I don't think we'd be happy going 1-15 if we had an injury at one position. But other people have different philosophies. I'm just saying that the contrast to that example. I don't think that's really what we're trying to do."

And so, with that insurance policy in hand, the Patriots were able to approach the 2016 season with the knowledge that no matter how bad things got, they weren't going to go into a game with an unprepared Painter or overwhelmed Sorgi under center. Instead, they would have a guy who had been raised in the Patriots/Brady system. He wasn't Brady, but he would give them a chance.

As opening night drew closer, the veteran core of the team started to close ranks around Garoppolo and aimed to take a more active role in his development. One of the guys who reached out was special teams captain Matthew Slater. A perennial Pro Bowler and one of the most respected guys in the New England locker room, Slater had gone from a guy on the bubble as a rookie to one of the best special teamers in the league. Along the way, he had earned his bona fides as someone worth listening to. And so, in the days leading up to the opener, he had been spending more and more time chatting with Garoppolo, doing what he could to try and make sure he was as cool as possible heading into that night in the desert.

And whether it was the wisdom from Slater, the fact that he leaned on veterans like Blount, the fact he didn't throw a single pick, that he steered the ship in a way that allowed them to play excellent complementary football, or all of the above, it all came together in one of the more shocking wins of the Belichick/Brady Era.

On a beautiful September evening, just over nineteen months after Malcolm Butler stepped in front of that Russell Wilson pass toward Ricardo Lockette, the Patriots returned to University of Phoenix Stadium to take on the Cardinals. With the roof closed, the climate-controlled conditions were perfect for New England's season opener. Arizona won the toss and elected to receive, but punted it away after a stalled possession. On the Patriots' first drive of the year, Garoppolo found Edelman three times for 38 yards, and gave the ball to Blount to pick up another 10. That got them to the Arizona 37, where Garoppolo and the Patriots faced second and 4.

The young quarterback lined up under center, took the snap, and lofted one down the sideline in the direction of Chris Hogan, who ran a simple go-route past Xavier Williams, who expected help in the form of zone coverage that never came. The Cardinals had single-high safety coverage, which left Hogan free to cruise into the end zone with the first touchdown of the year for New England. The Patriots were on the board for the first time all season.

The two teams went back and forth for the middle two quarters, with Garoppolo hanging in and trading punches with Palmer and the Arizona offense. For New England, the highlight came in the fourth quarter. With the Patriots trailing 21–20, Garoppolo led them all the way back on a 13-play drive that ended with a 32-yard field goal from Gostkowski to give New England a lead. The best throw from Garoppolo on that drive came after a sack and incomplete pass; with the Patriots sitting on a third and 15 from their own 20, the quarterback took the shotgun snap. He saw Edelman in the right flat, and offered a sharp-looking pump fake. He bought some time with a quick scramble to his left as

Amendola shot over the middle near midfield. He fired downfield—just ahead of a hit from ex-teammate Chandler Jones—and located Amendola between three defenders for a 32-yard gain. It was the second longest completion of the night for Garoppolo, and put New England in position for a 32-yard field goal and the lead shortly after that.

It was a razor-sharp bit of execution for the young quarterback. Given the circumstances and stage, that drive and the throw to Amendola were more than reminiscent of the work of Brady back in 2001.

"We spent all night trying to get them in third-and-long, then they make that one," said Arizona defensive coordinator James Bettcher. "It was a big, big play."

In the end, Garoppolo stunned the football world with a terrific performance, going 24-for-33 for 264 yards and 1 touchdown while leading the game-winning fourth-quarter drive in the shocking 23–21 win. While there were some game-planning tweaks made by the coaching staff—and the Patriots were able to get their fair share of luck when a woeful group of Arizona special teamers botched what would have been a game-winning field goal from Chandler Catanzaro—it was the kid who made the difference. He didn't have Gronkowski, Lewis, Vollmer, Solder, and Ninkovich, but he wasn't overwhelmed by the moment. He bounced back after getting socked in the mouth by the Arizona pass rush. He didn't throw an interception. And he led the team back from a second-half deficit on the road against a team that made the NFL's Final Four the previous season.

Maybe the most remarkable thing was that in the days leading up to the game, there was plenty of talk about how the Patriots would seriously alter their playbook to make things easier on the young quarterback. But that certainly didn't appear to be the case. It was more a case of New England utilizing its usual approach as a game-plan offense that was able to exploit some of the mismatches they found in the Arizona defense. Garoppolo wasn't Brady. But he had enough Brady in him to guide the team to a win—and sound just like the veteran when he met the media after the game.

"Whoever is out there," Garoppolo said shortly after getting the game ball, "we have confidence in one another. And that's a good thing."

While the youngster wasn't overwhelmed by the moment, at the same time, he didn't seem to grasp the magnitude of what he'd accomplished until he finished a postgame interview with NBC's Michelle Tafoya. After he was done, he stepped back and let out a huge "WOOOOOOOOO!" after the victory, an exclamation point on one of the most unexpected wins in recent franchise history.

Edelman was asked by Tafoya if he had a message for Brady, who was watching at home.

"Love you, buddy. We're going to get a couple more for you. A few more," Edelman said.

And while the Patriots couldn't ignore the fact that Brady wasn't there, they were effusive in their praise of Garoppolo.

"He's incredible," Devin McCourty said of Garoppolo's performance. "All game, he went out there and made the plays he was supposed to make. We knew as a team, we believed in him. There was no doubt in this locker room that Jimmy could go out there and play. . . .

"Everyone can shut up now and watch the guy get better and grow and us keep improving as a team."

Next up? Miami. While New England was buzzing about the

season-opening win, the good feeling that powered the team home from Arizona was nowhere to be found the following Wednesday. Belichick was in *no mood* to revisit the victory. Instead, he was all too happy to remind the assembled media that the Dolphins were the team who upended the Patriots in the 2015 regular-season finale, denying them a shot at the No. 1 seed.

"It was sickening," Belichick added, referring to the death-by-a-thousand-cuts defeat at the end of the 2015 season.

"I don't know if you've had a chance to see [it] or not," he rhetorically asked a reporter. "It wasn't very good. Bad coaching. Bad playing. Bad, period."

It was classic Belichick. All of New England was celebrating and feeling good. Belichick? He was all too ready to pour cold water on things. And the win over the Cardinals was the best possible outcome for the coach, especially at this time of the year: They were able to go on the road and get the win, but it was not a perfect victory. There were plenty of things for him to go back and obsess over. There were multiple teaching points for him to hit on—penalties, negative plays, etc.—and several ways to keep his team humble, including the fact that the upcoming opponent had beaten them the last time the two teams had played.

These moments are where Belichick is at his best and most perfect as a coach and motivator. That Wednesday, not only did he get a chance to take a few shots at the media for daring to ask if he had any regrets about that game—only after he brought it up—but it also was a case of him using the media to get the message out to the 53-plus guys in the locker room, especially those who might be feeling pretty good about where they were at this point on the calendar. *Celebrate at your own peril, gentlemen. One win will not get you anywhere in this league.*

But McCourty was right: Garoppolo *did* get better. That Sunday, on an overcast, slightly humid afternoon in Foxboro, the youngster started blazing hot against the Dolphins, completing 10 of his first 11 passes against Miami on the way to an astounding 21–0 lead. A Dolphins team that thought it had a legitimate shot at winning the division with Brady on the sidelines for the first four games was shell-shocked. Three early touchdowns had Gillette Stadium dancing. *Tom, take all the time you need, buddy.* At that point, a 4-0 start without Brady seemed all but assured.

But then Jimmy the quarterback gave way to Jimmy the football player. Remember that near miss of a hit he took in the preseason against the Saints? He wasn't so lucky this time. With just under five minutes left in the first half and the Patriots up 21–0, the 2016 season was about to pivot again.

On a third and 9 from the Miami 26, Garoppolo escaped pressure in the pocket by slipping to his right. He locked in on Mitchell downfield. Garoppolo got rid of the ball quickly, but not fast enough to avoid a hit from Dolphins linebacker Kiko Alonso, who drove him to the turf, square on his right shoulder. He went down hard, and was gone for the rest of the afternoon, giving way to Jacoby Brissett. It would be the last significant snap of the season for Garoppolo.

One of the things that Bill Parcells tried to hammer home to Brissett during the pre-draft process was that he was always just a heartbeat away from playing. You *always* had to be ready. That's why, when he would text him, he wouldn't refer to him by name. It was always "One Snap." Turns out, Parcells knew what he was talking about.

"That's a *message*. He understood it," Parcells would recount later to MMQB.com. "I was trying to put his ears up like a German shepherd. Put your ears up; you are only one snap from playing.

"Sure enough, it happened."

If Brissett didn't get the urgency of Parcells's message before the draft, it was certainly driven home that afternoon. But he was ready, and he was smart enough to lean on the guys around him. Of course, it also helped when Blount ducked into the phone booth and changed into Superman. The veteran back embarrassed the Miami run defense over the course of the second half, finishing the game with 23 carries for 129 yards and 1 touchdown. The highlight came on a 26-yard run in the third quarter that included a leap clear over Dolphins defensive back Byron Maxwell on a dash down the sidelines.

"I don't know how he keeps doing that," Bennett marveled when asked about the vertical on the 250-pound Blount, who had turned the trick before. "[Maxwell] was standing straight up! Le-Garrette doesn't look like he can do that, then all of a sudden he does it. (He's) like Bambi."

Despite the work of Blount, the game flipped from a blowout to a close contest that was ultimately decided when Duron Harmon picked off a Ryan Tannehill pass in the end zone with 9 seconds left to give the Patriots a 31–24 win and a 2-0 record.

But now, Garoppolo was gone, lost with what the team was calling a shoulder injury. If the Patriots had a regular week, there was some thought that he could come back. But New England was facing a quick turnaround against the Texans—with J. J. Watt, Jadeveon Clowney, and Johnathan Joseph—in a Thursday night game at home. That meant it would be the rookie quarterback who would be called upon to try and get the Patriots to 3-0.

For what it's worth, his old mentor said Brissett's chances for success on a short week were exponentially better because he was in New England.

"I am glad that he is with Bill Belichick," Parcells told MMQB.com that week. "Because I know that gives him the best chance for success. I'm not going into an exposé about that. I'm just telling you I'm glad he is there, and I think Bill gives him an excellent opportunity to be successful."

While there would be more epic wins to follow over the course of the 2016 season, Week Three of the regular season was perhaps the best coaching moment of the year for Belichick. Earlier that week, NFL Network analyst Michael Irvin said that if the coach could find a way to beat the Texans with a third-string quarterback on a short week (*three days of prep work against one of the best young defenses in the league?*), the NFL should rename the Lombardi Trophy the Belichick Trophy.

That night, Belichick and McDaniels did just that. As they had done before when Brady was out of the lineup, they didn't try to pound a square peg into a round hole like so many other, more dogmatic coaches might have done. Instead, they found a way to maximize the strengths of Brissett and minimize his weaknesses. There were no deep balls, but lots of read option and reverse plays that got the ball in the hands of the likes of Edelman and Bennett. Gronkowski was back on the field relatively briefly, but was used primarily as a blocker. In the end, the Patriots—in their blue color rush specials for *Thursday Night Football*—got a smart and steady effort from Brissett, as well as stellar performances from the defense and special teams en route to a 27–0 win.

"We really asked a lot out of the team this week," Belichick said. "They responded. They never batted an eye."

Belichick may have praised his team, but it was the sort of wildly underrated coaching job that became routine for him in 2016. That wasn't only the result of Belichick and McDaniels, but assistant quarterbacks coach Jerry Schuplinski. Schuplinski had been a steady presence at Brissett's side that summer, working with him throughout camp and helping prep him for life in the NFL. Belichick singled out Schuplinski after the win with a game ball in the locker room, and he offered more on a conference call with the media the following day.

"Jerry's spent a lot of time with Jacoby," Belichick said. "Josh obviously spends a lot of time with all the quarterbacks, but again, there's times where Tom or Jimmy was going to be the starting quarterback, sometimes the second quarterback—whether that was Jimmy a couple of years ago or last year, or Jacoby this year— is on a little bit different scale in terms of their preparation."

"They have a fantastic coaching staff," Texans coach Bill O'Brien said with a sigh after his team had been run out of the building. "They have what I think is the best head coach in the history of the league. They do a great job."

"In my opinion, [Belichick is] the greatest coach to ever coach this game, so anything he says, I'm going to do," Blount said. "The results speak for themselves."

The New England defense didn't allow Houston to cross midfield until the late stages of the third quarter. Collins had a pick of a wildly overmatched Brock Osweiler. The offense got a thunderous performance from Blount (105 rushing yards, 2 touchdowns, 4.4 yards per carry). The offensive line protected Brissett from Watt, Clowney, Mercilus, and Wilfork for almost the whole night—the Texans had just one sack and one quarterback hit on Brissett. But this was a night for special teams, as that group forced a pair of fumbles on kickoffs and punter Ryan Allen put six of his seven punts inside the Houston 20. In short, the game plan and level of execution was almost flawless, especially when you consider the Patriots had a third-string quarterback starting on a short week against a team that had gone to the playoffs the year before.

"They did a good job," Watt said when asked about Brissett. "They never really put him in a situation where he had to be throwing the ball too much. They did a great job at the run game and did a great job all around, and he played well being in a tough situation."

When it came to the quarterback, he had the support of the locker room, particularly some of the key veterans. In the same way that Slater helped calm the waters for Garoppolo, Bennett was a veteran who helped ease the transition for Brissett. The two ended up carpooling to work on a few occasions—something Bennett did with some of his other teammates in 2016—and the veteran clearly had a soft spot for the rookie, talking about him in glowing terms both on and off the record. In the days leading up to the Houston game, Bennett was one of a few veterans who good-naturedly chided Brissett for the crime of "acting like a veteran quarterback," something that included him looking a little too blasé in meetings, crossing his legs while drinking coffee.

For what it's worth, Brissett certainly acted like a veteran quarterback that night, particularly when it came to ball security. The quarterback had been instructed all week to make sure maintained possession at all costs. Ball security is important, but with such a narrow margin for error against a playoff team like the Texans, it was even more paramount for the young quarterback. And while it wasn't quite something out of *The Program* where he was carrying a football around all week, it wasn't too far removed. *Don't give Houston the ball.*

Brissett wasn't overwhelming by any stretch of the imagination (11-for-19, 103 yards, 0 TDs), but was smart and protective of the football, and like Garoppolo, he continued to put the ball in the hands of the offensive difference-makers around him. His signature moment came when he ripped off a 27-yard scoring run on a play where he did an excellent job reading the action, waiting for things to develop, and utilizing a couple of nice blocks, including one from Mitchell. It was the longest touchdown run from a Patriots quarterback since 1967, and it would be the only rushing touchdown the team had during the regular season by anyone other than Blount.

After he scored, he brought the ball to the sidelines and gave it to Belichick.

"I was supposed to give him the ball. Make sure [the Texans] don't get it," Brissett said of his decision to hand it over to Belichick. "Make sure we get it. So I gave it to him."

For Brissett, it was a major triumph. Life is never easy for a third-string quarterback, especially a rookie, and during the summer, he had to sit and wait for Brady and Garoppolo to get their work in. Biding his time, he made the most of the opportunities he received and performed well when he was called upon. During training camp, he and a handful of youngsters were frequently among the last on the field, running sprints and getting extra work in. He ramped up his responsibility level when Brady left at the start of the regular season, but to be thrust into the spotlight and come out with a shutout win in his first professional start was impressive.

"I think he handled himself great last week, this week, all week every day. He's done nothing but come in here and work as hard as he possibly can—when we had three quarterbacks—to take his opportunities and learn from the other two guys, when it was him and Jimmy and then this week it was pretty much all him," Belichick said of the rookie quarterback, shortly after he returned the football to him.

"He's just a hard-working kid that is really dedicated to doing what's right for the team and trying to improve on anything that you tell him. He just wants to do what the coach tells him to do. I'm glad we have him."

By extension, if there was ever a moment that represented the triumph of the Patriots system, it was the win over the Texans. Since the start of the 2002 season, Belichick was 13-5 without Brady in the lineup. He won with Cassel, Garoppolo, and Brissett under center. Through three games in 2016, Brady, Lewis, Vollmer, and Ninkovich all hadn't played a snap. Gronkowski had only played 12 snaps. Hightower, the guy who was thought to be the new defensive centerpiece now that Wilfork and Mayo were gone, had played one of the three games. But the Patriots were 3-0. Belichick already had the inside track on Coach of the Year honors. And now, they had an extra few days to get ready for Rex Ryan and the Bills.

That's when Brissett's thumb entered the picture.

At some point in the win over the Texans, he suffered an injured thumb on his throwing hand; he was seen on the sidelines having his right thumb examined by the training staff after Wilfork landed on him in the third quarter. The fact that he finished the game was encouraging, but there was no word as to the severity of the injury, which appeared to be another obstacle placed in front of the Patriots over the first quarter of the season.

At some point, with Brissett potentially facing surgery and the Patriots looking like they were running out of quarterbacks, it was inevitable that people started to question the severity of the injury to Garoppolo. *Couldn't the kid take the needle? His team needs him? I played with shoulder injury like his when I was in high school, and I still managed to throw 3 touchdowns. Why can't he do the same?*

While Garoppolo was improving—the previous week, he couldn't lift his arm above his head, but the following Tuesday, he was back out at practice—it appeared more and more that week that the Patriots were content with figuring out a way to make it work against the Bills with Brissett (who had his wrist and thumb taped during practice), while Garoppolo could work as the emergency backup.

Ultimately, despite the fact that they were 3-0, between Brissett's thumb and Garoppolo's shoulder issue—which was described that week as a sprained AC joint in his throwing shoulder—the Patriots were in uncharted waters when it came to the quarterback position. With both QBs a question mark heading into Week Four, it inspired a sports-talk radio fever dream that included the possibility of Edelman lining up under center for the first time since he was a collegian. At the very least, he'd be considered a backup, something that wouldn't shock Brady.

"If that's the case, I'd expect Julian to go in there and the coaches to be comfortable with the plays they're calling for him," Brady told Westwood One. "He still talks about that touchdown pass he threw against Baltimore a few years ago."

The possibility also existed of the team signing a stopgap for a week out of the bargain bin. Names like Ryan Lindley, Jimmy Clausen, and (*ho ho ho*) Johnny Manziel were bandied about as possible one-week replacements. But none of the backup plans were ever taken seriously, however, as the team was wary of using a roster spot on a one-off signing for the week. That would mean someone would get cut, and with roster spots at a premium, the Patriots weren't about to make that sort of move.

But that all contributed to the level of drama; in the week leading up to the game, no one was quite sure who was going to be taking snaps for the Patriots. In his conference call with the Buffalo media, Edelman was asked by "Walt Patulski" of *The Buffalo News* if he was going to play quarterback. Only Walt Patulski was actually Rex Ryan.

"I'm going to do whatever the coaches ask me to do," said an unsuspecting Edelman. "If they ask me to go out and give a glass of water to someone on the sideline, I'm going to do that with a smile on my face if it helps our team win. You can ask our coach about that."

Ryan/Patulski quipped, "All right, buddy. I will."

Edelman wasn't the only potential quarterback in the locker room. In the spirit of trying to wring a different sort of quote out of Collins, the media asked him if he could play quarterback if the team needed him. The hyper-athletic linebacker—who had previously lined up at tight end at times in practice—didn't hesitate to respond.

"Yeah, I'll play," Collins said with a completely straight face. "Whatever it is. I don't care what the level is. I don't care what the level is. Whatever it is they need me to do, I'm doing it."

Wait, really?

"Nah," he replied. "I ain't even see myself as a quarterback in the NFL."

(Truthfully, at that point, Collins at quarterback wasn't that crazy an idea. He played some quarterback in high school, and in his senior season, he rushed for over 1,200 yards and threw for over 1,000 yards on the way to an appearance in the state championship game. He also played receiver, safety, and linebacker.)

That wasn't the only odd Q&A that day at Gillette Stadium. The Patriots usually had Brady go to the podium for his session with the media at some point during the week, but with no Brady and the quarterback position still up in the air at this point, the day started with a message from the team that neither of the quarterbacks on the roster would be available to speak with reporters. But things evolved over the course of the morning to a point where both quarterbacks were speaking to reporters at their own lockers—dual press conferences, less than fifteen feet apart.

Despite the odd look, neither one of them revealed much. In his first session with reporters since his shoulder injury, Garoppolo said he was "getting better by the day," and added that he needed to be smarter when it came to evading pressure.

"I mean, it's football and stuff is going to happen like that. But [you] have to be smart in those situations," he said, referencing the play where he got hurt. "After it's all said and done, it's easy to say that. But it's one of those things; you're in the heat of the game. Bottom line? I have to be smarter than that."

He also said that he didn't feel he was being pressured to play by the team, a roundabout way of denying the report that some in the organization were leaning on him to get back out there.

As for Brissett, he was similarly vague in his responses: the thumb was "fine," and he hoped to play Sunday.

Roughly a half hour later, the two were back out at practice and seen throwing passes during the relatively brief peek afforded to the media. Those windows are unbearably small for reporters and rarely include anything more than stretching, but can be an effective tool for the team when it comes to disseminating information. Simply put, nothing around Gillette Stadium ever happens by accident, and by having their two quarterbacks out there throwing in full view of the media—which reported as much that afternoon—it forced the Bills to continue guessing who would be lining up at quarterback that weekend.

Although Edelman took some quarterback snaps in practice that week, that Sunday, it was Brissett. (Garoppolo was ultimately one of the inactives.) On the way out to the field, the Bills appeared to goad Brissett into a scuffle. The young quarterback said it didn't impact him, but the 16–0 loss—a game where the Patriots went with Brissett, but Edelman ended up getting a few wildcat snaps at quarterback—was probably the low point, at least over the first four weeks. New England couldn't get any sort of offensive traction on the afternoon, as Brissett was 17-for-27 for 205 yards while taking 3 sacks. Bennett did have 5 catches for 109 yards, but Blount was bottled up, ending up with 13 carries for 54 yards. Meanwhile, Buffalo quarterback Tyrod Taylor was pretty good, going 27-for-39 for 246 yards and 1 touchdown.

In the least eventful game of the season, the Bills put up a first-quarter touchdown and added 3 field goals for the difference. When it was all over, Ryan strutted off the field while pointing and laughing at New England fans who were hooting at him.

"One-for-12 on third down," crowed Buffalo linebacker Jerry Hughes on the way off the Gillette turf, referencing the job of the Bills defense. "*That's* how you play fucking football."

After the game, Ryan chortled that he knew who was playing quarterback all along for the Patriots, saying that he had a mole inside Gillette who told him it would be Brissett.

"How about that?" Ryan grinned. "I'll stir some stuff up. 'Who was it?' Who was it? I don't know who it was.

"It's satisfying, but let's face it, they had a player out," Ryan added, making an obvious reference to the suspended Brady. "They had a player out, and we had our team, so we expected to win."

But even in the loss, the Patriots found a rallying cry. The pregame fight stuck in the craw of several New England players, who believed that Buffalo deliberately went out of its way to try and rattle Brissett. Several veterans, including Bennett, took exception to that idea.

"I wasn't out there," Bennett said when asked after the game about the incident, going from his usual bright and cheerful demeanor to stern distaste. "It would have been different if I was out there. I don't let that shit happen."

At the same time, the response from the players who were out there was certainly noticed by the veterans. Brissett was jogging alongside Mitchell when it happened, and Mitchell didn't back down from Buffalo safety Robert Blanton. When Blanton shoved Brissett, Mitchell shoved Blanton, and the two quickly got in each other's face. New England coaches, including wide receiver coach Chad O'Shea, intervened and the whole thing was done within fifteen seconds or so. But the fact that Brissett and Mitchell responded the way that they did was encouraging to the vets in the locker room. *The kids are all right.*

"At the time, I did what I thought was best," Mitchell said after the game. "Am I right or wrong? I don't know."

The way the Patriots had responded to some early adversity was encouraging, and the fact they finished the first four games with a 3-1 record was really the first sign the mental toughness of the 2016 Patriots was not something to be trifled with. The fact that they were able to neatly respond to the challenges of the first four games of the regular season without Brady, Ninkovich, Gronkowski (he missed two), and Lewis (who didn't return until November) was a sign it wasn't your usual group. The near-disarming practicality that was shown by the rest of the roster when faced with a challenge became its calling card. There was always a way around an obstacle. It just took time, smarts, and resources to figure everything out.

The upshot of the whole thing? The rest of the league got a good enough look at Garoppolo for two weeks, and the film on him was good enough for some to suggest that in a quarterback-starved league, he could draw a first-round pick in return. The fact that his audition came as the result of Brady's four-game suspension represented a cosmic evening of the scales in the eyes of many.

Another plus that came out of the first three games was the fact that they knew they had the perfect back for their offense in Blount: a smart, cost-effective vet who was more than capable of carrying the load, as well as executing in a four-minute offense. Through the first three games, Blount had had the third-most productive start to a season of any running back in franchise history, with 75 carries for 298 yards and 4 touchdowns. That trailed only the three-game stretch from Dillon at the start of the 2004 season (66 carries for 323 yards and 1 touchdown) and Tony Collins in 1983 (43 carries, 312 yards, 3 touchdowns).

With Blount, it wasn't so much how many yards he got, but when. Through the first three games of the season, 219 of Blount's 298 rushing yards came in the second half of games, usually at the most important times. That included a whopping 94 second-half yards on the ground against Houston that helped drive a dispirited Texans defense into the dirt. Overall, in the first three games, he had 31 first-half carries for 79 yards, a 2.55 yards-per-carry clip. In the second half, he had 44 carries, 219 yards, and a 4.98 yards-per-carry average.

In the wake of the Week Four loss to Buffalo, there was a huge "Yeah, but . . ." feeling in the building. *We lost. We got embarrassed at home. We suffered our first defeat within the division.*

"Yeah, but . . . You Know Who comes walking back into the building on Monday."

"Look, we're 3-1 right now. I mean, nobody is panicking," said Bennett after the Buffalo loss. "We just keep doing what we've been doing, getting better and focusing and [doing] what we need to do. Come in and get corrections. We've been doing well with whoever has been under center, and [when] Tom comes back, we'll continue to do the same things we've been doing in the games before.

"We had a loss right now. They were the better team today," Bennett added. "But we're *still* the Patriots."

There was no way of realizing this at this point, but when the horn sounded at the end of the loss to the Bills, it marked the final significant snaps of the season for both backups. But given what they did over the course of the first four games, their performance went a long way toward putting the Patriots in the best possible position to win. Think about it: If Garoppolo seized up on the big stage in the opener against the Cardinals or Brissett was overwhelmed by Watt and the Texans, given the narrow margin for error down the stretch, there was the very real chance New England would have been chasing the Raiders or Chiefs for the top seed in December instead of the other way around. But the kids were all right. They did their job. Now, Brady was back. The season was just about to get good.

4. ALLOW ME TO REINTRODUCE MYSELF

Thanks to Roger Goodell, Tom Brady is going to kill us all.
—One NFL assistant coach to Mike Freeman of
Bleacher Report, on the possibility of the rest of
the league facing an angry Brady in 2016

It's Tom Brady. You don't expect anything less.
—Julian Edelman after Brady passed for 406 yards
and 3 touchdowns in his first game back in 2016

For the Patriots, the most anticipated chapter of the 2016 regular season began the Monday after the 16–0 loss to the Bills. Brady was back in the building. The team tried to keep things as normal and low-key as possible; in the week leading up to his return to the field, the quarterback didn't speak with the media. The team was able to exploit a roster loophole because the quarterback wasn't on the roster yet—the league had granted them an exemption—and didn't need to add him officially until the day before the game.

In his place, Rob Gronkowski went to the podium. The tight end had gotten better and more expressive in his sessions with the media. He started out merely tolerating the exchanges, but had become increasingly more comfortable. He wasn't going to give any state secrets away, but by 2016, he had reached a point where he could provide at least one quality sound bite per session. (He preferred to stick at his locker, but with Brady's absence at the start of the year, combined with his growing star power, he was more of a regular at the podium in the media workroom than ever before.) Asked for his thoughts on the return of Brady, the gleeful exclamation he offered that morning told you all you needed to know.

"Tom's back at quarterback, baby!" Gronkowski said with a smile. "It's exciting to get TB back, man."

The game was against the 0-4 Browns—the lone winless team in the league. It was the perfect way for Brady to ease back into the NFL grind. But in addition to the return of Brady, there was a heightened level of excitement in the building because, for the first time in almost a year, the Patriots would get a chance to have Brady, Edelman, Gronkowski, Solder, and Blount—as well as newcomers Bennett and Hogan—all together on the field at the same time. For the first point in the season, nearly the full capability of the 2016 New England offense had a chance to be realized. Asked about the opportunity to face the Patriots at this stage of the season, Cleveland coach Hue Jackson gave a straightforward response.

"Not fun at all," he said.

Meanwhile, the feeling among the fan base was simple: *Let the FU tour commence.* (One popular meme had a picture of an angry Brady with the caption: "You haters had a four-game head start.

Now I'm coming for my fifth ring!") A vengeful Brady would be a productive Brady, according to Hall of Famer Brett Favre.

"It doesn't bode well for everyone else, starting with Cleveland, because I feel like Tom is going to take it out on everybody who he faces," Favre said in the days before the Browns game on his Sirius/XM Radio show. "You know, the guy is incredible. He's a heck of a player, and he is such a competitor. To me, as I've watched him over the years, that's what's been most impressive is that the fire seems to get bigger each year, and that's hard. To me, the competitive fire and spirit that he shows is at a level each year that is surprising to me.

"With this situation, not that [Brady] needs an edge—nor Belichick needs an edge because he coaches with an edge, he's always looking for an angle to approach his team with," Favre added. "Tom's sort of that type of player, and he's got that edge now and he's going to take it out on everyone in his way. So that's not good for everyone else."

Brady had always done well to harness his emotion. Playing with a chip on his shoulder was simply part of the competitor he was; he spent the bulk of the 2007 season raining thunderbolts down on the rest of the league like Zeus on Mt. Olympus for several reasons, not the least of which was the fact that he believed his team was unfairly maligned because of Spygate. But he was older now, and while he still occasionally felt the need to exact payback on an opponent, it was more about picking and choosing his battles at this stage of his career.

For his part, Brady wasn't talking about revenge. He found his motivation in other ways.

"It was great to be back in the building," Brady said in an

interview with Jim Gray on Westwood One the day he walked back into the building. "It was certainly great to be back to work. It's been a long four weeks for me, but I'm excited to get started on my preparation for Cleveland. I'm anxious for the week ahead. I want to get back on the practice field. It's what I love to do, and now I have an opportunity to do it.

"I was motivated seventeen years ago, and I'm motivated today," Brady added. "I'm motivated to win for my teammates. I'm motivated to go out there and represent our city well. None of that's changed."

As his return drew closer there were more Brady sightings in and around New England, and thanks to social media, they took on a sort of breathless quality that got people fired up. On September 30 he filmed his part of a Beats commercial at Milton Academy, and New England fan Billy Lacey caught video of him throwing. (In the latest saga of the Patriots fans vs. ESPN, the four-letter network asked permission to use the video, and Lacey responded angrily via Twitter: *"No chance ESPN, you all started Deflategate, do not use my video."* So much for a potential thaw in the relations between the Patriots' fan base and ESPN, a long-running cold war that still existed.)

Two days after that, video of a Brady workout at Dexter South-field School in Brookline showed up on the Twitter feed of local football writer Tim Whelan. Despite the fact that the Patriots were shut out that afternoon by the Bills, the video of Brady served to hearten New England fans. They were quick to dissect the brief segment, Zapruder-film style. *Look at the form! Look at the footwork! He's back!* That feeling stretched to Gillette after the quarterback returned to work with the team.

"I didn't notice any difference. It was four weeks—it felt like it went fast," McDaniels said the week of Brady's return. "Tommy is ready to go, and looks ready to go."

There was well-founded optimism that came with Brady's return. The Patriots had survived the first four weeks of the regular season without Brady and a host of others, but were sitting at 3-1. Only one AFC team—the Broncos—made it through the first four games undefeated, so New England was in very good shape when compared with the rest of the field. With one quarter of the season down, the Patriots were tied with the Steelers, Texans, Ravens, and Raiders.

But just as there was the same general level of uncertainty around the position at the start of the regular season, there was some now as well. This was new territory for Brady—since 2001, he'd never been dropped into the starter's role in the middle of a season. The veteran was away for a month, and as Belichick said on several occasions, you can't just run around a track a few times and hope to be in "football shape." You need to hit and get hit and fundamentally get callused up in preparation for game action. No one was doubting Brady's physical bona fides, but to be expected to go from zero to sixty in one afternoon—even against Cleveland— would be asking a lot for anyone, much less a thirty-nine-year-old quarterback.

Then there was the belief around the team that it would take more than just one guy to get them to where they needed to be. As great as he was, not even Brady could wave a magic wand and make everything perfect. The rest of the roster would have to, in Belichickian terms, *do their job* if they wanted to continue to win football games.

"Football comes down to every individual executing their job to the best of his ability to help out his team," said Slater in the days before the game against the Browns. "If Tom comes back and does that at a high level—but you have forty-five other guys that are dressed on Sunday that [don't] do it—it doesn't matter. We've all just got to focus on doing our individual job so that the team can have overall success. That's all we can control."

(In an odd happenstance, it was a Cleveland-Boston sports weekend, as the Red Sox and Indians were meeting in the ALDS at the same time. The same day Brady was set to return, the October 9 playoff game between the two teams was set to take place back in Boston, but it was rained out, allowing the full attention of the New England sporting populace to be trained on Brady's return.)

In Cleveland, it was a sunny, bright, beautiful October morning when Brady and the Patriots arrived at FirstEnergy Stadium on the shore of Lake Erie just before 10:00 A.M. The quarterback spent some time on the field for a few minutes, looking around the empty stadium before going in to dress. He warmed up underneath the stands, stretching and working with resistance bands tied around his waist. Around noon, when he trotted onto the field with Garoppolo, there was a huge cheer, as chants of "BRA-DY, BRA-DY" broke out from the Patriots fans who made the trip. He looked up and pumped his right arm in their direction.

At kickoff, it was 58° with a slight wind out of the north. New England won the toss and deferred, and after a three-and-out from Cleveland, the quarterback ran onto the field with the rest of the offense to another loud cheer. The Browns might as well have been playing on the road.

It wasn't the Ravens in January or Seahawks in February. But considering the fact that he had been away for an extended stretch, that afternoon marked one of the most notable performances of his Hall of Fame career. From the first drive until he ceded control of the offense to Garoppolo with just over six minutes left in the game, Brady was in complete control. He hit his first 3 throws—his first two to Edelman and Gronkowski—and four of his first five, with the incompletion a drop by White. At one point midway through the second quarter, he had just two incompletions, both of which could have been classified as drops. He ended up going 28-for-40 for 406 yards with 3 touchdowns (all to Bennett), 0 interceptions, and a remarkable passer rating of 127.7.

Along the way, there was *some* emotion. An arm pump toward the Patriots fans in the Cleveland stands as he began warm-ups. There was a Usain Bolt–style celebration on the sideline after careening for a first down. And hugs and head butts for Gronkowski and Blount after big plays.

"Tom always brings the ampness to the table," Gronkowski explained.

The Patriots ended up winning, 33–13, to move to 4-1 on the season. After the game, there was no talk of revenge. No talk of *sticking it to the man*. No talk of playing for the quarterback. It was an October win. A starting point on the way to a much bigger goal.

Brady simply appeared happy to be back.

"I thought the team played really well," Brady exhaled. "It was fun to be part of it. It's been a fun week to get ready to play, and be back doing what I love to do."

Asked about what the win meant after sitting for the first four games, Brady shrugged.

"This isn't the time for me to reflect," Brady said. "I've just moved on, man.

"It's been a fun week getting ready to play and back to what I love to do. And 4-1 is a pretty good place to be right now."

Brady had hit the ground running with his old friends like Edelman and Gronkowski. But the most impressive aspect of what he did against the Browns was his ability to do such a good job with the new faces in the offense, namely Bennett and Hogan. Bennett had a team-high 6 catches and 3 touchdowns for 67 yards, including a 7-yard grab where he was so wide open he literally walked into the end zone. (That one was punctuated by an awful spike.) Meanwhile, Hogan had 4 receptions for a team-high 114 yards, including a 63-yard thunderbolt in the second quarter that was the biggest gain of the day for New England. In all, the new guys (Bennett, Hogan, and Mitchell) accounted for 12 of his 28 completions. For a team that had had trouble in the past integrating new faces into the offense, it was a perfect ratio.

Of course, Brady wasn't the only one back in the lineup. Ninkovich saw his first action of the season after his own four-game ban. And while it was Brady who garnered most of the headlines, Ninkovich was just as happy to get back out on the field.

"I missed it a lot," Ninkovich said after he played 24 snaps in the easy win. "I was ready to stop changing diapers and get back to football. My wife put me to work there. I'm just really happy to be back; happy to come into work and just practice. Little things that you miss out on. I'm super pumped to be back and look forward to this coming week."

It was a good time for Brady to jump back into the fray, quite frankly. As much as the Patriots publicly built up the Browns in the week leading up to the game, Cleveland wasn't going to pose much of a threat, especially with Brady returning to the fold. It was a good opportunity for him to get his legs back underneath him, get some quality reps with the likes of Bennett, Hogan, Edelman, and Gronkowski, and help him get ramped up for the greater challenges that would loom over the next quarter-plus of the season.

It also needed to be said that given the way the first month-plus of the regular season was going, the league was happy to have him back as well. While the NFL was winning the ratings battles when stacked against other sports, the TV numbers were way down across the league to open the 2016 season. Things came to a head during a forgettable October contest between the Jets and Cardinals in Arizona on *Monday Night Football*. In the middle of another stoppage, play-by-play man Sean McDonough offered the clearest criticism of the state of the game when he went after the officiating.

"If we're looking for reasons why TV ratings for the NFL are down all over the place, this doesn't help," he said. "The way this game has been officiated is not something anybody wants to watch."

Part of that was due to increased oversaturation—namely, *Thursday Night Football* as a year-round event. As McDonough alluded, part of it was pace-of-game issues that arose because of officiating and mandatory TV timeouts. Casual sports fans were invested in the baseball postseason, while others were drawn to the most eventful presidential campaign in recent memory. And while some of the stats were anecdotal, a groundswell of support for a boycott of the league appeared to take hold on social media because of the Colin Kaepernick protests with the hashtag #boycottNFL.

But there was also the simple fact that the league was in a year with very few compelling teams that were also good enough to be considered genuine championship contenders. (The league that championed parity through balanced scheduling and a salary cap had seen it waste away because many teams were too stupid to keep up with the rest of the really good franchises.) By mid-October, it appeared that the field of elites had been narrowed to nine teams *at most* in the Patriots, Broncos, Steelers, Cowboys, Vikings, Seahawks, Panthers, Falcons, and Packers. Like every year, there was the possibility of a team coming out of nowhere and surprising people. (And teams like Minnesota and Denver would eventually fall off the pace before Christmas.) But at that point, there simply wasn't a lot of good football being played. And even some of the teams that were off to a hot start weren't all that compelling.

As much as some members of the league office loved to watch the Patriots squirm, the fact remained that the NFL needed them and Brady's star power. They are one of a precious few teams that move the needle; nationally, people tune in to New England games because they want to see the Patriots win big or get crushed. They are compelling, in the same way the Cowboys of the '90s were compelling. And while there was a curiosity factor around New England because people wanted to see how they would do with Garoppolo instead of Brady, Brady and the Patriots made people care about the league. In a time where there weren't many fascinating teams out there, the Patriots inspired emotion.

With Brady back at the helm, New England had returned to the forefront of the NFL conversation, and the victory over the Browns kicked off a four-game run of dominance for Brady that was as impressive as anything he was able to accomplish. In that stretch of contests—three of which were on the road—he had a 73 percent completion rate with 12 touchdowns, 0 picks, 1,319 passing yards, and a passer rating of 133.9. Along the way, the team won all four games by an average of 16 points. It was such a hot streak that it sparked legit comparisons to his 2007 season, an MVP year that was, at least statistically, the finest of his career.

The high point? The emotion that came with the first home game of the year against the Bengals. On that sunny October afternoon, when Gillette Stadium deejay TJ Connelly spotted Brady coming out for warm-ups, he hit the switch on Brady's traditional walk-up music for the first time in the regular season: Jay-Z's "Public Service Announcement (Interlude)," whose first verse opens with the line, *Allow me to reintroduce myself.*" When Brady said hello again to the folks in Foxboro, the place erupted with a big cheer.

In 2014, the Bengals were the opponents who got the season started in earnest, as the "On To Cincinnati" moment in the fifth game of the year was a touchstone for a team that would go on to win it all. This time around, there was no such bump from the Bengals, only a workmanlike 35–17 win for New England. Cincy actually had a 14–10 lead at the half, but 2 third-quarter touchdown passes (one to White and one to Gronkowski) and 1 safety from Hightower gave the Patriots more than enough separation.

"Once I got out there running around, it felt like football," said Brady, who completed 29 of 35 passes for 376 yards and 3 touchdowns in a contest that was marred by some late-game pushing and shoving.

"It's certainly an emotional environment for football," he

added. "There were a lot of people there when we ran out, and they were there all game, so it was great. And it was great to win."

The Patriots' regular season was over a quarter of the way done, and it had already been one of the more eventful stretches in recent franchise history: three quarterbacks, six games, five wins, and a return to the top of the standings in the AFC East. But you wouldn't know that things were all that wild if you talked to veteran defensive back Devin McCourty. McCourty was as even and understated as they come. Not much seemed to disturb the former first-round pick out of Rutgers, who was now the most senior member of the New England defense in terms of time in the system.

Over the previous five years, McCourty had been as steady a defensive player as the league had seen. He arrived in the NFL as a cornerback, and was a second-team All-Pro in his first season, coming away with 7 picks as a rookie and earning a Pro Bowl berth. After a rocky second season, he was moved to safety (he made the jump full-time in 2012 after New England traded for Aqib Talib), and the combination of his ball skills, athleticism, field vision, smarts, and leadership made it all click. The anchor at the back end of the Patriots' defense, when he hit free agency following the 2014 season, McCourty turned down more money elsewhere to return to New England. He wasn't necessarily recognized as a star, and so he wasn't one of the first guys you thought of when you started running down a list of players responsible for the Patriots' dynasty. But he was absolutely vital to what New England wanted to accomplish on defense.

"He's done such a great job for so long; I'm trying not to screw him up," safeties coach Steve Belichick joked when asked about McCourty midway through the 2016 season. "I always feel good when Devin is on the field."

McCourty had a varied skill set, but few were more practiced in the simple, semi-profane, four-word acronym that came to define a sizable part of the success of the secondary in recent years: Get The Fuck Back. Known as GTFB, it was the go-to default phrase among the New England defensive backs. *When it doubt, GTFB.* No deep balls. Nothing over your head. No big plays. There were fundamental debates over defensive backs and their technique and speed and footwork and hand fighting. But at the end of the day, the overriding philosophy was clear. *GTFB.*

And the results were clear: through the first six games of the 2016 season, no other team had held opponents to fewer pass plays of 40 yards or more than New England. (The Patriots would give up their first such play of the season the following week against the Steelers.) After the win over the Bengals, Belichick was asked about the impact of someone like McCourty, a coach on the field.

"Devin, again, as he normally does in the course of that type of a game, some of the comments and observations that he made affected some of the things we were thinking about doing. I think as usual he was right on the money with his observations, especially when you go back and take a look at the film a little more closely today," Belichick said. "You see what he saw. Then a couple of the things we tried to do after that, he was very helpful in kind of recognizing that and helping us steer some of those things in the right direction."

After beating the Bengals, McCourty and the Patriots faced

their first real road test of the season, a date in Pittsburgh. The Steelers were stumbling a bit coming into the game, but the fact that they were just a game behind New England in the rapidly developing AFC playoff picture made this one a must-win for a Patriots team that was hoping to gain some separation between themselves and the rest of the conference. The good thing for New England? It caught a break, as Roethlisberger—who had surgery for a torn meniscus the Monday before the game—wouldn't play.

As was the case before the game against the Dolphins, there was no time for Belichick to hit an optimistic note. *Five wins won't get you anywhere in this league, gentlemen.* That much was clear when the coach was asked for his thoughts on Le'Veon Bell, the Pittsburgh super back who was averaging almost 5.5 yards per carry in his first three games after returning from suspension.

"*Oh my God,*" he replied.

"Tremendous player. Great hands, catches the ball, very quick, makes people miss," Belichick added. "Bell's as good as anybody we'll play."

That Sunday in Pittsburgh, it was sunny and seasonal, perfect conditions for an October game between two of the best teams in the AFC. The two offenses struggled out of the gate with 2 fumbles and 1 interception in the first four-plus minutes of action. (The pick was well-timed, as Butler made a great play intercepting a ball in the end zone that was intended for Antonio Brown, a play that kept the Steelers off the scoreboard and changed the tenor of the game in the early going.)

But the Patriots' offense ground out an impressive 13-play drive, one that culminated with a 19-yard pass to White for the first score of the game. They stacked another impressive sequence on top of that, an 11-play sequence that finished with Blount punching it in from 3 yards out to make it 14–0 early in the second quarter. A Pittsburgh touchdown and 2 second-quarter field goals cut the Patriots' advantage to 14–13 midway through the third.

But that's when Brady and Gronkowski made like BRADY AND GRONKOWSKI. Midway through the third quarter, the Patriots took possession at their own 25-yard line. Runs of 11 and 25 yards from Blount moved the chains into Pittsburgh territory. On second and 10 from the Steelers' 36, Brady dropped back and eyed a streaking Gronkowski, who started in the slot and took off down the seam. He split the defenders, and Brady located him perfectly at the Pittsburgh 12, a step ahead of Steelers' safety Robert Golden. Gronkowski churned into the end zone for the score. It was a classic Brady-to-Gronkowski pitch and catch, and gave the Patriots more than enough of a cushion for the 27–16 win.

It also moved Gronkowski into a tie for the most touchdowns in franchise history with 68, which the big tight end noted gleefully after the game. *Uh-huh.* By now, everyone around the team pretty much knew about the importance of No. 69 for Gronk. It was his favorite number; he once taped it to the back of his practice jersey. He had also said that he enjoyed doing 69 push-ups as part of his workout. There was also an incident where he struggled to hold back his laughter when ESPN's Josina Anderson asked him in a 2015 interview about a situation where a teammate played 69 snaps and 69 percent of the game.

"One more and I got sixty-nine touchdowns," he smiled after the win over Pittsburgh. *"If you know what I mean."*

The most disconcerting news to come out of the win over the Steelers was the continued struggles of Stephen Gostkowski. After not having missed an extra point in a regular-season game for nine straight seasons, the veteran missed one for the second consecutive week against Pittsburgh. Toss in three missed field-goal attempts earlier in the season, and it had become tough sledding for Gostkowski. While the rest of the roster was flying high after a satisfying road win over a conference foe—and kickers around the league were having issues with the new extra-point rules—he wasn't pulling any punches when asked about his own performance.

"Right now," he said after the Pittsburgh win, "I stink."

"Nobody works harder than Steve. Steve's a very talented player. He's mentally tough," Belichick said after the contest. "We'll work through it. Again, this is a tough place to kick. I'm not making any excuses, but the kicker on the other side of the field had trouble, too. But we have to have to make them."

It was the latest part of a rough stretch for the kicker, who had missed an early extra point in the 2015 AFC title game that came back to haunt the Patriots at the end of regulation. The former first-team All-Pro had been pretty much money over the course of his career. But after a strong opening night against Arizona where he booted 3 field goals and pinned the Cardinals deep in their own end time and again on kickoffs (the performance was enough to warrant AFC Special Teams Player of the Week honors), it had been a bear of a season. It was not going to get any easier for Gostkowski, as the Patriots were headed to Buffalo the following week. New Era Field had always been a tough place to kick because of swirling winds. And so the kicker headed to upstate New York that week looking to reestablish the level of consistency he had enjoyed to that point in his career. Meanwhile, the rest of the roster was looking for a little payback.

In a year that some believed was defined by revenge, the Patriots certainly went into their October 30 game in Buffalo aiming for retribution. But things always tend to get a little weird for New England when it visits Buffalo, and this time was no exception.

The Bills Mafia is the most gonzo fan base in the AFC East, and one of the nuttiest in the league. (Take one serving of Oakland's Black Hole, mix it with a healthy dose of bitterness that comes from four Super Bowl losses, add some of the gnarliest parking lot tailgate videos you have ever seen, and set it against a backdrop of freezing cold temperatures nine months out of the year. Boom! You've got the Bills Mafia.) And when you combine the fact that the fan base has been driven mad by Brady having won 25 of his 28 career starts against Buffalo heading into that October contest, it was easy to see why the Bills' fan base was in a froth that afternoon. The usual variety of homemade signs were out and about—including a giant one on the side of an RV that read "TOM BRADY CHEATS . . . ON HIS BOYFRIEND!" In the end, the fan who would leave the biggest imprint on the game wasn't toting a sign, but a dildo. But more on that guy in a second.

The truth was that while it was fortunate enough to catch New England at the right time earlier in the season when the JV was on the field for the game in Foxboro, Buffalo was woefully unprepared to have to deal with Brady and the varsity this time around. The Patriots jumped to an early lead behind the quarterback, as well as Gronkowski and Hogan, who had the chance to celebrate at the expense of his old team.

In many cases, when new guys on the New England roster get the chance to face their old team, if the opportunity presents itself, the Patriots try to get those guys something of an extended run against their old club. Sometimes it worked, sometimes it didn't. In 2015, in his first game back in Buffalo, they tried just about everything to get former Bills tight end Scott Chandler a touchdown, but couldn't seem to make it work. But they were able to get it going that afternoon against Buffalo, which had foolishly given up on Hogan. Against the Bills, Hogan had 4 catches for 91 yards, including a beautiful 53-yard touchdown reception near the end of the first quarter. The catch undoubtedly had Buffalo fans lamenting the fact that while Hogan was little more than a complementary player in his time with the Bills, he had evolved into a dependable part of a team that was on the way to passing them.

Hogan was a really interesting piece of the puzzle. When he first arrived in Foxboro, people had often mistaken his skill set as being the same as any of the other receivers on the New England roster because he was, well, *an athletic white guy* who looked kinda shifty and was overlooked at one point in his career. But Hogan was really a lot different from Amendola and Edelman. Instead, he served as more of an intermediate and deep threat, filling the role that Brandon LaFell served for the bulk of the 2014 and 2015 seasons. Hogan spent a sizable portion of 2016 among the league leaders in yards per catch, and was as good a field-stretcher as there was in the AFC. That was the case on the 53-yard scoring strike, where he simply blew past cornerback Stephon Gilmore (who might have been expecting help over the top) on the way to the end zone.

That afternoon against the Bills, Brady finished 22-for-33 for 315 yards, 4 touchdowns, 0 picks, and a passer rating of 137. His four games back after the suspension were the finest four-game stretch for any thirty-nine-year-old quarterback in the history of the league: 98-for-134 (73 percent), 1,319 passing yards, 12 touchdowns, 0 interceptions, and a passer rating of 133.9.

With Goodell and the rest of NFL security (presumably) scrutinizing his every move, he rattled off one of the best four-game stretches of his career, and parlayed that into AFC Offensive Player of the Month honors for October. The suspension? It didn't slow him down. It didn't impact his prep. And it didn't make a dent in his overall performance. Overinflated footballs? Underinflated footballs? Water balloons? You could argue that the overall skills of the opposing defenses weren't exactly world-class. But at this point, it was more probable than not that he could beat you any way you want.

Of course, Brady used the fear of critics who would have tied a slow start to Deflategate-related issues as a spark. If he had spent his first four games back looking god-awful, it would have given ammunition to those who believed he needed some sort of competitive advantage to continue playing at a high level. *What's the matter, Brady? Football got too much air?* Instead, he looked like someone at the top of his game.

"I don't know if I've ever seen him better," sighed Ryan after the contest.

The 41–25 win over the Bills was highlighted by Gronkowski's 69th touchdown, which set a new franchise record for career receiving touchdowns and *wink-wink, nudge-nudge* action after the game. Gronkowski loved playing in Buffalo for several reasons, including the fact that he grew up in upstate New York and it was a chance to play in front of his family and friends. Most times the

Patriots come to Buffalo, there are more than a hundred people in Gronkowski jerseys milling about on the field after the game—a couple of years ago after a New England-Buffalo contest, a frustrated security guard tried to corral all of them. He started herding them toward the exits when the stadium was starting to close down, but none of them listened. Eventually, the guard threw up his arms and walked away.

In the postgame media interview room this time around, Gronkowski was asked initially about the record, and his thoughts on surpassing the mark set by the great receiver Stanley Morgan. But hot on the heels of his dissertation on the importance of his record-breaker, a reporter asked what he thought of the "marital aid" that was tossed onto the field during the game.

There was a pause. Those packed into the tiny workroom simultaneously smirked and held their breath waiting for the reply.

"I think that was for the Bills," Gronkowski said with a smile.

(The next month, at the end of the investigation, Bills VP of Operations Andy Major said that "luckily, nobody was hurt," before adding that "none of our players stepped on it and blew their knee out." *OK*. He added that the dildo thrower had been banned for life from New Era Field. The thrower, who wished to remain anonymous, appeared on a Buffalo-area podcast later to reveal that he had written "Tom Brady's dildo" on it with a Sharpie, and snuck it into the stadium by wearing two pairs of pants.)

"Only in Buffalo," Brady said on WEEI with a laugh the next day.

Brady, Gronkowski, and Hogan weren't the only ones who

found their form that Sunday against the Bills. Gostkowski was 2-for-2 on field-goal attempts (including an impressive 51-yarder) and 5-for-5 on extra points. It was a good starting point for the kicker, who would soon get on a roll heading into the postseason. He wasn't quite back to 100 percent just yet, but his outing against the Bills certainly inspired more confidence among the New England fan base.

"Man, we're very excited for Steve," said special teams coach Joe Judge the week after the Bills game. "I'll tell you what; *nobody* works harder than Steve. Nobody prepares better than Steve. We have all the confidence in the world in Steve. He's done it consistently for so long in this league. There is nobody I'd rather play with."

As for the rest of the roster, the Dildo Game marked the half-way point of the regular season. The Patriots were 7-1, and sitting on top of the AFC playoff picture. Despite all the off-season talk about New England's potential vulnerabilities, the season was pretty much playing out the way the rest of the conference thought it would: with the Patriots still in the driver's seat. As for the AFC East, it was already fundamentally wrapped up at that point, as the win over the Bills gave New England a three-game lead on Buffalo, Miami, and the New York Jets.

"I mean, it's the halfway point," Ryan said glumly after the game. "But I think in the division, it's unrealistic to think you're going to win your division when you just got beat by [16 points]. How many games are [the Patriots] up by? Three? Something like that? I don't see that changing."

New England's latest four-game win streak had moved it to 7-1 and the No. 1 spot in the conference, with the Broncos and Raiders (both 6-2) close behind. Meanwhile, the quarterback had righted the ship and appeared to put the team back on a championship course. The defense had done its part when it came to playing sound complementary football. And while there were a few nervous moments for the special teamers, things looked to be headed in the right direction as the second half of the season loomed.

But in truth, the Patriots' journey was only just beginning.

5. SPEED BUMP

I talked to my wife [Gisele] and she said I can't talk about politics anymore. I think that's a good decision, maybe for our family.
—Brady after being peppered by reporters about his relationship with Donald Trump

On to Seattle . . . Seattle. Seattle. Seattle. Seattle.
—Belichick responding to a reporter asking about a letter he sent in support of Donald Trump during his presidential campaign

I don't know nothing about Von Miller money. Nothing. It never came out of my mouth, never. Let's be smart. Let's all have some common sense.
—Jamie Collins, after he was dealt from the Patriots to the Browns. There was a report he had asked for "Von Miller" money from New England when it came to a new deal.

OF COURSE, NOTHING WORTHWHILE IS ever *easy*.

The 2016 Patriots were sailing along. Sitting at 7-1. Brady was back. Gronkowski was healthy. They were on top of the AFC and looking squarely at another big year.

That's when things really got nuts. Even for *them*.

It all started the day after the win over Buffalo when they traded Collins, shipping him to Cleveland in a deal that fundamentally amounted to them giving away one of their essential defensive chess pieces. The rumor was that Collins, who was set to be a free agent, was in the market for Von Miller money (a claim he later roundly denied). With the Patriots facing a handful of looming contractual questions, "Miller Money" for Collins seemed unlikely, even for a player of his caliber. And so, he was jettisoned to Cleveland, going from the Patriots to the Browns in a blink.

In New England, Collins was always a tough guy to get a read on. A freakish athlete—a picture of him as a collegian leaping to block a kick looked like it *had* to have been Photoshopped—the 6-foot-4, 250-pounder out of Southern Miss was the most dynamic defender on the roster. He could run with tight ends and backs in the passing game, all while also working as a blitzer. Only three defenders finished the 2014 season with at least 4 sacks and 2 interceptions: Collins, Green Bay's Julius Peppers, and Seattle's Bruce Irvin.

But he was quiet and pretty much kept to himself. He wasn't into self-promotion, and assiduously avoided talking with the media at *all* costs. (At the start of Media Day prior to Super Bowl XLIX—a situation where he *had* to speak with reporters—one asked him why they hadn't seen him in a while. "I've been busy," he replied with a smile.) He spent quality time with his teammates, but with the end of his rookie deal looming at the conclusion of the 2016 season, it was tough for outsiders to get a sense of where he stood. That didn't make him a bad guy. It was just tough to discern his loyalties.

There was a belief Collins wasn't following the game plan when it came to his responsibilities. (From the outside, it didn't help that it appeared he was at fault when it came to coverage on 2 touchdown passes from Peyton Manning to Owen Daniels in the 2015 AFC title game.) There were arguments to the contrary, but a look at the film from the win over the Bills in Buffalo—a game where he played fewer snaps than usual—seemed to confirm he was either willfully out of position or simply not where he needed to be in that moment. Was he freelancing? Was he upset? Did the Bills do something to create confusion on the part of the New England defense? Or was it, as Ian Rapoport of NFL Media indicated, the first sign he was going to be utilized in a part-time role going forward because of his perceived struggles against the run? No one really knew for sure. And Collins sure wasn't talking.

Then, a sign: The day after the win over the Bills—and hours before the trade deadline—Belichick was asked about the play of his defense in the win against Buffalo. He didn't single out Collins, but didn't seem overly thrilled when it came to the play of the linebackers against the Bills.

"I think overall, we had our ups and downs. At times we played well defensively," Belichick said. "At other times, not so well. It was good enough to win. It was good at times. And then, at other times, I think we really . . . I think we're all disappointed, so we really just need to do a better job. That's pretty much across the board—the running game, the passing game, everything. I mean there were some things that just, we need to do better."

"Ups and downs" was a fitting way to describe the 2016 season to that point for Collins. He was clearly at the top of his game in wins in Weeks One and Three—there were times where he was the most dominant defensive player on the field in both of those contests. At the same time, he appeared to struggle at times in Weeks Two and Four and was overshadowed in Week Five against the Browns by surprisingly sturdy rookie Elandon Roberts.

And so, he was gone, just hours before the trade deadline, shipped to the Browns for a third-round pick. It was the most shocking deal in the league on an otherwise slow day for trades.

Collins's performance wasn't the sole reason behind the move, but if Belichick didn't have the full attention of the locker room before he made the trade, he certainly had it now. The message was simple: Don't get too comfortable. If he's willing to ship out a guy like Collins—sending him from 7-1 to 0-8 in one afternoon—he's willing to ship out *just about anyone* who might not be totally and completely committed.

Belichick's history of shocking moves, either in-season or close to the start of the season, tended to send the team in one of two directions.

In 2003, they cut Lawyer Milloy shortly before the start of the season. That team took a brief step back before winning 17 of 18 and a second Super Bowl, going from *They hate their coach* to a parade down Boylston Street in the span of a few months. In that case, the 2003 team was rocked back on its heels for a few days, but managed to rebound for a few reasons, including the presence of veteran safety Rodney Harrison, who managed to stabilize a young group of defensive backs and work with other established vets like Ty Law. As a result, the secondary went from a colossal question mark to a position of strength by the end of the year. And Belichick's roll of the dice paid off.

In 2006, a trade that shipped popular veteran Deion Branch to Seattle ultimately robbed a team on the cusp of another Super Bowl of one of its most valuable options in the passing game. Without Branch, Brady carried the passing game on his back down the stretch and into the postseason, making do with the likes of Reche Caldwell and Doug Gabriel, all while veteran Troy Brown played the bulk of the season on one good knee. If Branch had stayed with the Patriots and remained healthy (and Harrison hadn't suffered a knee injury after sustaining a cheap shot from Tennessee wide receiver Bobby Wade late in the regular season), there was every reason to think Branch would have been the final piece of the puzzle that would have allowed them to get past the Colts and Bears. Instead, New England ran out of gas in the AFC title game.

In 2009, a September trade of Richard Seymour to Oakland was part of a series of moves that ultimately doomed that year's team. Like the Branch deal, losing Seymour played a sizable role in the fact that team came up lacking when stacked against some of the New England teams of the past. In the case of both the Branch and Seymour trades, however, their impact went beyond the numbers. Both were key parts in the on-field success of the team, but their impact as leaders was tough to replicate. The Seymour deal also came in the midst of a period where the team also saw guys like Harrison, Mike Vrabel, and Tedy Bruschi all depart. Ultimately, the personnel losses sustained through that stretch were too great, particularly on the defensive side of the ball, and the result was the most disappointing season of the Belichick Era in New England.

And in 2010, the Patriots dealt Moss to the Vikings in October and replaced him with a supposed downgrade in Branch, who made a much-heralded return to Foxboro after almost four years in Seattle. It was part of a much larger reset for the New England offense: having added a pair of preternatural tight ends in Gronkowski and Hernandez that off-season, the Patriots' passing game was evolving. The Patriots responded with a memorable run toward the postseason, and in hindsight, they chose the perfect time to get out of the Moss business. While the moves didn't necessarily bear immediate fruit—New England lost in a divisional playoff showdown with the Jets that year—Belichick's move toward a two-tight-end set created all sorts of new matchup issues for its opponents. That move ultimately ended up as a plus for the Patriots.

How would they respond to another in-season deal? The Collins deal would be another challenge.

"I think we'll see," said Brady, days after the decision was made. "You can sit up here and say yes or no, or think of all the different hypotheticals. I think that we're going to have to wait and see. We as players, it's not our choice. We don't do anything about it. At this point, we've just got to do what our job is, and that's to go out there and try to make improvements this week. And then, get ready for next week."

New England did make a move the week beforehand to acquire another linebacker, Kyle Van Noy, from Detroit, an athletic defender who could provide some depth and could at least help fill the void left by the loss of Collins. In addition, more would likely be asked of Roberts, Mingo, and McClellin. But as teams like the Patriots started to gravitate more and more toward using nickel-and-dime packages as their base defenses, the guy who would be asked to do more would be Hightower. Fewer and fewer traditional linebackers would be needed going forward, but that rock in the middle of the New England defense was still going to be the Alabama product.

In the context of the bye week, the recent defensive struggles, and the Collins trade, it was interesting to hear Belichick talk about the opportunities that the extra few days afforded them. Not only could you spend plenty of time resting up and getting prepared for the second half, but you also needed to engage in a long, hard look at your own roster. If something wasn't working, the bye week gave you a few days to try and change things up.

"You have to answer that question every week, not just the bye week. You do something that doesn't work out well, what are your options? Get rid of it or continue to do it and see if you can improve it," Belichick said, days before the Patriots broke for the bye week. "That's the judgment you make. If you really feel convicted that you can do it well, then you put resources into it and try to improve it.

"[But] at some point, if it doesn't go well, you might decide that we've tried, we've invested a lot of time, we've invested whatever we have to invest in this and it's still not working, maybe it's time to move on to something else."

Then things *really* got interesting.

The night of November 7, Donald Trump was campaigning in New Hampshire. He whipped out a letter. He told the crowd it was from Belichick, and he started to read aloud:

"Congratulations on a tremendous campaign. You have dealt with an unbelievable slanted and negative media and have come out beautifully. You've proved to be the ultimate competitor and fighter. Your leadership is amazing. I have always had tremendous respect for you, but the toughness and perseverance you have displayed over the past year is remarkable. Hopefully tomorrow's election results will give you the opportunity to make America great again."

The crowd cheered wildly. In the same speech, Trump told the crowd his "friend" Brady had called him, and said that Brady gave him permission to tell his fans he would be voting for him. The perceived link between the Patriots and the presidential candidate was officially sealed.

It's not like anyone *shouldn't* have seen this coming; Trump had already aligned himself with the Patriots. For the last decade, he had been a presence for big games in Foxboro as a friend of Kraft's. (Trump had tweeted about his support of the Patriots in the past, including before one game against the Texans where he wished good luck to coach "Bob Belichick" and the rest of the team.) In return, Kraft said one of the things that cemented their relationship was the fact Trump came to the funeral of his wife, Myra, and the billionaire/reality TV star had called him once a week for a year after that.

"When Myra died, Melania and Donald came up to the funeral in our synagogue, then they came for memorial week to visit with me," Kraft told Gary Myers of the New York *Daily News*. "Then he called me once a week for the whole year, the most depressing year of my life when I was down and out. He called me every week to see how I was doing, invited me to things [and] tried to lift my spirits. He was one of five or six people that were like that. I remember that."

Deepening the relationship between Trump and the team was the fact that Belichick and Trump were photographed together in March after the two had dinner in Florida with Belichick's girlfriend, Linda Holliday.

Regardless, the timing of the release of the letter was odd. Belichick was willing to subject himself and his team to this sort of distraction during the week of the biggest regular-season game of the year? It seemed out of character for the coach. But Belichick confirmed the letter later in the week.

"I think anybody that spends more than five minutes with me knows I'm not a political person," Belichick explained. "My comments are not politically motivated, but out of friendship and loyalty to Donald."

Belichick also took pains to indicate he had developed friendships with Republicans *and* Democrats, saying Secretary of State John Kerry was in the locker room after the game a few weeks before.

"He's another friend of mine," Belichick said of Kerry. "I can't imagine two people with more different political views than [Kerry and Trump]. But to me, friendship and loyalty is just about that. It's not about political or religious views."

Meanwhile, the Trump Question created a tough situation for the quarterback. He had been friends with Trump since the early days of the twenty-first century when he was asked to judge one of Trump's beauty pageants, and the two had maintained a cordial relationship ever since. Brady, being loyal to a fault, thought nothing of sticking a "Make America Great Again" cap in his locker, in full view for everyone to see in 2015. He said a Trump presidency would be "great."

But as the campaign continued, it became a larger and larger issue for him. The ugliest moment came at the end of an October 12 press conference when a reporter yelled out a question for Brady: "Tom, you have kids of your own. How would you respond if your kids heard Donald Trump's version of locker room talk?"

"Thank you, guys. Have a good day," Brady replied and walked off the podium.

For the bulk of his life as a celebrity, Brady had done well as a human Rorschach test. People saw what they wanted to see in him, and that was one of the reasons why he had largely managed to avoid the whiff of scandal. He was adept enough at avoiding serious topics, and so, people didn't have to choose sides when it came to talking about Brady as a public figure. Fans rooted against him, sure. You could dislike the Patriots. But when it came to his personal life, there wasn't much to hate on. The simple truth was, despite the fact he played for one of the most polarizing franchises in recent NFL history, he wasn't in the moral crosshairs as often as the coach.

Some national fans used Deflategate as a referendum on Brady and his legacy as a player. (That argument was weak at best, as the people who loved Brady backed him even more, and the ones who didn't like him just doubled down on that dislike.) But the election/Trump stuff was different. Like other beloved athletes who were thrust into the political spectrum by their own statements, decisions, or actions—think Muhammad Ali and the Vietnam War or Michael "Republicans buy sneakers, too" Jordan—Brady found himself at a crossroads. After massive athletic success, if you lean one way or another on a volatile political topic, you risk losing or alienating some of your fan base. And while he caused a flap when he missed out on the trip to the White House in 2015, this was the first real time where Brady was perceived as taking a stand on a wildly divisive issue. In his weekly sessions with the media that fall, he was visibly uncomfortable on the subject.

Always one who was careful when it came to choosing his words, he was even more deliberate now. Asked by a reporter why he might have given Trump "permission" to let people know the quarterback had voted for him, he paused.

"Why did I give him permission?" he asked with a small smile, repeating the question. "So you're assuming that I gave people permission?

"I'm just going to talk about football this week," Brady said, adding later, "I just want to focus on Seattle. At the end of the day I don't . . . I have a lot of relationships with a lot of people. I don't think a lot of people are entitled to my conversations with friends of mine or people that I may speak with."

It's important to note his connection with Trump wasn't Brady's first foray into the political arena. He was a part of the team trips to the White House in the past. He appeared at George W. Bush's 2004 State of the Union speech, sitting in a box reserved for honored guests. He met Barack Obama in 2005, but later didn't go to Obama's White House after Super Bowl XLIX because he claimed he didn't get enough advance notice when it came to the trip, which apparently clashed with a family commitment that had been planned for months.

But the Trump Question left some New Englanders—namely, football fans living in the bluest state in the union—uneasy. Every county in Massachusetts voted for Hillary Clinton. Could you root for a team if it appeared you were diametrically opposed to the politics of the owner, coach, or star player? In 2016, it didn't appear to be a sizable problem. In the simplest terms, it was soon clear that Massachusetts football fans who might have voted for Clinton and backed Brady and the Patriots had become adept at separating the art from the artist. They were OK appreciating the talents of a player without worrying about who he might be supporting politically. Whatever barometer you wanted to use—TV ratings, merchandise, ticket sales—it certainly didn't look like left-leaning Patriots fans were rejecting their team based on the political views of Brady.

Ultimately, for Brady, it didn't appear to necessarily break down along party or political lines. It was a question of loyalty. The quarterback had always been an exceedingly loyal individual. Trump had been in his corner since the early days of 2002. When he put the cap in his locker, he was just doing a favor for someone he considered a friend. He wasn't thinking about the political ramifications; honestly, not many were when it first happened. Many longtime Brady watchers believed that the quarterback initially saw the cap in the locker as nothing more than a gesture of goodwill. But when it happened, and Gillette became the intersection of sports and American politics, it marked an occasionally uneasy period for the quarterback, one he would have to navigate the rest of the 2016 season.

Ultimately, for the Patriots, who had routinely been part of a soap opera of some kind or another the previous dozen-plus years, the election was simply another distraction. The Trump Question hung over the team all year, even after November 8. It stuck all the way to the Super Bowl, where Brady would come under heavy fire for the relationship.

At the same time, one of the things that managed to distinguish the 2016 team was the fact that while there were outspoken factions who took strong stands on multiple issues, it didn't impact the final product. In October, eight of the fifty-three guys on the roster were thirty or older. Ten guys on the roster were in the league eight years or more. If this were a younger team, those sorts of distractions would have rocked them. But in the locker room and on the field, those things were hardly an issue. The election was discussed among the players. There were Democrats and Republicans dressing alongside each other. But it was never the sort of issue that would divide the team. The locker room wouldn't allow it to become a problem.

It's not to say it *wasn't* an issue. It's just to say Brady isn't the sort of guy who would stop throwing to Bennett because the quarterback supported Trump and Bennett publicly voiced support for Clinton. That is what grown-ups do, and this roster was full of grown-ups. The bottom line? Ben Roethlisberger, Matt Ryan, and Julio Jones had a far greater impact on what happened to the 2016 Patriots than Donald Trump.

"I think you have a lot of respect for the guys—and I certainly do that I've always had—in the locker room," Brady said. "We're all on the same team. We're all from different places, different backgrounds, different ages, races, ethnicities, beliefs. But when you come into the locker room, you're all trying to put your feelings you have about anything aside, and try to accomplish a common goal.

"I think we talk a lot about distractions, because that takes away from what your goals may be. But we have a very close locker room, and it needs to be that way."

While the captains and other vets were able to create a positive locker room infrastructure both before and after the election, the Long/Bennett combination was particularly vital in helping the franchise navigate any potential land mines. They both carved out a niche as substantial on-field contributors but off the field as well, particularly when it came to navigating the finger-wagging #stick-tosports culture of social media in the wake of the election.

During the Belichick/Brady Era, the Patriots had endured all sorts of things that could be classified as distractions for an NFL team. There was the strange and sad saga of Aaron Hernandez. In addition, the arrival (and subsequent departure) of high-wattage football celebs like Tim Tebow, Randy Moss, and Chad Ochocinco contributed to the circus. And the soap opera nature of Spygate and Deflategate certainly made 2007, 2014, and 2015 interesting. While they weren't blind to whatever real-world issue might be just outside the walls of Gillette Stadium, the proof of their ability to ignore the noise was seen in the run of success. Simply put, they did a better job putting on the blinders when they came to work than just about anyone else.

All that being said, in the Belichick Era, the locker room had never really had to deal with any sort of overtly *political* issue. No one was marching, protesting, or speaking out against governmental policies. This was a place where individuals of diametrically opposed political beliefs played alongside each other and won together. There were discussions that acknowledged the outside world, but that sort of outside noise never became an issue between teammates.

But 2016 was different. It wasn't just the election. It started with the Colin Kaepernick protest in August, and that was one area where Long and Bennett distinguished themselves as leaders. In an interview with ESPN Radio in mid-September,

Long—who had a rep as being socially active and self-aware of his surroundings—expanded on the topic of the protests involving Kaepernick and other players, saying that it was a "complicated" issue: while he respected the anthem and would never kneel, he said he understood those who would, and believed there was "a lot of truth" in the message.

"I've had a lot of thoughts about it, and it's hard, because you want to talk to the media, you want to say something about it. As you know with the media, it's a long conversation and if you talk about it for a few minutes, they might take ten to fifteen seconds out of your quote and take you out of context, and run with the narrative."

Long added: "But I'll make it pretty clear: I support my peers in exercising their right to protest. This is a wonderful country, and I think everyone agrees on that, but there are things in our country that can improve. I don't think that by acknowledging as a white male that America isn't the same for me, maybe, as it is for everybody, the same great place, that we're complicit in the problem or that we're saying America isn't a great place."

Long also discussed the fact that when it came to those sorts of issues, he was sometimes better off stepping back and listening to his teammates.

"And listen, I'm just going to listen to my peers because I respect those guys, and I can't put myself in their shoes," he said. "I play in a league that's 70 percent black and my peers, guys I come to work with, guys I respect who are very socially aware and are intellectual guys, if they identify something that they think is worth putting their reputations on the line, creating controversy, I'm going to listen to those guys."

As for Bennett, he was already one of the best quotes in the fifteen-plus years of the Belichick Era. One of the reasons why he was allowed to be so free and open with the media was because he was an established veteran who continued to do exactly what the team needed him to do. If the team needed a pass catcher, Bennett caught passes. If they needed him to block, he did that. If the team needed him to be a complementary piece to Gronkowski, he willingly played that role. If a younger teammate had a question, he was there to answer it.

But while he carved out a niche as the funniest guy on the team—he nicknamed himself "Captain of Fun" for the New England locker room—he also drew praise for his toughness. Sure, he was quick with a joke, but he was also extremely durable. Despite a whole host of injuries, he played in every game, powering through shoulder and ankle injuries, the latter of which included a cracked bone. There were moments where his outsized personality might have gotten on the nerves of some of his teammates (there were a few calls for him to turn his music down over the course of the season), but for the most part, that was overlooked. His durability, production, and good nature were always welcome in the locker room, with both his teammates and the media.

And Bennett was like Long in that he wasn't about to #sticktosports. That side first revealed itself to New England fans prior to the regular-season opener against the Cardinals in Arizona. In front of a national audience still trying to wrap its collective head around the Kaepernick protest, he and McCourty could be seen raising their fists at the end of the national anthem. After the game, both discussed why they did what they did.

"I won't go in deep detail, but really just to start the conversation, to get people to take notice," Bennett said. "Some things people just brush under the rug, under the water, under the bridge.

But it's big. It doesn't just affect one family—it affects all families. From the moments when you're riding in the car, and there's a Young Jeezy song on, you hear it, and you hear the sirens in the background of the music, you panic, and you freeze while you're driving. When it comes to that point, it's really time to start having a conversation."

McCourty was equally adept at navigating the occasionally tricky waters of the era, bringing nuance and context to an uncomfortable conversation.

"Around the NFL, a lot of guys are doing different things," McCourty told reporters, referencing the protests. "It's all for the same cause: different social injustices. We've talked as players throughout the league trying to make change in our communities one by one using our platform, not just doing it on Sundays and game days. We've talked about different things we're going to try to do to help the country and help our communities out.

"[On Sunday], I wore socks with the American flag. I believe in this country. I love this country. My father was in the Army. My older brother was in the Army. Those men and women go out there and put their life on the line. I respect that. That's the reason why I didn't do anything during the anthem because I respect it. You talk to people about how much respect they have for the flag. That's why they believe. That's why they go fight. Nothing but respect for that."

Ultimately, it was also really important to remember that when it came to the Trump Question—or the Kaepernick protests, for that matter—it wasn't like the fifty-three players, the entire coaching staff, and the rest of the front office were all of like mind. The responses of Long, Bennett, and McCourty all made that clear. It also become clear as the season wore on, particularly when it became evident that the Patriots were going to go deep in the playoffs and the question arose of whether or not each player would visit the White House if they won the Super Bowl. In the days leading up to the Super Bowl, several players indicated they would not go if New England won. McCourty, Bennett, Hightower, Blount, Branch, and Chris Long were all very forthright when asked if they would go. And while saying they would respect the decision of any of their teammates who chose to make the trip, they all said no. (Long and McCourty appeared in a video later that spring explaining their decision.)

In the wake of Trump's victory, Bennett fired off a series of Tweets explaining why he had supported Hillary Clinton, including one that simply read: "I'm with her." The day after the election, Bennett was playing Tupac's "Keep Ya Head Up" and Kendrick Lamar's "Alright" in the locker room. Both songs have uplifting lyrics, and the two played consecutively at one point during the open locker room session. And a day after that, Bennett posted an open letter to his daughter on Instagram explaining his thoughts on what lay ahead.

In the locker room, there was discussion about the election among players, but it never reached a crisis point. Distractions are for weak teams, an excuse for teams that aren't mentally tough enough to succeed in the NFL. Despite the volatile nature of the election, that wasn't going to happen in Foxboro.

With the election done, for the Patriots, it was on to Seattle, a game that was eagerly anticipated for several reasons, not the least of which was the fact that it was a rematch of Super Bowl XLIX. There was the chance for New England to dismiss the claim that it hadn't beaten a quality opponent to that point on the calendar. There was also the opportunity for the Patriots to really see how they would stack up against one of the best teams in the league at the start of the stretch drive.

And then there was the quest to overtake Milt Plum.

Wait . . . who?

The former Browns quarterback was one of the most accurate passers in the league in 1960, when he went the first nine games of the season without throwing an interception. Now, eight games into the season and going up against one of the best pass defenses of the modern era, Brady and the New England quarterbacks were one game away from tying Plum's old mark. Plum was well aware of what was going on with Brady and the Patriots.

"I'll be watching on Sunday night," Plum said when reached by phone at his home in North Carolina. "I'm a football fan, so I don't think that'll be a *concern* of mine. I mean, if he breaks it, he breaks it. . . . I didn't know they had records for that kind of thing. I really wasn't thinking about it much at the time. Peyton Manning broke one or two of my records before. Now, they have records for everything: How many times do you go to the bathroom during a game? They know everything."

The tone for the tough, edgy game was set right from the start. This would be big-boy, prime-time football at the start of the stretch drive for both teams. Late in the second quarter, Brady found Gronkowski down the seam for what looked to be a big gain, but the tight end was rocked square in the chest by Seattle safety Earl Thomas. The hit was a savage shot on Gronkowski, one Thomas delivered with his right shoulder. It was distinctive for a few reasons, not the least of which was the fact that it was a completely clean hit. In an era where defenders felt the need to go high or go low on Gronkowski, the textbook "Hawk Tackle" style was a reminder that quality defenders can still get the job done when it came to bringing him down. That said, it was later revealed that Gronkowski suffered a perforated lung on the play, but stayed in the game to finish.

The fallout from Thomas's tackle on Gronkowski continued for the next week-plus, with the two exchanging appreciative Tweets. "Nothing but respect for Gronk. One of the best I've lined up against. Hoping to see him back on the field sooner than later," Thomas tweeted. Gronkowski replied in kind: "The respect is mutual man, you got the best of me on that one. The grind is real, you showed the fans a real football hit."

(In the wake of the game, the only case of bad blood came from Seahawks coach Pete Carroll, who implied that the New England fans might have gotten a little too complacent, and as a result, Gillette had become a little too quiet. "It's not a great place," Carroll said of the New England stadium a couple of days after the game in a radio interview. "They weren't nuts. It's because they're so used to winning. There was a time when they kicked their last field goal to go ahead, and it was like a round of applause for a nice effort. Gosh, our guys would be going berserk. We're so hungry for it.")

Then, there was the low hit Brady took from Kam Chancellor. That shot, which happened early in the third quarter, drew a roughing-the-passer penalty on Chancellor and left Brady limping and flexing his knee after the play. In a bang-bang moment in real time, it looked an awful lot like the one that Bernard Pollard delivered on Brady that left the quarterback on the shelf for the bulk of the 2008 season, so it was easy to understand why Gillette went quiet after it happened.

The quarterback flexed and appeared to be OK. Like Thomas's

hit on Gronkowski, you could argue that it might have warranted a flag. But Belichick wasn't necessarily buying it.

"On a football field it's hard to judge intent," he said the next day. "I don't think the officials can judge intent. I think that's too difficult. They're taught to judge what they see and call what they see, so that's their job. They made a lot of calls last night. We had some that favored us. We had some that didn't, but that's their job and really I'm focused on our job, which is to prepare to play better than we played last night."

For Brady, the knee was a nagging issue that continued to dog him the rest of the year. The biggest takeaway? It underscored the delicate nature of the process. The quarterback goes down? The whole house of cards collapses.

It was a great contest—truthfully, in a year that didn't have a whole lot of classic matchups, this was one of the best NFL games of the season. There were *seven* lead changes, as Brady and Russell Wilson dueled late Sunday night in front of a national television audience. Blount put the Patriots on the board with a 1-yard plunge at the end of the first drive to make it 7–0, but 2 Steven Hauschka field goals and 2 touchdown passes from Wilson to Doug Baldwin gave the Seahawks a 19–14 lead at the half. Compounding the level of concern for New England fans was the fact that Brady threw his first pick of the season, a floater midway through the second quarter that was picked off by DeShawn Shead. (The interception meant that Plum got to keep his record, but the team did set a mark for most pass attempts to start a season, breaking the mark of 251 pass attempts by the 2008 Redskins. Brady got them all the way to 258 to open the year.)

Midway through the third quarter, Blount darted around left end for his third touchdown of the night, putting the Patriots up by 2, 21–19. The Seahawks answered when Wilson found Baldwin to give Seattle a late lead. Despite the fact that there was no Marshawn Lynch, the similarities between this game and Super Bowl XLIX were hard to ignore: two of the best and most physical teams in the league, slugging it out late in the game in front of a national television audience, with a big catch (in this case, an over-the-shoulder grab from Gronkowski) setting up a first and goal from the 2-yard line with less than a minute to go in regulation.

Brady went up the middle for a yard to get to the 1-yard line. But Blount was stuffed on second down, and Brady lost the handle on a quarterback sneak on third down. A back-corner fade from Brady to Gronkowski with Chancellor in coverage on fourth down was off the mark. (*Why are they throwing on the goal line?*)

On the play, it looked like Gronkowski and Chancellor got tangled up going for the football; was there enough contact to warrant pass interference? These were the sorts of plays that had consistently been an issue for Gronkowski the last few years, as some officials had been accused of holding him to a different standard from other pass catchers because he was so big. He had seen a sizable spike in offensive pass interference calls against him in 2015, and while those numbers had dropped off a bit in '16, there was still a double standard when it came to Gronkowski. Defenders could drape themselves all over him and not get flagged, but he could deliver a subtle push-off and it would draw a quick OPI penalty.

After the game, Gronkowski—who ended up tied for the league lead in offensive pass interference calls in 2015, more than almost any team in the league—was asked about the disparity in the way penalties were called when it came to him versus other tight ends.

"That's a tough question. I've had problems in the past with that, last year and a couple times this year," he said. "But I'm not here to make excuses and say that was a [penalty]. I just want to— we just lost a game—I want to give credit to the Seahawks. They played a good game. It was a well-fought sixty-minute game on both sides of the ball. But I mean, I'm not trying to get into that discussion right now."

But this time around, there was no call. And in the end, the Patriots suffered a narrow 31–24 defeat that dropped them to 7-2 on the season.

"We've just got to do a better job. It starts with me," Belichick said with a sigh at the end of the longest week of the season. "Coaches, players; I mean, we've just got to do better.

"Seattle is tough. They force you into some mistakes. They do a great job. Not to take anything away from them, but there's just some things we've got to do a better job of. Those showed up to-night. We need to work harder on them and be able to perform better in these kinds of situations."

Even with the last-minute loss to the Seahawks, New England was still running away with the division, and was also ahead of a rapidly developing field of conference rivals in the race for home field. At the same time, the Patriots hadn't done much to assuage critics who said they were a phony title contender who had fattened up on lesser competition because they couldn't hang with the powerful Seahawks. The Seattle loss was an indictment on their championship chops; an indication that they weren't true Super Bowl hopefuls. *King of the Tomato Cans. They haven't played anyone! What's going to happen when they face real competition?* The reported rumbles of discontent that echoed throughout the locker room in the wake of the Collins trade to Cleveland were reminiscent of the train wreck of 2009. How was the rest of the roster going to deal with the loss of Collins? That was a season that started with all the promise in the world but ended on a sour note, as that group was eventually revealed to be the most mentally soft team of the Belichick/Brady Era.

But in hindsight, there was going to be a striking similarity between the 2001 and 2016 teams in that the last loss of the regular season came in a prime-time contest at home against a powerful NFC opponent. The '01 team had St. Louis. After that one, they wouldn't lose again. They didn't know it yet, but the '16 team was about to jump on the same magic-carpet ride.

6. WON'T GET FOOLED AGAIN

I don't think you win over 200 games by just doing one or two things right. You do a lot of them; he does.
—Belichick on Tom Brady breaking the
NFL record for most quarterback wins

As many issues as Patriots fans had with the league over the year-plus, the 2016 schedule really broke in their favor. Opening without Brady, they still had three of their first four games at home. They had their bye smack in the middle of the season—the perfect time. They had stayed relatively healthy, and had started to take advantage of the fact that they were a good team in a relatively down year for the rest of the league.

But as November gave way to December, things were still a little . . . *unsettled*. At least outside the locker room, anyway. They had yet to register what some critics could point to as a signature win. (They had beaten the Steelers in Pittsburgh without Roethlisberger. They had beaten Buffalo when the Bills didn't have LeSean McCoy. And they beat the Texans while a hobbled J. J.

Watt was days from going on season-ending injured reserve.) The trade of Collins and the talk of the election had left them as the most-questioned 7-2 team in football. The thinking was that they were a talented group, but were only sitting at the top of the AFC because they had taken advantage of a soft schedule.

In particular, there was some heat on defensive coordinator Matt Patricia. In late October, they had dealt their most dynamic defensive player to the Browns, and they had just given up 31 points at home to a team that came into the game struggling on the offensive side of the ball. Events like this caused former Patriots cornerback Ty Law to go on Fox Sports that week and say that the New England defense should "show some damn pride" if they wanted to start doing its part to carry the team.

"They need to fix it. Still, the old adage is defense wins championships and it's going to carry over. So right now, the Patriots are so good at offense, and I think they're putting everything in Tom Brady's hands. . . . If you got a guy like that you got to put the ball in his hands. You got Gronkowski, you got Edelman, you got all these offensive weapons that can move the ball pretty much against anybody.

"Defense, I think the philosophy right now is bend-don't-break, because we have [Brady] back. But I think as a defensive unit, regardless of what's going on, what we're talking about in the media, what the coaches might be saying. But the defensive locker room, kick the coaches out. Let's get together amongst ourselves and say this is what we got to do. It's not just Tom Brady, Bill Belichick, and everybody else. You got to have some damn pride, and go out there and make something happen.

"So I'm waiting to see who's going to be that guy. Because you didn't have to have that in our locker room. You had Willie

McGinest, myself, Tedy Bruschi, we had guys that will step up and play, Lawyer Milloy, Rodney Harrison, we had outspoken, vocal, competitive people, we competed amongst ourselves. So that's what they have to find, that magic that we had back then because it wasn't about just the offense. It was more of a defensive team. And then Brady became Brady, but at the time he didn't have to carry the load. So the defense, in my opinion, needs to start taking it personal with all the criticism that they're getting right now."

OK, then.

Over the course of the Patriots' run of success, several players would transition to TV after their on-field careers were done. On the national level, that was a group that included McGinest, Bruschi, and Harrison. (Law, Troy Brown, and Matt Chatham were among those who worked more on the local level.) When they would be forced to speak ill of their old club, it initially caused some consternation in the New England locker room. *Who is he to say that about us? He knows what we go through down here. Why wouldn't he have our back when he goes on TV?*

But as that generation of stars got older and the current players started to drift away from that group—the only guy left in the locker room who was a teammate of Law's in New England was Brady—it had become less of an issue. That didn't mean it didn't make some waves among the roster. When the Patriots arrived for work the day after the comments were made, they were ready for their critics, including Law. How could the defense turn things around? The answer was simple.

"Play better. We can hoot and holler and yell and scream, but leaders have to play better," McCourty said with a shrug. "It starts with us. If we play better, usually the whole defense plays better.

Leadership comes in different forms, and at times, you have to do different things to lead. But the best way to lead is to go out there and play good football and lead the team and give them an example to follow.

"All the veteran players and the leaders on this defense have to go play better. I think that's what we think as a team in all phases. Bill says it all the time: If you're a leader on the team, it starts with you. You go out there and play well, the team will follow."

That week on the conference call, Patricia was asked by the estimable Tom E. Curran whether or not he was disappointed in himself that he couldn't get as much out of the defense as he might have hoped. Patricia responded by saying it was a "negative question," but added that he was going to try and spin it into a positive. Patricia's thinking was simple: It's a long season, and this team—like every other team before it—is a continuous work in progress. And to this point in the season, Patricia liked the progress his defense had showed.

"It's a season that is continuously evolving. If you look at the teams through the course of the different seasons that have played that have wound up in the end where you want to be, I'm sure those teams have gone through a lot of different things throughout the season. We're just kind of in that mix.

"It's getting towards Thanksgiving. We're going to try to play our best football here moving forward with whoever is out there and try to get better no matter what. Certainly, me as a coach, I'll answer that one. I always look at myself first. And I'll always try to make sure I'm doing everything I can to help our team prepare to win and do the best job I can week in and week out, which is what I really try to do."

Patricia was a great example of the new generation (post–Charlie Weis and Romeo Crennel, anyway) of Patriots assistants: a whip-smart individual who traveled a unique path to Foxboro and steadily climbed the ladder. The bearded Patricia got a bachelor's degree in aeronautical engineering from Rensselaer Polytechnic Institute, and had spent time coaching at his alma mater, as well as Amherst and Syracuse, before joining New England. As was required for many young assistants in Foxboro, he started out on the lowest rung of the coaching ladder and learned to game-plan and scheme on both sides of the ball before evolving into a coordinator. He started in 2004 as a low-level assistant, then worked as an assistant offensive line coach before flipping over to the other side of the ball and coaching linebackers and safeties. He eventually became the full-time defensive coordinator in 2012, and had generated some serious buzz the previous off-season, interviewing with the Browns for their head-coaching vacancy.

In the wake of the loss to the Seahawks—as well as some other occasionally underwhelming performances over the first two months of the season—it was thought that his image had taken a bit of a hit. But in many ways, that conference call was the defining moment for him that season. He was supporting his guys. The trade wasn't his decision, but the call to move forward without Collins was a sign of faith in the rest of the roster that they could win without the linebacker. Now, all they had to do was roll the dice and take their chances.

The good news? Their next three games were against the Niners, Jets, and Rams, three teams that allowed them to hit the reset button and do some things and try out some different combinations against lesser competition. And so, they discovered that Roberts, Van Noy, and McClellin could do some rotating at linebacker in place of the departed Collins. None of them had the freakish skill set of Collins, but they were all relatively steady. They realized that Mitchell could play a little bit, and worked him into the receiver rotation. And they found that, in his first action back in almost a full year, Dion Lewis still had that sort of electric speed and dynamic presence that put untold amounts of stress on opposing defensive coordinators.

Making things more challenging was the fact that the Patriots kicked off the stretch without one of their better defensive linemen in Jabaal Sheard. The veteran had a rough couple of weeks, and had followed a similar arc to that of Collins; Sheard saw a sizable dip in playing time the week before against the Seahawks (he went from playing 73 percent of the snaps against Buffalo to just 23 percent against Seattle). But he wasn't on the injury report all week. After New England took off Friday for San Francisco, an Instagrammed shot from the Celtics game popped up on Sheard's feed, and when he was announced as one of the inactives ninety minutes before the game, it was clear he had landed in the doghouse.

The first of the three games—against the Niners in San Francisco—was a unique one for Brady, as it would be the first regular-season game of his sixteen-year career in the Bay Area. (He missed New England's previous trip to San Francisco in 2008, as it came while he was sidelined with a knee injury.) It wasn't exactly Candlestick Park—which Brady often spoke of reverently—but for the Northern California native, it was a welcome opportunity to play in front of his family and friends.

"For the first chance to ever do that, it was very special," Brady said. "I felt it in pregame warm-up, and it carried right to the last play of the game. It was pretty great."

It was a gloomy day with rain in the forecast as the Patriots kicked off against the Niners, but after a bit of a shaky start—the Patriots led just 13–10 at the half—it was smooth sailing for New England the rest of the way. Brady threw a touchdown in each quarter and ended up 24-for-40 for 280 yards with 4 touchdowns, 0 interceptions, and 1 sack. Meanwhile, the Patriots were able to bottle up Kaepernick, who was sacked 5 times (including once each by Butler and Patrick Chung) and ended up going 16-for-30 for 206 yards and 2 touchdowns.

While there were certainly bigger games and more important scores, Brady got major style points on his last 2 touchdown passes of the day. In the third quarter, he barely slipped away from DeForest Buckner's attempt at a shoestring sack; with Ronald Blair bearing down on him, Brady fell backward as he nailed a 5-yard scoring strike to Amendola for a 20–10 lead. In the fourth, he zipped a laser to Mitchell after just avoiding an oncoming Ahmad Brooks. Mitchell took it all the way, weaving through traffic for a 56-yard touchdown reception to make it 27–10.

While there were others who distinguished themselves through-out this stretch, maybe the most pleasant discovery the team made in that three-game run was the fact that Mitchell could *really* play. In those three games, he had a combined 17 catches for 222 yards and 3 touchdowns. (That included 2 touchdowns at the expense of Darrelle Revis in the win over the Jets.) Trying to find the next great young receiver had become an eternal quest for the Patriots, and while they had managed to augment their offense with a well-placed free agent or two, several pass catchers who had been drafted (or acquired via free agency) had come to New England with the best of intentions, but had been spooked for many reasons, not the least of which was the fact they suffered a crisis of confidence somewhere along the way. They didn't want to be the guy who let Brady—and, by extension, the New England offense—down. That was clearly the case with Ochocinco when he arrived. (The cowed veteran once compared his first day with the Patriots to the opening scene in *Full Metal Jacket*.) And to some extent, that was also the issue with Dobson, who was a smart and talented receiver, but had confidence issues.

As the season went on, it was clear that wasn't the case with Mitchell, who had a quiet assuredness about him. Whether it was his background, his mental wherewithal, or his ability to go above and beyond as needed, he was able to distinguish himself as a positive presence throughout his rookie year. Mitchell's final regular-season numbers (32 catches, 401 yards, 4 touchdowns) wouldn't quite equal the first-year output of the likes of Julian Edelman (37 catches, 359 yards, 1 touchdown in 2009) or Deion Branch (43 catches, 489 yards, 2 touchdowns in 2002), but the fact that he was even in the conversation was a good sign.

"I've just been impressed with him since the day he came in," Brady said of Mitchell following the win over San Francisco. "He's a very positive person, and he made a great play today, made a lot of great plays. He's growing along with everybody else. It's been really great to see."

The three-game stretch wasn't all easy, as they had to sweat out a November 27 win over the Jets in North Jersey. The Jets were a miserable mess at this point in the season, with a 3-7 record and no one to play quarterback. But they lived up to their rep as a semi-regular pain in the ass for the Patriots to have to deal with, sticking around until late in the game. The Jets had a 17–16 lead, but a classic Brady drive led to a Mitchell touchdown with just under two minutes left. Things weren't secured until Long strip-sacked Ryan Fitzpatrick late in the contest, for a 22–17 victory.

In that one, however, the Patriots were again reminded that nothing good is ever truly easy. Early in the game, Gronkowski—in his first on-field appearance since the Seattle loss—suffered a back injury. With 4:55 left in the first quarter, the Patriots were facing a third and 7 from their own 47. Brady went deep down the right side, but the pass was off the mark, and the big tight end fell to the ground awkwardly. He left the game, and shortly after that, he was escorted to the locker room.

It was the last action Gronkowski would see in 2016; while there was some hope that he might be able to make it back if the Patriots could stay alive deep into January, later that week, New England removed all doubt by placing him on season-ending injured reserve.

Life Without Gronkowski figured to hamstring one of the league's best offenses for the rest of the way. Because of season-ending injuries in 2011, 2012, and 2013, whenever he went down awkwardly, when he fell or twisted his knee and stayed on the ground for an extra beat, there was a sudden sense of dread. Was this going to be it? Would that be the injury that brings his Hall of Fame career to an end? He would go down, wait a second, and everyone would wait a beat . . . until he got back up again. Compounding things was the fact that many defenders believed the only way to bring down Gronkowski was to take a shot at his knees. After all, you don't bring down a redwood by chopping at the midsection. You work on the base. And so, every time a rogue defensive back went low on Gronkowski, football fans from Bangor to Bridgeport held their breath.

When it came to Gronkowski, there was an injury history. While he'd be the last guy in the league to be classified as fragile, health issues in college were a major reason why he was available in the second round of the draft back in 2010. But it was also worth noting that when he got to Foxboro, he had more placed on his shoulders than just about anyone else on the offensive side of the ball, save the quarterback. When he was on the field, he was the primary focus of the defense on just about every snap. He was either blocking or being hit. And while no one would weep for Gronkowski—the 6-foot-6, 265-pounder could overwhelm a defense when given the chance—it took a massive toll, at least physically. Ultimately, he didn't necessarily require the football IQ of the quarterback or the durability of an interior offensive lineman. But when you would add those two traits, no one on the offensive side of the ball rated higher than the big tight end.

The Thursday after he prematurely left the Jets game—and the day before he underwent surgery on his back—the team and the Gronkowski family issued a joint statement indicating he would be out for the rest of the season:

> During the Seattle game on November 13, Rob sustained a hit to the chest that resulted in a pulmonary contusion to his lung. Rob was examined by several specialists at Massachusetts General Hospital as directed by the team, as well as an independent physician. He received medical clearance to return to play two weeks later for the New York Jets game

on November 27. After a hit early in the Jets game, Rob began to experience significant back and leg pain. This injury forced him to leave the game and he did not return. With the help of the Patriots medical staff, along with the consultation of several medical experts, it has been determined that it is in Rob's best long-term interest to undergo surgery to address his lower back injury. Rob is expected to have surgery tomorrow. We do not expect that he will be able to play for the remainder of the 2016 season, but will await the results of tomorrow's surgery before making a final determination. Rob has always been one of our hardest workers and was voted captain for the leadership he provides on our team. We are deeply saddened any time a player is lost to injury. We are committed to assisting Rob throughout his recovery and look forward to his return to playing football for the New England Patriots.

The fact that statements like this were issued by the team in conjunction with the Gronkowski family always seemed to raise some eyebrows. But by this point, it was pretty much standard operating procedure. It was unique, sure. Given his on-field performance and off-field worth, Gronkowski had been elevated to his own brand, one that many people had a hand in helping shape. There were allowances made for Gronkowski that were simply not made for anyone else on the roster, save the quarterback.

But even with all the uncertainty around his health and all the baggage that came with Gronkowski, he was worth it. *By God, he was worth it.* In the mind of the Patriots, it was *all* worth it. There was a reason he hadn't played in a preseason game since 2012. You could argue about the relative worth of Edelman or

Solder or anyone else. But at the end of the day, outside of Brady, a fully operational Gronkowski was the most precious offensive asset they had. When he was 100 percent, he was not only one of the best tight ends of the modern era, he was one of the most overwhelming offensive performers in the recent history of the league.

And while the self-created GRONK party image of a lovable lunkhead was one that made him some money, he never let that get in the way of the work. Look, we're setting the real-world bar low here, but in the context of today's NFL, it's important to remember that in his first seven years in the league, he never showed up drunk to practice. He never scrapped with teammates. He didn't rack up fines or suspensions or take cheap shots at the opposition. (Unless you count old friend Sergio Brown getting thrown out of the club a few years back.) There was never an issue with police. And he developed a very quiet rep as being one of the most conscientious guys on the team when it came to charity appearances and hospital visits. To utilize a popular Belichick-ism, no one worked harder than Gronkowski.

Since he arrived in the NFL, he hadn't always made the right decisions. There's been some boorish, juvenile behavior. And to the general public who might not be completely cognizant of his larger record, a large part of the optics around Gronkowski's booze cruise are less than flattering. But the amount of goodwill he's built with the team and the attention to work when it was time to get down to business, combined with his All-World talent, allowed him leeway to do some things that, say, other players might not get away with. By way of example, when Tebow was with the Patriots in 2013, he reportedly went to Belichick regarding a potential endorsement opportunity that would have made him

$1 million. Belichick apparently put the kibosh on the deal. There were, apparently, no such qualms about Gronkowski's booze cruise.

Gronkowski could also do some of that stuff because he was one of the smartest players on the roster. In the New England offense, the tight end needs to understand not only the responsibilities for his own position, but also the work of the wide receiver and running back, all while being mindful of the wishes of the quarterback. It's an incredibly complex position, one that demands a high football IQ, and Gronkowski was able to handle it all.

When he arrived in the NFL, it was something he seized upon fairly quickly. He *had* to pick it up quickly, because the only other option was not getting the ball. After all, Brady is a demanding boss. In a story Gronkowski told Andy Benoit of *Sports Illustrated* in 2016, he recounted one of his early encounters with an angry Brady.

"Tom wanted me to get outside leverage on this flag route, and I just couldn't," he said. "I just kept going inside. And he just flipped out on me about it. He said, 'All right, the ball's not going to you then.'

"I remember that," he added. "So finally I just started learning, All right, I've got to get outside."

It sounds simple, but it's an adjustment that not many are capable of making—or willing to make. But it's been par for the course for Gronkowski. There's GRONK the cartoon character. But there's also Gronk, football savant.

"Probably other than the quarterback, the tight end position—in our offense—is the hardest to play," Belichick said of Gronkowski in 2015. "You have all the protections, all the [work in the] running game, and you have routes from sideline to the middle of the field to occasionally even in the backfield. There are really no plays off mentally for that position. [Gronkowski's] work ethic, his ability to work with his teammates, whether it's the quarterback, the offensive tackles, the other tight ends or even with the defensive players, is good.

"Rob does a great job in the running game, too," Belichick added. "He's one of our best run blockers, period, at any position. I'd say for me, him and [Mark] Bavaro, they're the two best [tight ends] I've ever had, on a consistent basis, for all the different things they have to do, not just one particular block or something like that."

(For some Patriots fans who came of age in the early days of the twenty-first century, the Bavaro-Gronkowski comparison is an innocuous, throwaway line that likely means little. But Bavaro was a frequently invoked name by Belichick, and meant as the highest of compliments. The former New York Giant was a rough-and-tumble tight end who was as comfortable throwing a block as he was hauling in a pass from Phil Simms, and a durable and steady presence who was a key part of a championship team. He might not have had had the flashy stats of modern-day tight ends, but Belichick considered him as good as it gets. Basically, for him to compare any current player to a member of his old Giants' teams of the 1980s was high praise indeed. It happened occasionally over the course of the 2016 season, including one time where he drew a line between Dion Lewis and Joe Morris. But given all the bouquets that had been thrown at Gronkowski in his first seven years in the league, that one should arguably be at the top of the list.)

The third thing about Gronkowski that was completely unique among everyone on the roster was the fact that he didn't seem to engender as much ill will among opposing teams and/or fan bases as other Patriots stars in recent franchise history. If you were a fan of another team, it could be easy to work up a level of hate for Belichick. Likewise Brady, or Kraft, or anyone else associated with the franchise. But it was awfully tough to really *hate* a guy like Gronkowski, someone who not only appeared to take great joy in playing the game of football, but was an ebullient and outgoing character off the field as well. He got a side gig as the host of a kids' show on Nickelodeon called *Crashletes. How can you hate on a guy who hosts a kids' show?*

But if history were any indication, the loss of Gronkowski would put a crimp in their Super Bowl plans. In previous years that ended short of a title—including 2011, 2012, and 2013— Belichick would later lament the fact that if they had only had a fully healthy Gronkowski at the end of each one of those seasons, they might have won it all.

"The two big factors in those seasons, in the ultimate end of those seasons, were [Gronkowski's] lack of availability, and our overall ability to play defense in some critical situations," Belichick said in the NFL Films documentary *Do Your Job.*

"It was obviously good enough to get to the Super Bowl or the AFC Championship games. But just the improvement in the overall defensive play, that was one thing that we wanted to continue to try to build on," he added. "Had Rob been healthy in any of those three years, as close as those outcomes were, it might have made a difference."

And so, when Gronkowski went down and was later ruled out

for the year, it was only natural to wonder about the impact the injury would have on their title chances. There was, however, some reason to be optimistic that 2016 would be a little different from '11, '12, or '13. The truth is the Patriots offense was better equipped to deal with the loss of Gronkowski because it was more multifaceted than it had been in previous seasons when he departed prematurely. The inclusion of Bennett, the arrival of Hogan and Mitchell, the steadying presence of Edelman, and the resurgence of backs like White and Lewis in the passing game all allowed the Patriots to take a chance on a more versatile approach than the years past when Gronkowski was lost for the duration.

At the same time, the margin for error as a true Super Bowl contender had just gotten thinner. Bottom line? The 2016 Patriots would have to end the season without the two guys who started the season as the leading playmakers on each side of the ball: Gronkowski and Collins.

The day after the surgery, Gronkowski posted a video to Instagram, revealing the fact that he was up and around. He sounded a little punchy and looked stiff as he maneuvered down what looked like a hospital hallway with a walker next to his father after surgery.

"Step One: We get the kid on his feet," you could hear his father Gordy say as he followed Rob down the hall. "He's back in action."

"Dance floor tomorrow night, here I come," Gronkowski said, teetering down the hall.

"We're going to pimp it out. Throw some lights on that shit," the father said of the walker.

"Pimp Daddy Rob," responded Gronkowski with a goofy smile.

Rob Gronkowski's off-season had begun.

The high point of their three-game tune-up for the stretch run came on December 4. A late-season clash against Jeff Fisher and the woeful Rams isn't usually the sort of game you'd circle on the schedule. Frankly, you knew it wasn't a compelling matchup if the Patriots were playing a game Sunday at one o'clock at that point in the season. But it was the sort of milestone contest that would ultimately make it a memorable afternoon in Foxboro.

When it comes to the greatness of a quarterback, wins are a much-disputed measuring stick. Dave Krieg has more career wins than Bart Starr, and no one is rushing to call Krieg a better quarterback. Like victories given to a pitcher in baseball, they can be a wildly imperfect stat, because—and let's face it—sometimes there are other people more responsible for the victory. But the win over the Jets had put Brady at 200 career wins (including the postseason), and 201 would break the all-time record for most regular-season wins for a quarterback, allowing him to edge past Peyton Manning.

Set against the backdrop of a weekend-long celebration of the 2001 team—the group was being honored as part of the fifteenth anniversary of New England's first title—it gave some depth to an otherwise forgettable game that saw the Patriots feed the Rams through a woodchipper. New England won, 26–10, in a classic not-as-close-as-the-final-score-would-indicate sort of contest.

The Rams had some talent on both sides of the ball, but the core was simply in over its collective head in this one. (Los Angeles' roster didn't inspire laughter, but their coach did. Jeff Fisher was seen at one point on the sidelines struggling to find his red challenge flag. Told about the awkward moment after the game, one Patriots veteran rolled his eyes at the story.) The Patriots took a 17–0 halftime lead on the strength of touchdowns from Blount and Hogan, as well as 1 field goal from Gostkowski.

In addition, Sheard, who had been benched for the Niners contest, had one of his best games of the season that afternoon against the Rams. He had an early pressure of Jared Goff that led to a Van Noy interception, and he nearly had a pick of his own late in the fourth quarter when he dropped deep into coverage. In all, he played 55 percent of the defensive snaps that afternoon against Los Angeles, and appeared to be back in the good graces of the coaching staff.

At halftime, the 2001 team was honored as part of the celebration. A handful of former Patriots addressed the crowd, including Troy Brown, who shouted, "Fifteen years ago, we took on the greatest team on turf. That made us the greatest team on fucking Earth." The crowd went nuts. Somewhere, Marshall Faulk was undoubtedly gritting his teeth.

The sight of so many former players on the field from the roster that jump-started the whole thing was the realization of a dream for the franchise, one that it had been striving for for several years. Now, with success spread across multiple decades, there was clear evidence of a generational culture that had been created in Foxboro, not unlike what had been created in Pittsburgh and Dallas, as well as schools like the University of Miami. When you put on a Patriots jersey, there was an obligation to play the game a certain way. *To carry the banner.* Not just for your current teammates and coaches, but to live up to the tradition and history. If you didn't do your part, you'd face the wrath of the likes of Law and McGinest and Bruschi. (In the case of some of those guys, that wrath would rain down upon them in the form of scorn on national television.) For those guys, it *meant* something to be a Patriot. Woe to the current players if they didn't carry themselves appropriately and play the game the same way.

While the weekend was a chance to wake up the echoes and remind people just how remarkable the 2001 team really was, it was also an opportunity to marvel at the fact that while many members of that championship team were now in their late forties and early fifties (cornerback Otis Smith had just turned fifty-one at the time of the celebration), Brady was still out there, grinding every day. The quarterback—who was older than some of the retired New England players who returned for the weekend—was the now the oldest position player in the league. (Only a handful of special teamers, like kickers Adam Vinatieri and Matt Bryant, were older than Brady.) How did he do it?

"I think Tom [Brady] does the things he's always done; he prepares hard on and off the field physically, mentally. He studies film, knows how to game-plan, knows the opponents, [and] he's got great experience," Belichick said of the quarterback after the win over Los Angeles. "Every game, he has a couple of plays out there that are, I'd say, just made on experience. Just kind of sensing something or doing the right thing in the right situation and he's got a lot of poise. Guys are flying around all around him but he's able to keep his eyes downfield and focus on the target and does a great job in the pocket of sensing the rush."

The league acknowledged the record-setting win with a Tweet, while Brady received a congratulatory video from Brett Favre, and later revealed he got a note from Manning. With his contemporary now retired from the game and working as a company pitchman, it was one way for Brady to one-up his rival.

"[Manning is] someone that I've always been in touch with for a long time," Brady said in his weekly spot on WEEI. "I've known him for sixteen years. He sent me a very nice note. I have a lot of respect for him and all that he accomplished, too. He's a great guy. We've shared a lot of things in common and I've just always appreciated him as well."

There was no note or statement from the commissioner.

"I wouldn't expect that anyway, so that's fine," Brady told Westwood One the following Monday. "He probably has plenty of other important things [to do]."

Brady said there were many things responsible for his lengthy career: diet, nutrition, an exercise plan. He was also a big sleep advocate, and late in the season, started pitching his own line of Under Armour sleepwear. However, he wasn't always about avocado ice cream and magic pajamas. Drew Bledsoe, who was in town that week for the celebration for the 2001 team, recalled a different Brady when he was younger.

"When Tommy was young, he was just like the rest of us. I could even get him to have a beer or two back in the old days. We had some good times," Bledsoe said with a smile. "But I think that's something he's learned to develop over time as he's gotten older. I do remember as I've gotten older in my career it took a lot more work to feel the same and I think Tom saw that coming, and that's where that change has come from."

The fact that Brady was able to recognize that he needed to make a change if he wanted to continue playing is one of the reasons he's had the success he's had in his thirties.

"The fact that Tommy is still playing at the level he's at is pretty impressive," Bledsoe said. "You guys know, you wear everybody out talking about his diet and exercise regimen, but it's working. That, combined with the fact you can't hit the quarterback anymore these days, has allowed him to play a lot longer.

"Watching the deal with Cam Newton and he has a list of hits he wants to talk about with the commissioner and I'm like, 'OK I've got a list of about 150 hits I'd like to discuss with the commissioner.' These guys used to try to rip our heads off. But I think Tommy can play for a long time. He takes good care of himself. He's been a great leader for this organization, and I think he can go for a while now, which will be interesting."

Brady was enjoying a bounce-back stretch, both on and off the field. He had cooled slightly from the breakneck pace he had at the start of his season, but was still in the conversation when it came to MVP candidates, along with the likes of Atlanta's Matt Ryan, Oakland's Derek Carr, Detroit's Matthew Stafford, and Dallas' Dak Prescott, and Ezekiel Elliott. In addition, a new commercial the quarterback taped when he was sidelined premiered the week after the Seahawks game. The spot, for Foot Locker, showed a slice of self-deprecation: Two fans walk into a diner after buying shoes and wonder how Foot Locker is able to keep its "Week of Greatness" *so* great every year. They sit next to Brady, who overhears them and launches into a wild rant about their "unfortunate mind-set."

"Just because something's great year after year doesn't mean anything's going on. Why can't some things just be great?" he barks at the pair.

"It's just a question," one fan says.

"It *starts* with questions. And then questions turn into assumptions. And then assumptions turn into . . . vacations.

"So why would you punish the Week of Greatness for something that never even happened?"

And so, armed with big stars like Brady, Edelman, and Hightower hitting their stride and complementary players filling their roles perfectly, the Patriots were now 10-2. They had made some personnel adjustments on the fly and figured out some of what it would take to survive the rest of the season without Gronkowski. They quieted some critics, and secured a spot in the upper echelon of the AFC playoff picture. They had also won three straight games over the second half of the season, setting them up for a nice little bounce at the start of the stretch drive. Was the level of competition exactly world-class? Not by a long shot. But they had taken advantage of the scheduling gift they had been given, and there was no shame in that.

7. THE 12 DAYS THAT DEFINED THE 2016 PATRIOTS

I think [that period is] a good example of what kind of team this is. They're tough. They're physical. And they just grind it out.

—BELICHICK ON THE THREE-GAME STRETCH
FOR THE TEAM IN LATE NOVEMBER THAT
PRODUCED THREE WINS IN TWELVE DAYS

Those three games in that stretch . . . it said a lot about who we were. Not only physically, on the field, but mentally to be able to get through that and win out.

—SPECIAL TEAMS CAPTAIN MATTHEW SLATER
ON THE SAME THREE-GAME STRETCH LATE
IN THE REGULAR SEASON

Three games in twelve days is a lot, obviously. You have to be mentally and physically tough to handle something like that.

—LEGARRETTE BLOUNT

IN EACH ONE OF THE Patriots' campaigns under Belichick, there was a line of demarcation—usually one that came late in the season—that really served to reveal something about that year's team. Since 2001, every team was in the hunt as November turned to December. (Since the start of that season, every single regular-season game the Patriots have played has had postseason implications. The only two years they didn't make the playoffs—2002 and 2008—they were eliminated from postseason contention following the regular-season finale.) But if Belichick used the first month of the season to really try and get a handle on his team, the Thanksgiving-to-Christmas stretch always revealed the true character of the roster.

In the 2001, 2003, 2004, and 2014 seasons, New England was able to put the hammer down during the stretch drive, revealing championship character that was usually forged by overcoming a difficult challenge late in the year. All these years later, it's still remarkable to think the '01 team didn't lose a game after Thanksgiving, riding a wave all the way to the first title in franchise history.

The '03 and '04 teams were as hardened as they come; they were the last to win back-to-back Super Bowls and one of a handful of teams in NFL history to win thirty-plus games over a two-year span. It seemed like there was very little that team couldn't overcome, and that paid off with big moments in the biggest games late in the regular season. A mixture of All-World talent and toughness, they were, to lift a phrase from former Celtic Kevin Garnett, all grit and balls.

The '14 team was perhaps the ultimate example of a work in progress. There was very little that was impressive about them over the first four games of that season, a stretch that culminated with one of the ugliest losses in franchise history against the Chiefs in Kansas City. That was the come-to-Jesus moment for a team that was about to hit its stride. Turns out, they were "On to Cincinnati" and bigger and better things; their defining moment came near the end of the season in a brutal six-game stretch that saw them rise to the occasion again and again against the Broncos, Colts, and Chargers (among other teams), a test that ultimately served as the perfect preparation for a memorable postseason run.

Conversely, that same late-season period often showed some cracks in the armor that would later be manifested in the form of an earlier-than-anticipated elimination. There were a myriad of challenges that proved to be too much. In 2007, the pressure of the perfect season eventually brought them down. In 2009, they weren't very mentally tough; the damning scene in the Belichick documentary *A Football Life* where the coach was talking to the quarterback in the waning moments of a November blowout loss to the Saints in New Orleans told you all you needed to know about the reality of that team.

"I can't get this team to play the way we need to play," Belichick lamented.

In 2010, the core was still in the process of hitting the reset button. And in 2006 and 2013, a combination of age, injury, and roster turnover would combine to do them in.

Now, the 2016 team stood at a crossroads. The three previous wins had allowed them to take care of business against lesser competition, fatten up their statistical totals, and increase their lead on the rest of the conference, all while figuring out some personnel questions. A 10-2 record was a good place to be, but in some ways, it was similar to 2015. After a 10-0 start and the possibility of potentially perfect season looming, there were four losses in the last six games that saw them go from being an un-defeated juggernaut to a 12-4 finish. The low point was the regular-season finale, where they completed their gag job with an ugly loss to the Dolphins in Miami that ultimately left them with the second seed.

That memory was scalded onto the cerebral cortex of every member of the Patriots who ended up returning for 2016. The failed stretch run and the humiliation of having to watch the Broncos raise a Super Bowl trophy when they could barely beat a hobbled New England team in their own building? Inconceivable. They were going to do whatever it took not to have that happen again.

And while there was no *singular* moment when everything clicked, the defining stretch for the 2016 Patriots came in late December. That's when they came away with three wins in twelve days, including victories over traditional rivals Baltimore and Denver. It was a thunderous closing kick that showed the football world the true character of the '16 team.

Through that three-game stretch, the Patriots *never trailed*. They outscored their foes 87–29. They forced 8 turnovers and al-lowed just 2 touchdowns, and the defense solidified its position as one of the best in the league and one of the best of the Belich-ick Era.

On offense, Brady had a 60 percent completion rate, 808 yards, 6 touchdowns, 1 interception, and a passer rating of 102.9. Without Gronkowski, the success of the offense relied on Edelman, Bennett, Blount, and Lewis, and all would have their moment in the spotlight.

On special teams, Gostkowski didn't miss a single extra point or field-goal attempt. In his first game back in Denver since missing an extra point in the AFC title game the year before, he connected on field goals from 45, 40, and 21 yards out.

And the team would put the hammer down on the rest of the league, going from 10-2 and second place in the race for home field to 13-2 and the inside track on the No. 1 seed.

The first of those three games would come Monday, December 12, against the Ravens in Foxboro. While the Jets were a potential pain in the ass every time you'd face them (in North Jersey, anyway), Baltimore was pretty much a sure bet to push New England just about every time they met. The Patriots had their occasional run-ins with the likes of Denver, Pittsburgh, Indy, and others, but if we're going with the understanding that a true rivalry includes a healthy amount of wins from both sides, then New England and Baltimore had one of the more underrated feuds in the NFL, one that was renewed on a semi-regular basis. Baltimore had beaten Brady and the Patriots twice in the playoffs in Foxboro (in the wild-card round in 2009 and the AFC title game in 2012), and came within a dropped pass/pass breakup and missed field goal from another postseason win in the 2011 AFC championship game at Gillette Stadium.

The ironic thing? The two teams shared a lot of the same characteristics; like New England, the Ravens placed a premium on mental and physical toughness, and that attitude had served them well in several playoff runs under head coach John Harbaugh. Baltimore GM Ozzie Newsome learned his trade while working with Belichick in Cleveland, and a phone call from Belichick to Ravens owner Steve Bisciotti was one of the factors in helping Harbaugh land the head coaching job in Baltimore. With that in mind, it's no wonder that they occasionally found themselves competing for the same available free agents, like Steve Smith Sr., who said he nearly signed with the Patriots before joining the Ravens prior to the 2014 season.

Their most memorable battle took place in the 2014 AFC divisional playoff game, a contest where New England fell behind by 10 points, but managed to jump-start things with some trickery that included an unbalanced offensive line—a completely legal maneuver, but one that flummoxed the Ravens. Instead of calling time out, stepping back, and reassessing the situation, Baltimore complained about the move both during and after the game. The Patriots then shocked the Ravens with a double pass from Edelman to Amendola, which helped propel New England into the AFC title game.

"Nobody's ever seen that before," argued Harbaugh after the game when asked about the unbalanced line. "It's not something anybody's ever done before. The league will look at that type of thing and I'm sure that they'll make some adjustments."

"Maybe those guys [have] got to study the rule book and figure it out," Brady said of the move, which had in fact been tried on multiple occasions in college and the NFL over the last year-plus. "We obviously knew what we were doing and we made some pretty important plays. It was a real good weapon for us. Maybe we'll have something in store next week."

After the season, when it came to the Patriots-Ravens rivalry, all that anyone could talk about was the unbalanced line. That off-season, Baltimore pushed for and won rules changes that felt like a sour-grapes move, and it added another layer of intrigue to the rivalry. But Baltimore was more worried about its place in the AFC playoff picture, as the Ravens were 7-5 coming into the game, and needed to get a win to keep pace.

This one started with a bang on a clear and seasonally cool

night in Foxboro. New England went up 16–0 in the first half behind 1 safety from Malcom Brown, a 1-yard run from Blount, and a 6-yard touchdown pass from Brady to Mitchell. There was also a 19-yard scoring play to Bennett that came in the third, and was only approved by the officials after he wrestled the ball away from linebacker Zach Orr in the end zone.

"I had it. I had it," Bennett said of the catch, his fifth touchdown grab of the year. "Sometimes there's one slice of pizza left and there's two hands that reach into the box. I'm always going to get the last slice.

"Unless it's my wife's hand. Then I'll let her get it."

But those pesky Ravens hung around, and the Patriots needed some late-game magic from the combination of Brady and Hogan to pull away. A 3-play sequence from New England really underscored the difference between the two teams.

With the Patriots holding a 23–17 lead with just under eight minutes left in the fourth, Joe Flacco had engineered a Baltimore drive that saw the Ravens' offense reach the Patriots' 12-yard line. Mindful of Flacco's ability to occasionally engage in some theatrics in Foxboro, New England needed a negative play. On third and 4, a Ninkovich sack pushed Baltimore back to the 20, forcing Baltimore to settle for 1 field goal to make it 23–20.

After White brought the kickoff back to the New England 21, Brady and Hogan connected on the difference maker on the first play from scrimmage. Brady opened in the shotgun, and after a play-fake to Blount, he spotted Hogan, who had started in the slot and just *kept on running*. Veteran safety Eric Weddle, who froze after the fake to Blount, was caught flat-footed as Hogan raced past him. Brady hit him in stride, for the final score of the night, as a Gostkowski extra point followed to make it 30–23 and send everyone home happy.

"It was one mistake," Weddle lamented to Greg A. Bedard of *Sports Illustrated*. "You play great all game, making plays and he's the type of quarterback . . . a lot of quarterbacks wouldn't do that. They'd overthrow it or not even see it. You have to credit them."

The Patriots finished the night with 496 yards of total offense, the most allowed by the Ravens in a non-overtime game since they gave up 525 to the Saints in a 34–27 win on November 24, 2014. Brady ended up going 25-for-38 for 406 yards and 3 touchdowns. (It was the most passing yards allowed by Baltimore since Denver had posted 445 yards on September 5, 2013. In addition, it tied the regular-season high for Brady on the year—he also had 406 against the Browns.)

As Bedard said after the game, New England broke Baltimore's defense.

"They deserve the victory," Harbaugh said after the game. "They played winning football, and they made the plays they needed to make."

(The loss put the brakes on a streaking Baltimore team that had won four of its last five, including a 38–6 victory over the Dolphins. In truth, it was the beginning of the end for the Ravens, who ended up dropping three of their last four to finish out of the playoff picture.)

The only black mark against the Patriots that night came on special teams, specifically, the return game. Rookie Cyrus Jones was working as the punt returner in place of an injured Amendola, and the poor kid was so in his head that there were multiple occasions where he was *running away from footballs*. One time, a ball bounced off him, giving the Ravens prime field position. He was pulled after that gaffe, and when Lewis came in for the ensuing kickoff and took a knee, he got a big mock cheer from the crowd.

Going to Denver. On a short week. In December. It was maybe one of the least palatable scheduling equations in the NFL.

Denver had been a tough place to play for the Patriots for several years. The Broncos were almost always pretty good, so you start from there. But it was almost always an incredibly uncomfortable place to play. The stadium was standing-on-a-runway-next-to-a-jet-engine loud. There was occasionally some sort of bizarre weather event; the 2013 and 2015 AFC title games, both in late January, were 60° and sunny. There was the thin air of the mountains. It all lent itself to some strange days for the Patriots: Brady had his worst career road mark in Denver. Jamie Collins got turned around by Owen Daniels. Calls never seemed to go their way. And that was just the last few years. Even with the 11-2 Patriots holding an edge in just about every department on the suddenly reeling Broncos, there was always a sense of dread heading into Denver, which was 8-5 and still hanging around the outer fringes of the AFC playoff picture.

"That felt like we had the yips or something when we went in there," Slater recalled of the struggles in Colorado against the Broncos. "We couldn't get it done."

For the Broncos, this was their Super Bowl. The ineffectiveness at the quarterback position and the ill-timed injuries seemed to ensure that there would be no back-to-back Super Bowl trips. But Denver could still do its part to derail New England's attempts at landing home-field advantage. Beating the Patriots? That was always awesome.

"Bring it, New England. The Broncos are ready to go down swinging," wrote Mark Kiszla in *The Denver Post*. "This is a broken and bleeding champ's last hurrah. In front of a home crowd, against the one formidable foe that defensive lineman Derek Wolfe and everybody else in Denver love to hate, the Broncos have more than a puncher's chance to put a big hurt on Handsome Tom and the Pats one more time."

But on a short week on the road, it was New England that delivered the knockout blow. The Patriots fundamentally eliminated Denver from the playoff picture with what turned out to be a pretty convincing win, all things considered, shaking off some of the old ghosts and smothering the Broncos. New England finally got over the hump in Denver with a 16–3 win over the Broncos that featured one of the most dominant defensive performances of the season for the Patriots.

Denver's young quarterback Trevor Siemian was 25-for-40 for 282 yards, but a big chunk of those yards came late when New England backed off to protect its 13-point lead. The exclamation point came late in the contest when McCourty delivered a crushing blow to Demaryius Thomas on a fourth-down pass play, knocking the ball loose and giving the ball back to the Patriots on downs. After hearing about how they weren't a championship defense for the better part of the season, New England took some time to enjoy the moment when the game was over.

"We were doubted all year," cornerback Logan Ryan told reporters after the game. "You all said we sucked, and we heard about [the Broncos'] secondary and their defense. So we wanted to come out here and prove something."

Ryan had earned the right to talk some smack. Working as a complementary corner over the first few seasons of his career, he frequently operated in the shadows of higher profile teammates like McCourty, Butler, or Darrelle Revis. However, he had really come on strong at the end of 2015, and he kept that momentum rolling into 2016. In the final year of his contract, he had emerged as a consistent No. 2 corner who could be counted on to work in tandem with the likes of Butler. That afternoon against the Broncos, he led New England with 7 tackles, and also delivered one of the signature plays of the day.

With the Patriots and Broncos tied at 3 at the start of the second quarter, the Denver offense was driving. Siemian had steered the Broncos deep into New England territory, and was sitting on a third and 3 at the Patriots' 14. *Just don't turn the ball over, and Denver comes out of the situation with a lead.* But after taking the snap, Siemian stared down Emmanuel Sanders in the left flat, so much so that Ryan knew exactly what was coming. He stepped in front of the ball and took it all the way back to the Denver 46-yard line. The turnover led to the only touchdown of the day.

"How [the Broncos] ended our year last year, man, this was definitely a personal game for us," Ryan told reporters. "I don't care what anyone says. We wanted to come out and play well. We felt like we played well last year, too, but we didn't play well in the red area. We wanted to come out here and completely dominate the game, make the quarterback look like a young quarterback."

But the guy who got to exorcise most of those demons that afternoon against Denver was right tackle Marcus Cannon. Cannon was swallowed whole in the 2015 AFC title game by the Broncos pass rush. Fair or not, he was the one who stood out the most in that loss, and heading into that off-season, everyone outside of Gillette wanted him gone. But much to the consternation of a large portion of the fan base, he not only stuck around, but the fact that Vollmer had spent the whole season on the reserve/physically-unable-to-perform list opened the door for Cannon to become a full-timer once again.

Since the start of the year, he had performed extremely well for three primary reasons: one, he was back working with Scarnecchia. Two, he lost weight, and the reshaped body made the transition from guard to tackle that much smoother. No one was going to step up and say exactly how much weight he'd lost, but it's worth noting that his pre-draft profile had him at 358 pounds, while the 2016 Patriots roster had him listed at 335. Truth be told, Cannon was a guard playing tackle last year for a few reasons, not the least of which is the fact that he was a little more solidly built than most tackles. And three, he was able to develop good consistency and continuity with the rest of the offensive line, as he started fifteen regular-season games and all three playoff games at the same position.

"Marcus is having a good season. He's been a good player for us," Belichick said of Cannon in late November. "Marcus has always done a solid job for us whenever he's played. I'm glad we have him going forward. He works hard. A quiet kid, but he's very dependable [and] team-oriented. He's done a good job for us in the running game and the passing game. He's been a good player."

"Just changed some stuff here and there," Cannon said when asked about his weight loss. "We have a great strength and conditioning coach; he helped a lot. Just put some good people in my corner and helped me be the best I can be."

Cannon wasn't the type to say a lot, but his performance in

2016 spoke volumes, especially that afternoon against the Broncos. In the 2015 AFC championship game, Miller racked up 5 tackles, 2.5 sacks, 4 quarterback hits, and 1 interception. Almost a year later, against the same opponent, Miller finished with 4 tackles and nothing else.

"Those two really were matched up a lot," Belichick said after the game when asked about the Miller-Cannon showdown. "But I thought Marcus did a real solid job for us, as he always does. Sometimes he was on Miller, sometimes he wasn't—he was on defensive ends or combination blocking the linebackers and so forth. But they certainly saw plenty of each other. I thought Marcus competed well. Our offensive line competed well against that front seven, which is a very good group."

The best tribute to Cannon probably didn't come via the contract extension from the Patriots, or the performance that Sunday against Denver. Instead, it was when the 2016 Pro Bowl rosters were announced the following month; the fact the TCU product was snubbed for the honor got several New England fans upset. It was hard to imagine another member of the Patriots' roster taking the same journey in such a relatively short span. But the recognition from the fan base was a well-deserved honor, and a sign he had come a long way in a relatively short period of time.

"Marcus has just become more consistent each week, each year that I've had an opportunity to be around him," Josh McDaniels said. "I think he's just trusting his preparation and playing—he always plays as hard as he possibly can. He prepares hard, he practices hard, and it means a lot to him to do his job."

While the best game statistically wasn't the win over the Broncos, it was one of the most satisfying victories of the season on both a team and an individual level. It moved the Patriots to 12-2, and secured the Patriots a first-round playoff bye. It also managed to seal Denver's fate and remove at least some of the mystique for the Patriots around playing in Colorado, much to the chagrin of Kiszla.

"The champs are dead," he wrote of the Broncos after the game. "Long live the champs."

Meanwhile, the win had allowed the Patriots to take another step on their own championship journey. The victory clinched the AFC East title for New England. It was a hat and T-shirt game; first named by former linebacker Tedy Bruschi, he called it that because after you got back to the locker room, there were new hats and T-shirts waiting in your locker. Through the years, the team had mixed emotions about celebrating a division champion milestone. In 2001, it was a monumental event. In the years since, the reaction had moved to something sort of lukewarm. That's not to say there wasn't a certain level of appreciation. It's just that when you win eight straight division championships and fourteen in sixteen years, it becomes part of the routine.

But there seemed to be a resurgence of emotion the last few seasons. And whether it was the emotion of the year, the joy associated with a big road win over a rival, or the fact that they had simply completed the first step on the road to a Super Bowl, it was a loud locker room.

Once everyone had returned from the freezing cold field, across the room, Belichick spotted Butler.

"You look good in that hat!" Belichick exclaimed.

"Yeah!" Butler replied with a smile.

"You can't BUY these!" shouted Slater, holding a shirt that read HOLD DOWN THE EAST. "You've got to EARN these!"

Meanwhile, some of the new guys who were headed to the

"It was *embarrassing*," said Jets wide receiver Brandon Marshall. "You guys are smart. You saw the game. It was just *embarrassing*."

While New York was forced to shuffle quarterbacks because of injury and ineffectiveness, the defensive standout was Butler. That afternoon, he didn't allow a single reception in coverage. He also picked off 2 passes: The first was a Bryce Petty offering for Robby Anderson midway through the first quarter, and the second came when he intercepted Fitzpatrick on a ball for Quincy Enunwa late in the third quarter. He also recovered a fumble early in the second quarter after teammate Elandon Roberts delivered a big hit on Khiry Robinson. While you could argue there were better single-game performances over the course of the season, it was easily his finest statistical moment of the year.

The other star of the show after the game? Backup tight end Matt Lengel, who stepped into the lineup when Gronkowski was lost for the season. A practice squad refugee from Cincinnati who was signed away by New England in early November, he had his first career reception on a touchdown pass from Brady on Christmas Eve against the Jets, an 18-yarder.

The last guy in the NFL who was part of Northeastern University's football team—he was a redshirt freshman in 2009, the last year of football at the school—it was a long road to that point for Lengel. He transferred to Eastern Kentucky after the Northeastern program shut down, but between his transfer and injuries (he battled through multiple knee injuries), he ended up spending six years in college. He had spent the majority of the two previous seasons on the Bengals' practice squad before he was signed by the Patriots after injuries to Gronkowski and Greg Scruggs. And on Christmas Eve, he became a cult hero of sorts, coming out of nowhere to catch a touchdown pass from Brady and inspire football fans everywhere to wonder *Matt Who?* (Lengel's unlikely star turn was augmented by his brother Mike, who became a semi-celebrity on social media after he tweeted during the game: "MY BROTHER JUST CAUGHT A TD FROM BRADY!")

"The first catch of his career, and it's from Tom Brady," marveled CBS broadcaster Ian Eagle. "A memory forever."

"Merry Christmas, Matt Lengel," added CBS analyst Dan Fouts.

Forty-one points and a story like Lengel's is always a good thing, but the biggest aspect to come out of the Jets game was the continued dominance of the defense and the statistical trend heading into the postseason. Through fifteen games, the defensive splits between the first half and second half of the year for the Patriots were staggering. There were several different things that went into the improved totals, but however you wanted to break it down, they were certainly trending in the right direction as the playoffs loomed: Since the Collins trade, the Patriots' run defense had gone from allowing an average of 101.6 rushing yards per game to 89.5 rushing yards per game. The pass defense went from allowing 253 passing yards per game to 240. The points per game allowed went from 16.8 to 15.7. And since the bye (seven games), they had 11 takeaways, including 3 against the Jets. That was after 9 takeaways through the first eight games.

Two important things: one, *it wasn't all because of the trade.* And two, you had to take the totals with a grain of salt because of the level of competition that was faced over that stretch. But the before and after splits, as well as the level of execution, provided ample evidence the Patriots had hit on the right combination.

When it came to measuring mental toughness, three games—and three wins—in twelve days at the end of the regular season was a big statement. New England was 13-2, with one game remaining, a New Year's Day date with the Dolphins in South Florida. (Miami had flipped the script on its early-season woes, and had become the hottest team in football, winning nine of its last ten games.) But a game up on the Raiders in the chase for home field with one week to go, the Patriots were playing their best football of the season, fueled by the memory of last year's choke job. For New England, it was time to focus and finish.

"We feel like we're playing our best ball now, and last year we weren't at this point," Logan Ryan said after he and the rest of the Patriots defense systematically dismantled the Jets. "We just have to continue to not take anything for granted—just like we didn't take the Jets for granted—and go out and practice in these frigid temperatures. And it's going to help us [come game time]."

The Patriots had ground through the toughest stretch of their regular-season schedule. They had answered their critics, winning three games—two on short weeks—in twelve days. They were days from securing home-field advantage, one of the primary steps on the road to a championship. At home on Christmas Eve, they were exactly where they wanted to be.

8. "WORK FUCKING HARD EVERY FUCKING DAY"

And, when you want something, all the universe conspires in helping you to achieve it.

—PAULO COELHO, *THE ALCHEMIST*

UNDER BILL BELICHICK, THE PATRIOTS have frequently leaned on slogans as a rallying cry. *Do Your Job. Fresh As Lettuce. On To Cincinnati. Tonight, We Are All Patriots.* Some are more organic than others, while some feel like they were ripped right out of a motivational guide. Regardless, by the end of most seasons, there's usually some sort of catchphrase that's been slapped on the franchise as an identifier about who they are and what they might be capable of accomplishing.

And while the 2016 Patriots were indeed riding high heading into late November—they were on the short list of genuine Super Bowl contenders at that point—they still lacked that all-encompassing slogan that defined who they were.

Their most memorable catchphrase over the previous few years was *Do Your Job*, the three words that came to embody the 2014 season. NFL Films utilized it as the title of the championship film on that year's team. It was an organic, three-word saying that was borne out of the language Belichick used when he would deliver a semi-profane tongue-lashing in the early days of his Patriots coaching career. Ultimately, it would come to embody a brand philosophy that's defined the Patriots and the way they do business.

"Maybe the one word that isn't in that's implied is 'Do your job . . . *well*,'" Belichick explained in the documentary. "It could be enough to make the difference."

Like all great catchphrases, however, it evolved over the years. In the early days of the twenty-first century, the phrase had a far saltier origin. When Belichick first arrived in Foxboro, it was more of a behind-the-scenes exhortation meant for the ears of players and coaches only. And instead of "Do your job . . . well," the phrase had a different wording.

"It was usually 'Do your fucking job!'" recalled one former player.

In the end, the Patriots took it, cleaned it up, and made it family-friendly enough to slap on T-shirts, hoodies, decals, caps, hats, and pins. The team thought so much of the philosophy that they even put it on the Super Bowl rings that year. (The final commodification of the phrase came last year when, like John Calipari did with "Refuse to Lose" and Pat Riley did with "Threepeat," they trademarked the phrase.)

In that same vein, for those who were casting about for some sort of all-encompassing saying that encapsulated the struggle and work ethic of the 2016 team, they found it in a November 27 conversation with Bennett following the win over the Jets. After a tractor-pull of a victory against New York, Bennett was asked why the team continued to *expect* success around every turn, despite any sort of long odds—the injury to Gronkowski, the suspension of Brady—that might be stacked against them. He shrugged and laughed.

"Because we work *fucking* hard every *fucking* day."

There was a pause.

"We work *hard* at this shit. Those moments, we work in those moments," he added. "They get paid millions of dollars to stop us, but we get paid millions of dollars to make plays. And we're going to make them."

Bennett's exhortation was just one of several memorable lines from the tight end over the course of the 2016 season. If you were a solo reporter working at a small outlet, you had to get quotes from him—he talked most of the time on Thursday or Friday during the week, as well as after games. He was always offering something for the media, even if it was a bit off the wall. There were sessions about bacon, his love for his wife, Gatorade, chips, Eastern philosophy, the state of the NFL concussion protocol, the book *The Alchemist*, his belief that he's the black Dr. Seuss or the Kanye of the NFL, and many other topics.

But this one hit it right on the head. The 2016 Patriots had carved out their identity with a simple R-rated phrase that pretty much spelled out their philosophy. They were true grinders. Their work ethic, focus, and attitude shaped their identity. And while other contenders started to fall away—Denver, Baltimore, and Indy—it was precisely that sort of drive that kept the whole thing moving right along.

Yeah, they had Brady and Edelman and plenty of emerging star power. But they were also a team that could suffocate their opponents. They weren't very sexy on the defensive side of the ball, especially after the trade of Collins. But the level of execution kept opponents out of the end zone. Over the last five-plus regular-season games, the Patriots' defense allowed a *total* of 6 touchdowns, including a stretch of ten consecutive quarters where they didn't allow a single touchdown to be scored.

The defense, derided as an underachieving and undisciplined unit in October, was now in position to become one of the best regular-season defenses in recent franchise history. It was an admitted long shot, but if they could manage a shutout of the Dolphins in the last game of the year, the New England defense would hold opponents to 236 points for the 2016 regular season. That would set a new franchise mark in terms of the fewest points allowed in a sixteen-game season, as well as a franchise record for fewest points per contest allowed in a sixteen-game season at 14.7 points per game.

Even if they couldn't pull off the shutout against the Dolphins, the growth exhibited by the New England defense over the course of the season was astounding. As Matt Patricia indicated midway through the year, it was a work in progress. By late December, that work in progress looked pretty good. Late in the season, Belichick attributed the improvement to a group that was simply dedicated to getting better each day.

"We've improved on a daily basis, really. Going out to the practice field and getting better on a daily basis," Belichick said of the 2016 crew. "We've had some players that are playing quite a bit for us now that either weren't on our team or weren't playing that much at the beginning of the year or in training camp. I think that's come together."

There were plenty of reasons for the defensive success, but it was hard to look past Hightower, who had become an elite off-the-ball linebacker. He was continuing to struggle with injury, but more and more, he had begun to emerge as the go-to guy for a generation of New England defenders.

"I'm just ready for whatever they put on my plate," he said late in the season, "whether it's loaded or not, and just try to do what's expected [of] me. There has been times where it worked and times where it hasn't. It's part of the learning curve, and that's just something that comes with football and life, and I'll just keep trying to move on that and keep trying to hold my spot as well as I can for my teammates."

Then there were the complementary guys like defensive lineman Alan Branch, who rode a wave throughout the season. Several of his teammates (including Hightower) called Branch, who was one of the guys who was having an eventful season but didn't get near the amount of respect he warranted, one of the unsung heroes of the defense in 2016. The big guy, who was cut loose by the Bills in August 2014 after a DUI, had become an increasingly important part of what the Patriots did defensively; he was strong, smart, durable, versatile, and cost-effective. Basically, he was the classic type of veteran defensive lineman the Patriots had utilized for over the last dozen-plus years, a talented pickup in the second half of his career who was hoping to finally nail down a ring in New England.

He had a strong finish to the 2014 championship season, and after bouncing from Arizona to Seattle to Buffalo over the first few years of his career, was happy to sign a two-year deal with the Patriots in the months after Super Bowl XLIX. There was another strong season in 2015, and as he became more entrenched in the New England system, he served as something of a mentor for younger defensive linemen like Malcom Brown, as well as 2016 draftee Vincent Valentine.

As the season wore on, Branch, Valentine, and Brown became part of a rotation along the defensive line, with Trey Flowers working along the interior, as well as getting some reps at defensive end. In the New England defense, the rewards for defensive linemen are few—the group isn't called upon to do much penetration. Instead, it's about trying to occupy multiple offensive linemen and free things up for the linebackers and defensive backs. (That's not to say they aren't responsible for getting after the quarterback. Brown and Branch picked up their share of tackles for loss in 2016, with Brown netting 1 safety in the win over the Ravens. Meanwhile, Flowers led the 2016 team in sacks. It's just that it's usually not their ultimate priority.) And few were more effective at it than Branch.

But there was trouble for Branch when it was revealed on November 21 that the veteran was going to be suspended four games for violating the league's policy on substance abuse, a troubling story on a number of levels, including the fact that Branch had been suspended by the team for an unspecified incident in August, one he had no interest in expanding upon when he returned to the locker room.

"If Bill [Belichick] isn't telling you, I'm not saying a damn thing," Branch said with a smile after he returned following a weeklong ban. "I guarantee that. If you're looking for something from me, it isn't happening."

But Branch won his November appeal—his agent Blake Baratz said it was "rescinded"—and the Patriots' interior defense never missed a beat. That was true on the field as well as the sidelines. Branch, who had the sweetest dance moves of anyone at 350-plus pounds, was frequently seen boogeying on the sidelines during the occasional stoppage in play. (He seemed to have a particular affinity for Whitney Houston's "I Wanna Dance with Somebody.") And as the 2016 season went on, the Alan Branch Sideline Dance Party became a thing. The big man, who occasionally bragged about his break-dancing career, continued to show each week that he had the moves necessary to help carry the interior of the New England defensive line back to another title.

On offense, they had learned to survive without Gronkowski. They were far less personnel-dependent than they had been in previous years when he had been prematurely lost for the season. Ultimately, it meant more work for the likes of Hogan, who replaced part of the downfield element that Gronkowski brought to the field over the first half of the 2016 season. It meant more was on the shoulders of Mitchell and Amendola and Edelman. And Bennett played a huge role as a blocker and pass catcher when it came to picking up slack in the wake of Gronkowski's injury. They wouldn't get to where they needed to be without him.

Ultimately no one ended up spreading the wealth in the passing game in 2016 better than the Patriots. The 2016 team was the first of the Belichick Era in New England to have five different receivers finish the year with 500 or more yards receiving. Part of it was because of the void created by the loss of Gronkowski, but the fact that the Patriots had Edelman (1,106 yards in the regular season), Bennett (701), Hogan (680), White (551), and Gronkowski (540) all clicking is an impressive display of versatility and multiplicity. No other team in the league had more than five pass catchers finish the season with 500-plus receiving yards.

One thing many opponents saw down the stretch and into the postseason was an increased reliance on backs in the passing game. For its occasional struggles in finding young receivers who could mesh with Brady, New England had an excellent track record when it came to identifying pass-catching backs. From Faulk to Danny Woodhead to Shane Vereen, all of them had emerged as serious threats who could do damage in space. Now, that torch had been passed to White and Lewis. And while White had emerged as a dependable presence in the passing game at the start of the 2016 season, the return of Dion Lewis augmented the passing attack, and gave Brady another option. Lewis had returned in late November, and provided depth and veteran savvy. He also allowed the Patriots to give Blount a bit of a breather, as the big back had already hit career highs in carries, yards, and touchdowns by the time December rolled around. Lewis had a surprising number of between-the-tackles touches late in the year—over the last three games of the regular season, he averaged 15 carries and 65 yards a game, all while stepping in to work as an occasional return man. (By this point, rookie Cyrus Jones was struggling in the return game to a point where he was pretty much a nonfactor.)

Lewis was the sort of feel-good story everyone could get behind, even those who didn't like the Patriots. The 5-foot-8, 195-pound back had suffered multiple knee injuries, and had bounced around from Philly to Cleveland to Indianapolis before he was signed as one of a handful of potential replacements for Vereen prior to the start of the 2015 season. But he beat out a bunch of candidates—including White, who was a rookie—for the job of third-down back that year, and quickly established himself as an electric performer with make-you-miss shiftiness, a trait that's absolutely vital at the position in New England. Just three games into his career with the Patriots, he had already impressed (including 120 yards from scrimmage in the opener against the Steelers) to a point where he agreed to a contract extension. Eventually, he was on pace for a season with more than 500 yards rushing and 500 yards receiving before going down in a heap with a knee injury in a November win over the Redskins.

Now, he was back to something close to full strength, and the Patriots weren't shy about finding ways to get their two backs on the field at the same time, preferably matched up against linebackers. If they could locate a positive matchup involving White and/or Lewis, chances were good Brady could find them and create positive yardage.

(Lewis also gained a sizable measure of notoriety for his remarkable streak: since he had joined the Patriots prior to the start of the 2015 season, every time he played, New England won. He played the first seven games of '15 before going down with a knee injury, and the Patriots started that year 7-0. Now, since he had returned in November, New England had not lost. Lewis would eventually keep his streak alive through the end of the regular season and into the postseason. After Super Bowl LI, his streak had reached seventeen straight wins with the Patriots.)

Lewis was one reason they managed to thrive without Gronkowski. Granted, they weren't the consistently overwhelming offensive presence they had been with him in the lineup. But in some ways, with a plethora of make-you-miss guys, they also became more difficult to defend. Veteran defensive back Eric Weddle faced the Patriots with and without Gronkowski over the years, and told Greg A. Bedard of *Sports Illustrated* in December that matchups New England deployed without Gronkowski in the lineup could be a nightmare, particularly when it came to accounting for the backs in the passing game.

"They spread you out a lot more," Weddle told Bedard. "With those backs, they're like receivers. You saw [White]. Put him out at No. 1 and he runs a slant for 60 [yards] when we're playing man and we're doubling [Edelman] and we're playing 2-man away so it's like, you can only take away so many [options] and they made a great play. That's just the matchups that they present on a play-to-play basis. Very rarely do they give you a chance to take advantage."

In addition to the backs, one other guy who was coming up big again and again in the passing game was Amendola. He had been bumped down the depth chart over the last year-plus, but every time Brady threw in his direction, he seemed to catch it. From the start of the 2015 season through the first eight games of the 2016 campaign, he was one of the most dependable receivers in the league. Since the start of the 2015 season, Amendola and Seattle's Doug Baldwin were the only two wide receivers in the league who were targeted at least 100 times and had a catch rate of 75 percent or better in regular-season action, according to Pro Football Reference—Amendola had 81 catches on 107 targets (75.7 percent) and Baldwin had 116 catches on 154 targets (75.3 percent). Amendola didn't get near the amount of targets in the New England passing game as Edelman or Gronkowski, but his dependability was an overlooked aspect of the Patriots offense.

Amendola's value would pop up at random times. He played a major role in one of the more significant moments of the 2014 postseason when he was on the receiving end of an Edelman pass in the divisional playoff game against the Ravens, a thunderbolt of a play that changed the complexion of the game. He was also

huge in Super Bowl XLIX with 5 catches for 48 yards and a touchdown. And along with White, he was maybe the most consistent
offensive performer from start to finish in Super Bowl LI. (His
absence late in the 2016 regular season because of a foot injury
also underscored his special teams skills, as New England struggled to find a replacement.) For a guy who had to take multiple
pay cuts between 2013 and 2015 to stay on the roster, he had a
knack for rising to the occasion in the big moments.

But the fact that the offense was clicking without Gronkowski
was in large part a tribute to the work of Josh McDaniels. He had
been gifted with a supremely talented group of individuals on offense, but using more and more of the quick passing game and
smallish receiving corps was a way to minimize the weaknesses
and maximize the strengths of the New England attack. And
based—at least partially—on his work over the second half of the
season, his name started popping up as a potential head coaching
candidate again. The truth was that McDaniels was a perennial
possibility, and this past year was no exception. In January, his
name would be linked to the open Niners job, but McDaniels had
the good sense to pull his name from consideration before things
ever got too serious. McDaniels, who washed out after two mostly
down years in Denver, had to be very picky when it came to his
next head coaching opportunity. Coaches only get so many bites
at the apple, and a sub-.500 record would make it awfully hard to
get another head coaching gig. The situation in San Francisco—
where the Niners were looking for their fifth head coach since
2010—certainly didn't appear to be set up for success.

"They did a great job with their presentation," McDaniels said
of his meeting with San Francisco. "[I'm] humbled to be included
in that process. At this time, it's just best for my family and myself

to remain here in New England, and focus on this year's playoffs and finish out the year however it turns out."

On the other side of the ball, a year after he got head coaching consideration from the Browns, Patricia drew the attention of the Chargers and Rams. But like McDaniels, it wasn't a good fit for him, at least at this point in his career.

"I'm so sick and tired of everyone talking about Coach Belichick. Yes, he is great," Jets receiver Brandon Marshall said late in the season. "But the reason why I'm so sick and tired of everyone talking about Coach Belichick is because they think he does everything, and he's the only one in the building that's working. They have a defensive coordinator by the name of Matt Patricia in New England who's awesome. He has the best third-down defense, and it's not because of statistics. It's because of the creativity."

"I think both Josh and Matt are great coaches," Belichick said in November. "[They] should absolutely be on any head coaching list. I can't imagine that there are many other coaches that could present a résumé equal or comparable to theirs. They've done a great job here for a sustained period of time so a great track record. I think, I personally think, that a list of head coaching candidates that didn't include them would be incomplete."

The coordinators were on a roll, and were a sizable part of one of the most astonishing stats of the 2016 season: From the second half of their win over the Jets on November 27 through the first quarter of the Super Bowl, the Patriots didn't trail at all. A lot of that was because they were able to get up on teams early and make them one-dimensional. But there were also several occasions where they were able to wear down their opponents by playing smart and physical football for all sixty minutes.

They had also managed to stay lucky when it came to maintaining relatively good health. There was the season-ending injury to Gronkowski, the fact that Lewis didn't return until midway through the season, as well as the fact they had to learn how to live without their starting right tackle (Vollmer) pretty quickly. But when you stacked them against some of the team's primary competition in the AFC, the Patriots were fortunate. Oakland quarterback Derek Carr (broken fibula), Denver running back C. J. Anderson (meniscus), Houston defensive lineman J. J. Watt (back), and Kansas City running back Jamaal Charles (knee) were some of the high-profile stars in the AFC who missed a significant stretch because of injuries. While the Patriots had their share of health issues, they had cut down on the health problems that had plagued them in 2015, when they were the NFL team that ended up losing the most man-games due to injury. Because of the health issues, they were forced to roll the dice at the end of the year as they tried to balance health vs. momentum. The result? They came up snake eyes in pursuit of home-field advantage.

But with one game left in the regular-season, it was a different story in 2016. There were a few reasons behind the difference. There was simple luck, but there was also a focus on "soft-tissue injuries," which are frequently a function of training, hydration, nutrition, and rest.

"A broken bone or an impact hit that causes a problem, it's hard to prevent those. Some of those are going to happen, although I do think there is an element of training that comes into play there, too," Belichick explained late in the season. "But noncontact injuries, injuries that occur from, again, pulled muscles, from dehydration or fatigue or whatever happens, those are the ones that

I think as a coach and as a staff you look back on and say, 'Could we have done things differently there?'

"So yes, some of that involves the individual player, his specific body composition and skill set and demands, and some of it is probably the training that we put him through and so forth, and how we best prepare the players for the workloads that they're going to have on game day. It's a long conversation, and one that we've spent a lot of time on."

In late December, the NFL regular season was winding down. The Patriots were just one of several teams that had gotten separation from the rest of the field, and while there were some playoff spots up for grabs, most of the teams were already counting down the days to the off-season, the Senior Bowl, and the start of the new league year and free agency in March. Sitting in New England, where postseason football had simply ceased to become a privilege and was more just part of the calendar, it was easy to lose sight of the fact of how good life was. For much of the NFL, the optimism that most every team had around Labor Day had dissolved to a sobering reality: They weren't going to the playoffs. In fact, many of the teams would be hitting the reset button when it came to the coaching staff and the front office. *Again.*

A handful of coaches had already gotten fired, as teams started to get a jump on the work of the off-season and begin the process of beating the other teams to The Next Great Young Coach. Heading into the final week of 2016, Jeff Fisher (Los Angeles) and Gus Bradley (Jacksonville) had already been fired. And on December 27, the Bills pulled the plug on the Rex Ryan Era after almost two seasons and just thirty-one games. There would be more firings, but the news of Rex's being let go by Buffalo gar-nered the greatest headlines in New England.

The Ryan-Belichick relationship always seemed contentious; perhaps it was because Ryan had both of his head coaching jobs in the AFC East, where he was guaranteed to meet Belichick and the Patriots at least twice a year. But while they came at their jobs from two distinctly different viewpoints, there was a real respect. Products of football families, they made their bones as defen-sive coordinators before moving on to head coaching gigs. While Belichick was publicly supportive of the thirty-one other coaches in the league, you could tell there were guys he genuinely re-spected. For the most part, Rex was one of those guys.

While Belichick didn't offer much of a comment on Ryan's firing when he initially met the media, other than a quick "Yeah, just worrying about Miami," he expanded on that a bit later on.

"There's not too much I can do about it," Belichick told WEEI. "Every situation is different. I don't know exactly where every-body else is. I try and dedicate my time and energy into the situation I am in. I can't really comment on what is going on with every-body else.

"There's a lot of change," he added. "It's frequent, and it seems like it's coming earlier and earlier every year. I don't think person-ally that's the best way to manage a team, but that's really not my call. Some of these guys, they just do whatever they do. I can't worry about it—just make the best decisions for our team, and get ready to go here."

While it was easy to overlook, one of the things that had dis-tinguished the Patriots from the rest of the AFC East since 2000 was an unprecedented run of stability. From 2000 through the end of the 2016 regular season, the Patriots had one head coach:

Belichick. While some coaches had been rehired in that time—like Bowles, who was an interim head coach in Miami before he took over as head coach of the Jets prior to the start of the 2015 season—twenty-three different head coaches were employed in the AFC East. (That was including the Bowles move, as well as the move from Ryan to interim Anthony Lynn that was made in late December by the Bills. Buffalo's off-season hiring of new head coach Sean McDermott pushed it to twenty-four.)

That's not to say the New England coaching staff hadn't been touched by change in that stretch. Since 2000, Belichick has had three different offensive coordinators (Charlie Weis, Bill O'Brien, and Josh McDaniels) and three different defensive coordinators (Romeo Crennel, Dean Pees, and Matt Patricia). In addition, positional coaches like Brian Daboll, Patrick Graham, and Pepper Johnson have come and gone. But when it comes to overall continuity and consistency, the example set forth by the Patriots is stunning. Belichick has been in charge since 2000, and the only coaches who come close to him in terms of longevity are Marvin Lewis (in Cincy since 2003), Mike McCarthy and Sean Payton (in Green Bay and New Orleans, respectively, since 2006), and Mike Tomlin (in Pittsburgh since 2007).

There are several reasons why Patriots fans should treasure these days, but the fact that the Patriots have had the same coach and quarterback in place since 2001? That gave them an instant edge, one that only a handful of other teams (Green Bay, New Orleans, Pittsburgh) could even think about matching. Brady freely admitted that it had given them an edge over a sizable portion of the competition.

"Continuity is huge in the NFL," Brady told WEEI late in the year. "I've been in the same offense for seventeen years and played for just a couple coordinators, one head coach. Our system's been in place."

The team-building process never stops. The midseason acquisition of Van Noy was one indication the Patriots were willing to do some tinkering in the middle of the season. But the Van Noy pickup was a blip on the radar compared with the fanfare that came with the acquisition of wide receiver Michael Floyd. He was released by the Cardinals on December 14 following a DUI arrest, and signed by the Patriots the next day. Floyd already toted plenty of baggage into Foxboro, and things got considerably more complicated when a video of the arrest went public. (In February, he would plead guilty to extreme DUI, and was sentenced to twenty-four days in prison and ninety-six days of house arrest.)

Belichick said there would be structure in place to deal with some of the challenges that came with adding a player like Floyd.

"We have a lot of things on our team to handle a multitude of things that players, coaches, and anyone in our organization can come up," Belichick said the Wednesday following the emergence of the police video. "There are a lot of things outside of football that we will deal with. It's a long, long list. We provide a lot of resources for everybody. So, yeah, absolutely. Without a doubt."

One thing he didn't have to deal with? The Curse of Number 17. The Patriots had a run of bad luck when assigning that number to wide receivers. Aaron Dobson, who was released just prior to the start of the regular season, had No. 17. Prior to that, Greg Salas had it when he was in New England for a spell in 2012, but had no catches in the one game he was a part of. In addition, Taylor Price had it for almost two seasons (2010 and part of 2011), but the third-round pick out of Ohio had just 3 catches in his time in New England. Before Price, it was another underperforming receiver—Chad Jackson—who had No. 17. The former Florida standout had just 14 catches in two seasons (2006 and 2007) with New England.

Floyd traveled with the team to Denver for the game against the Broncos but did not play. Instead—while wearing No. 14—Floyd suited up for the first time on Christmas Eve against the Jets, and had 1 catch for 6 yards. On and off the record, his teammates said he worked hard, listened, and was a good teammate for the final month-plus of the season.

And in the best example of the fact that it took everyone on the roster to ensure a championship season, even a late arrival like Floyd managed to get his time in the spotlight. In the regular-season finale against the Dolphins, he caught his first touchdown as a member of the Patriots, a 14-yard reception from Brady where he fought his way into the end zone, battling through the last few would-be tacklers before scoring to make it 14–0.

His signature moment—and one of the signature moments of the season for the entire roster—came midway through the third quarter. Miami had cut the lead to 20–14, and the memories of the 2015 flameout in the regular-season finale were briefly rekindled. New England had a third and 7 at its own 23-yard line when Brady hit Edelman on a quick out. The receiver slipped one tackle, and headed toward midfield. Just before he hit the 50, Edelman and Floyd worked together to find the perfect angle on defender Tony Lippett. Floyd lined up Lippett and *KAPOW!* He knocked him sideways.

"I didn't see him at all," Lippett said when asked about Floyd's block after the game. "I was trying to make a play on Edelman and he basically blindsided me. It was a good hit by him."

The block allowed Edelman to race to the end zone for the score, and New England would go on to the 35–14 win. The play provided the exclamation point on the regular-season finale, and provided the clearest example that when it came to a finishing kick, no one was going to be able to keep up with the Patriots. As for Floyd, it was the highlight of his relatively brief tenure with New England.

"Unbelievable," Edelman said of Floyd. "Mike came in here, he has been here for, like, two weeks, and he had a big opportunity this week to come in and help us and he made some plays. He's tough. He's physical. He can be in the room anytime I'm here. I like him."

Even if it was only for a handful of plays toward the end of the season, the Patriots' offense needed contributions from the likes of Floyd and Engel to keep the whole thing moving, because after Gronkowski was lost for the season in late November, the margin for error was perilously slim. Not so much in the "We're not going to make the playoffs" sort of slim. More like the "We're going to have a hard time winning the Super Bowl" sort of slim.

Gronkowski or no, they arrived on the doorstep of the playoffs playing their best football with seven straight wins and home-field advantage. The regular season was done, and with the win over Miami, they continued to burnish their résumé as one of the most mentally tough teams in recent memory; they ended the year as only one of nine teams in the history of the NFL to win eight regular-season road games in one year. But that won't get you anywhere in the playoffs.

"Gotta keep grinding," Belichick said with the regular season done. "Just keep getting better. There are a lot of things we can still improve on. We'll work on some of those this week, then we'll find out who we play, and then we'll start getting ready for whoever that team is. This team, we've got a good opportunity to work on some things, get better at some things we need to get better at. So we'll try to use that time productively and do it. We have a good opportunity to work on some things."

The real season? It was about to begin.

9. THE DRIVE FOR FIVE

We spotted those assholes a day and a half . . . so be it. We'll be ready for their ass.
— Steelers coach Mike Tomlin, in a speech to his team that was caught on Antonio Brown's Facebook Live stream in the moments after a division playoff win over the Chiefs that set up an AFC title game contest against the Patriots in Foxboro

I'm not sure, Gary. I don't know.
— Brady in the days before the AFC title game, asked by Gary Myers of the New York *Daily News* as to why the Patriots seem to elicit such a strong response

I don't know. Go ask Dallas and Kansas City.
— Belichick on any help the Patriots might get in the AFC title game because of home-field advantage

I don't give a shit about his social media. I don't follow him. Send some followers my way, Antonio. I've got better content.
—BENNETT ON ANTONIO BROWN'S SOCIAL MEDIA GAFFE FOLLOWING PITTSBURGH'S AFC DIVISIONAL PLAYOFF WIN OVER THE CHIEFS

I mean, shit, I don't know. I like cake a lot, and every time I get a new slice, I'm just as happy.
—BENNETT ON WHY PATRIOTS FANS HAVE BEEN ABLE TO MAINTAIN THEIR PASSION AFTER SO MANY TRIPS TO THE POSTSEASON OVER THE LAST DOZEN YEARS

WHILE THE REST OF THE league opened the postseason on January 7, in New England, the Patriots got to sit and wait for a week. Through the first weekend of the playoffs, there was some down time for the players. But for Belichick and the coaching staff, heading into wild-card weekend, it was full throttle.

"We're in the home stretch right here," Belichick said. "I don't think this is the time for the coaches to back off, or anybody for that matter. This is what it's all about. This is the highest level of competition that you can have. It's the best teams."

He added: "Regardless of who we play, there are things that we need to do. But then, we also need to know as much as we can and be prepared for the players when they come back in to give them the best information and the best scouting report and the best game plan we can to give them the best chance to win. That job isn't done yet. We've still got a lot of work to do."

It was a fun stretch for the Patriots, who had worked hard to claim the No. 1 seed, and had the weekend to enjoy the fruits of that labor. Players were mindful of the challenge ahead, but at the same time, the free weekend allowed them to heal up and be as ready as possible for the divisional round, all while armed with the knowledge they would be able to stay at home throughout the AFC playoffs.

"Our bye week was a long time ago, so this is the first time we've had off in quite a while," Brady said that week. "A lot of guys have been fighting through different kind of bumps and bruises over the course of the season, so you try and take advantage of that as best you can to feel good, because we're going to need everybody a week from Saturday to be at their very best."

It was in stark contrast to 2015, when New England entered the playoffs on a bit of a skid, with numerous personnel questions because of injury, four losses in the last six regular-season games, and the second seed as opposed to the top spot and home field.

On wild-card weekend in the AFC, things became clearer for New England: The Raiders, without Carr, were predictably smooshed in Houston by the Texans, 27–14. Meanwhile, the Steelers—who snuck into the playoffs after a dramatic win over the Ravens in the regular-season finale—crushed the Dolphins at a freezing Heinz Field, 30–12. That set the stage for the Patriots to host Houston and the Steelers to travel to Kansas City for the divisional round.

There were a lot of teams that could get the blood boiling when it came to a divisional playoff game. The Ravens provided the opposition for an epic divisional round showdown two years before. The Colts and Jets would have also whipped the New England fan base into a froth. But the Texans? Something felt . . . *lacking*. Maybe it was because they were one of the worst division champions in recent memory. Maybe it was because half the Houston coaching staff had New England roots. Maybe it was the fact that the Patriots had croaked the Texans 27–0 earlier in the season with Brissett at quarterback. Hell, you couldn't even mock the fact that Houston was going to sport letterman's jackets to the game, a stunt they pulled a few years back before a game against the Patriots. Frankly, in a year where it seemed like there was inherent drama packed into every week for New England, it was a bit of a letdown.

Regardless of the reason, when Belichick and Brady met the media that week, it wasn't the usual media horde. There was no buzz. No hate. No playoff energy. When it came to postseason buildup, it was the least-hyped postseason contest of the Brady/Belichick Era in New England.

But there was still plenty to celebrate when it came to the play-off opener, and Brady in particular. When the ball was kicked off against the Texans that chilly January night in Foxboro, the quarterback continued to add to his most unassailable record. It was his thirty-second career postseason start, far and away the most in the history of the league. (It's remarkable to consider that by the end of the postseason, the total represented an extra two-plus seasons on top of what he had already played.) And while the game and the NFL playoff format have changed over the years—and while so many careers are ending prematurely—it's the closest thing he has to a DiMaggio-esque fifty-six-game hit streak.

That being said, things got off to a slow start for Brady and the Patriots that night, as the Texans were able to hang around for a sizable portion of the first half. In the first two quarters, Brady was 8-for-13 for 145 yards with 1 touchdown, 1 (gasp!) interception, and 2 sacks. The quarterback, who threw just 2 picks in the regular season, saw one of his passes intended for Floyd tipped and eventually picked off by Houston cornerback A. J. Bouye. (Bouye might have had an in—he confessed after the game that in the week leading up to the game Denver corner Aqib Talib shared some of his personal notes regarding how to best defend Brady.) It was also one of the last plays of the year for Floyd, who was inactive for the last two postseason games for New England.

At the start of the second half, with the Patriots holding a surprisingly slim 17–13 lead, you could forgive a New England fan for wondering: *What the hell is going on here? How have the Texans managed to become such a colossal pain in the ass?* For its part, Houston did an excellent job disguising some defensive looks and shuffling some of its pass rushers, placing terrors like Clowney and Mercilus over the guards and center to try and get a push up the middle on the quarterback. Ultimately, Mercilus might have been one of the best defenders New England faced all season long. He got good, consistent pressure up the middle in the early going, including one play in the second where he came flying up the gut, spun neatly off a block, and corralled Brady on a play that ended up knocking the Patriots out of field-goal range. He also ran with the backs deftly in the passing game, knocking away one ball in the first half that was intended for Lewis. In all, he had 4 tackles, 1 sack (4 yards), 1 tackle for loss, 3 quarterback hits, and 1 pass defensed.

The net result was borne out in the final numbers, as Brady finished 18-for-38 (the worst postseason completion rate of his career) with a pair of interceptions. Basically, while the final score was a 34–16 win for the Patriots, it was nowhere near as dominant as some people thought it could be or should be.

The guy who had the most eventful night was Lewis, as the

running back became the first player in NFL postseason history to have a rushing touchdown, receiving touchdown, and kick return touchdown (for 98 yards) in a single game. After the contest, he didn't want to hear any praise, however, as he was torn up about the fact that he also fumbled away a kick return.

"I feel like this [was] my worst game ever," Lewis sighed.

(A few days later at a rainy practice, Belichick could be overheard saying, "Great day for ball security. Right, Dion?")

Lewis's gaffe aside, it was one of the best games of the year for special teams. Punter Ryan Allen dropped four of his six punts inside the Houston 20-yard line, and did more than his share of work when it came to tilting the field in New England's favor, especially when the Patriots' offense was struggling in the early going. Overall, he averaged 40 yards a punt on the night, with a long of 55 yards. Gostkowski was perfect, hitting on field-goal attempts of 19 and 43 yards and connecting on all four extra-point attempts. And Lewis's kick return for a touchdown was the first special teams touchdown of the year for the Patriots.

It was also a pretty good night to be a defensive back out of Rutgers, as Ryan, Harmon, and McCourty all picked off Houston quarterback Brock Osweiler. While they were all big plays, the interception from Ryan came at the biggest moment, and effectively ended all hope of a Houston upset. With thirteen minutes to go in the fourth quarter, Osweiler and the Texans were down by 8, but they had the ball at their own 11, thanks in large part to another dynamite punt from Allen. On Houston's first play from scrimmage, Osweiler fired a deep ball down the middle for DeAndre Hopkins, but it was tipped and Ryan made an acrobatic dive for the ball, coming away with it at the Texans' 29-yard line just before it hit the ground. He then got up and had the presence of mind to take it back to the Houston 6-yard line. Two plays later, Lewis scampered over from the 1 to turn a one-score game into a 31–16 contest.

It was not aesthetically pleasing, but the Patriots had dodged a bullet. In the end, Slater summed it up in the locker room.

"Survive and advance. That's the name of the game," Slater said when asked about the playoffs. "And that's what we did. We survived, and we're going to advance."

And truth be told, it was a hell of a lot better than the alternative. After all, not all No. 1 seeds were so lucky; the NFC's top-seeded Cowboys had suffered a shocking home loss to the Packers, and would be watching their conference championship at home instead of playing for a shot at the Super Bowl.

"There's an old saying," said Edelman, who had 8 catches for 137 yards and became the franchise all-time leader in playoff receptions. "An ugly win is better than a pretty loss."

Bennett put his own distinct spin on Edelman's take.

"An ugly date is better than no date," the tight end said with a shrug and a smile.

No worries. There would be plenty of time to celebrate the following weekend because of events on *and* off the field.

In terms of off-field activity, January 21, 2017, was probably the most eventful Saturday of the season for the Patriots.

First, the Curse of Deflategate claimed a new victim when the Colts announced they had fired GM Ryan Grigson. Indy had posted a perfectly mediocre 16-16 record in the two years since that memorable night. The blame fell to Grigson, who had struggled to put together a team around Andrew Luck that was worthy of the young quarterback's talent level. Grigson was also one of the central figures on helping jump-start Deflategate, alerting the league that he believed there was something up with the air pressure in the footballs. Of course, Grigson and the Colts weren't the only ones who had issues since that postseason. Baltimore, who apparently alerted the Colts about the football situation, was also 13-19 in that span.

(The bad mojo would continue: one month later, Colts linebacker D'Qwell Jackson was released; he was the guy who picked off the Brady pass, and upon returning to the Indianapolis sideline, the air pressure was measured and the results reported to the NFL.)

And second, in the wee hours of Sunday morning, the Steelers had to evacuate their hotel when a drunken Patriots fan pulled a fire alarm. Dennis Harrison, a twenty-five-year-old East Boston man, was the one who pulled the alarm at the Pittsburgh team hotel early Sunday morning, forcing the team and other guests to evacuate.

According to reports, Harrison was reportedly at a party in Revere that night when some friends dared him to pull the alarm. So they got in a car and headed to the Hilton Boston Logan Airport Hotel. Harrison entered the hotel, walked to the second floor, and pulled the nearest alarm. He ran out of the hotel and toward his car, but not only was the friend who'd driven him gone, so were his car keys. Harrison began walking away from the hotel, but was stopped by police. Allegedly, he initially told them he was waiting for an Uber ride, but after a little more questioning admitted he had pulled the prank, and offered the now memorable confession, telling a state trooper, "I'm drunk. I'm stupid. I'm a Pats fan," when he was apprehended.

"Harrison informed me that he knowingly and willingly activated the fire alarm system with the sole purpose of attempting to disrupt the Pittsburgh Steelers football team," Massachusetts State Trooper Bryan Erickson wrote in a report.

That all served as the prelude to an AFC championship game that had built to a head over the course of the week, thanks to another Pittsburgh postseason gaffe. In the moments after the Steelers' playoff win over the Chiefs—which set up a New England–Pittsburgh AFC title game—receiver Antonio Brown took to Facebook Live and starting rolling, direct from the locker room. He was initially hoping to give fans a taste of the vibe from behind the Steel Curtain. Talking excitedly with teammates about a return trip to the AFC championship game, he was soon shushed by some noise on the other side of the locker room. Pittsburgh head coach Mike Tomlin had started to address his team, and Brown's managed to catch a few disparaging words from Tomlin. The Steelers coach referred to New England as "those assholes," and added that they had to quickly turn their attention to the Patriots, as New England had a day-plus to start prep work, because the Patriots' game was on Saturday night and Pittsburgh's win came Sunday evening.

In truth, it was nothing out of the ordinary for postgame locker room chatter. But in the context of another Patriots-Steelers postseason showdown, it added another story line. Some reporters tried to make something out of nothing. When Edelman replied to a question about the video, they simply took notice of the fact that Edelman said, "That's how that team is run." They didn't take the full quote in context: "Hey, people have different rules. That's how that team is run. I personally don't think that would be something that would happen in our locker room. But, hey, whatever.

Some people like red and some people like blue. Some people like tulips and some people like roses, whatever."

There was some history to consider, because it wasn't the only time a Pittsburgher stuck his foot in his mouth before a big game against the Patriots. In the days before the 2001 AFC title game, the Steelers were seemingly preoccupied with Super Bowl prep work instead of being focused on the Patriots. And in 2007, rookie defensive back Anthony Smith guaranteed a win over New England. On both occasions, it blew up in their faces like a cartoon cigar. And when you add the recent amount of bad blood between the two teams, and the enmity that grew out of what happened in the 2015 regular-season opener when Tomlin hinted the Patriots messed with their headsets, you had a recipe for another bitter battle with a longtime conference foe.

When it came to the on-field stuff, New England was fairly confident going into the game for a few reasons. In years past, you would ask the Patriots about the Steelers' defense, and inevitably, the response would be some variation of, "They do what they do." It's a compliment in the sense that Pittsburgh's consistent approach has managed to work for decades: big, tough, physical football. They've won a ton of games that way over the years. That, combined with the *aura* that exists around the Steelers, is usually enough to overwhelm most teams. But it was also New England–speak for, "We know *exactly* what they're going to do."

The simple fact is that while the once-mighty Pittsburgh defense was still really good at the end of the 2016 season, it was nowhere near where it needed to be. With the talent they had, they could execute the same type of physical defense at a consistently high level. Most of the time, that would be enough to wipe twenty-five teams off the face of the earth. The Steelers finished the regular season tenth in the league in points allowed, and were middle of the pack defensively in most major categories. Basically, they got by on rep, swallowing up weaker teams.

The problem came when the Steelers would face the likes of Brady. Knowing that Pittsburgh had been fundamentally operating some variety of the same defensive system for the last twenty-plus years, the New England quarterback would pick them apart. Despite all the bluster from Pittsburgh, Brady had almost always dominated the Steelers. Coming into the AFC title game, he had never lost to Pittsburgh in Foxboro, and had completed 71 percent of his passes for 1,413 yards, 15 passing touchdowns, and no interceptions in those games. Over the span of his career against the Steelers, Brady had a 9-2 record with 3,148 pass yards, 26 touchdowns, and 3 interceptions. (It had been eleven years since Brady last threw an interception against Pittsburgh.)

So what happened? That afternoon, in the least surprising AFC title game in recent memory, the Steelers displayed none of the defensive ingenuity shown by the Texans. No outside-the-box thought. No ability to take what the Texans had shown them and build on that as a potential game plan to try and knock off Brady and New England. No, as usual, the Steelers *did what they do.* And Brady? He did what he did against the Steelers, going 32-for-42 for 384 yards with 3 touchdowns, no picks, and a passer rating of 127.5 on the way to a thunderous 36–17 win.

The Patriots never trailed, jumping to a 10–0 lead after one. In the second quarter, New England padded its lead with the play of the game. With just under eight minutes left in the first half and the Patriots holding a 10–6 edge, they were sitting on a first and 10 at the Pittsburgh 34-yard line. Operating under center, Brady delivered a clean handoff to Lewis, who took a few steps forward and then pivoted to flip the ball back to Brady after doing a great job selling the fake. The quarterback waited a few beats, and then hit a streaking Hogan, who had gotten separation from Pittsburgh defensive back Mike Mitchell on the play-fake, for a 34-yard touchdown pass. It was the second touchdown reception of the night for Hogan, who finished with 9 catches on 12 targets for 180 yards and 2 touchdowns.

"He's been incredible," Brady said of Hogan after the game. "He's made big plays for us all season. He made big plays in the biggest game of the year for us."

The play-fake was just the latest example of the Patriots being able to use the Steelers' hyperaggressiveness on defense against them at key moments in the game. The same was true back in the game in October, when a play-fake allowed Gronkowski to get open for what turned out to be the biggest touchdown of the game. And the same was the case in the AFC title contest, where Mitchell froze following Lewis's move, opening the window for Hogan.

The Patriots' level of execution was pretty much spot on all night, but there was something to the idea that the game undeniably changed when Le'Veon Bell left with a groin injury in the first quarter, one he had apparently been hiding in the days leading up to the championship contest. DeAngelo Williams took over for Bell and did as well as could be expected—he had 14 carries for 34 yards and 1 touchdown—but the Patriots changed their defensive focus from stopping the running game to contesting the pass, dropping the safety back and clogging up the passing lanes, a move that slowed the Pittsburgh passing game. Roethlisberger wasn't helped by a series of ghastly drops on the part of his receivers, including Sammie Coates and Cobi Hamilton. As for the social media star Brown? He had 7 catches for 77 yards, but was a nonfactor for much of the night and didn't talk to the media after the game.

"They are the champions of the AFC," Tomlin said ruefully during his postgame press conference. "Rightfully so."

He added: "They played their type of ball they normally play, and we *didn't* play the type of ball we normally play."

(Two months after the game, Bell said the contest would have been different if he had stayed healthy. "I think we beat them," Bell said of his team, which allowed an astonishing 431 yards on the night. "When I was out there, I wasn't feeling well at all. The fact I was out there [early in the game], their game plan was so different just because of the fact I was out there. If I go out there healthy and we go out there and do what we do, the way we've been doing it the whole season, especially in the playoffs, running the ball, running play-action, leaving [Antonio Brown] one-on-one . . . I think the outcome would have been different. We'll get back to that next year.")

The Patriots piled on in the third, stretching the lead to 33–9 after three and allowing for plenty of celebrating late. The team and the crowd were enjoying themselves: if it wasn't the sight of veteran defensive lineman Alan Branch engaging in a little side-line dancing, there was the "Livin' on a Prayer" sing-along conducted by Jon Bon Jovi himself from a luxury box.

The AFC title game was also a vindication of Belichick's skills as a GM: Hogan was signed as an under-the-radar, restricted free agent. Edelman, who had 8 catches for 118 yards and 1 touchdown, was a seventh-round pick. And the two guys who forced turnovers for the Patriots—cornerback Eric Rowe and linebacker Kyle Van Noy—weren't even on the roster in August.

Van Noy was acquired in October by flipping sixth- and seventh-round picks with the Lions, and the athletic linebacker became part of a rotation alongside Dont'a Hightower down the stretch and into the postseason. Rowe was acquired for a conditional fourth-round pick in September from the Eagles (who hadn't planned on re-signing him). While he wasn't always perfect over the course of the season, he eventually slid neatly into a complementary role, helping provide some steady play at the back end of the cornerback depth chart, an area that had been a bit of a soft spot in previous years. Both players weren't defensive centerpieces, but provided quality, middle-of-the-roster depth production down the stretch and into the playoffs.

Late in the game, radio analyst Scott Zolak was pictured on the video board leaning out of his broadcast booth with a sign he made earlier that afternoon: WHERE IS ROGER? The Gillette crowd picked up on Zolak's question, starting a chant that rang out through southeastern Massachusetts.

Where is Roger? Where is Roger?

Where was Roger, indeed? Instead of coming to Foxboro for the AFC title game, the commissioner avoided Foxboro at all costs. On divisional round weekend, he was in Atlanta with the Falcons, and then stuck around to see the Georgia Dome finale. (And you can't miss something like that.) The tone-deaf move on the part of the commissioner galled some New England fans, who were quick to remind people that it wasn't a coincidence that the commissioner hadn't shown up in Foxboro since Deflategate first broke— his last game as a fan in Foxboro came in the 2014 postseason. In October 2016, he was asked by Gary Myers of the New York

Daily News about the possibility of him ever seeing a game in Foxboro again.

"I have no . . . I don't know, Gary," said Goodell, who sounded thrown by the question. "I'll go wherever I need to go."

For people connected to the franchise, two years hadn't really dulled the emotion of Deflategate, and the idea of Goodell coming to a game in Foxboro sparked eye rolling on the part of many connected with the team. But the simple truth is that the commissioner either wasn't aware of the ill will between his office and the New England fan base or simply chose to ignore it. In his pre–Super Bowl press conference, he said that if he were invited to a game in Foxboro, he'd certainly go, and later agreed to an invite for the 2017 opener. But it was evident that if he had a choice, he wanted no part of Gillette Stadium. Forget about games in London: if the league goes intergalactic in the next few years and there's a choice between attending a game on the moon and a game in Foxboro, Goodell would prefer to be strapped to a rocket and fired into outer space rather than navigate Route 1. *Love the opportunity to connect with the 12's here on Mars! One of the most passionate fan bases in the league! Together we make football!*

But Goodell or no Goodell, the Patriots kept winning. They were headed back to the ninth Super Bowl in franchise history, and Brady was going for his fifth ring. And now, there was no escape for the commissioner.

"Goodell can't avoid the Patriots now," wrote Dan Wetzel of Yahoo Sports after the game. "The commissioner will be in Houston for the Super Bowl against the Falcons, where a potential delicious/uncomfortable (depending on your perspective) trophy presentation awaits. Brady could even accept the Super Bowl MVP trophy to conclude a season that began with a four-game,

Goodell-upheld suspension after an intense federal court battle between player and commissioner."

He added: "The juggernaut Goodell tried to kill just won't die. For the commissioner, there is no avoiding that now. Everyone knows where Roger will be on Super Sunday."

Back down on the field, the guy who seemed to be having the best time was Bennett. The tight end celebrated with his family on the field after the game—his wife shed tears when he told his daughter they were headed to the Super Bowl. He made confetti angels with his daughter. And he grabbed a pair of pom-poms and danced, T.O. style, with the cheerleaders while "I Wanna Dance with Somebody" played over the Gillette Stadium sound system. It was a sweet vindication for the veteran, who would now be headed to the first Super Bowl of his career.

Bennett had carved out a role as a Pro Bowl quote, and that earned him goodwill with the media. But over the course of the year, he had battled through serious shoulder and ankle issues, and still ended up playing 78 percent of the snaps in the regular season. (A report late in the season from the NFL Network indicated he played a portion of the season with a cracked bone and bone chips in his ankle.) That level of toughness was something of a public afterthought, but it was certainly appreciated in the locker room.

"He's been great," Brady said of Bennett. "He's been so productive for us and I really enjoy playing with him. You talk about a guy that's been out at practice every day; I mean, he's fought through a lot of stuff over the course of the year to be out there, trying to get better and improve. I think it shows a lot of mental toughness, but it's [also] showing up with his ability to produce on the field."

(In one of the weirdest things all year, it turned out that Bennett got tickets for Johnny Manziel, and Manziel—wearing a Brady jersey—documented the night via social media, posting updates on Snapchat. "He's my friend," Bennett told reporters who asked about Manziel after the game. "I mean, we're Aggies. Aggies stick together. You know we've got an Aggie brotherhood. He's a good kid.")

Manziel's appearance aside, the whole weekend was a celebration. Their enemies had been vanquished. They had survived turmoil, injury, and the threats from the rest of the conference on the way to another Super Bowl. And now, Brady, Edelman, Bennett, and the rest of the Patriots stood on the doorstep of immortality.

"It's an honor to get to go and play in [the Super Bowl]," Edelman said after the game. "This is what you fight for and this is what you train for and this is what you get hurt for and this is what you get yelled at for and prepare for and go through the ebbs and flows of a season. To get the opportunity to play in this game."

"We've won a lot of different ways under a lot of different circumstances," Brady said. "This mental toughness, man, that's what it's all about. And this team's got it. We'll see if we can write the perfect ending in a couple of weeks."

10. REDEMPTION

Revenge is never a straight line. It's a forest. And like a forest, it's easy to lose your way. To get lost. To forget where you came in.
                    —Hattori Hanzo, *Kill Bill, Vol. 1*

Like T. Swift says, players are going to play. Haters are going to hate. I'm just going to shake it off.
     —Edelman at a pre–Super Bowl press conference

Man looks in the abyss, there's nothing staring back at him. At that moment, man finds his character. And that is what keeps him out of the abyss.
                    —Lou Mannheim, *Wall Street*

I'M A CHAMPION, BRO!
          —Bennett to a reporter after Super Bowl LI

I didn't come this far to only come this far.
          —Brady, January 2016, quoting an
                              unknown philosopher

IN THE WEEKS LEADING UP to Super Bowl LI, there was a lot of discussion in New England about who would be the best Super Bowl opponent for the Patriots. While there were arguments to be made for and against each possibility, for much of the fan base, it boiled down to four simple words:

Anyone but the Giants.

When it came to irrational fears regarding a potential Super Bowl opponent, it began and ended with New York. It didn't matter that virtually the entire roster and coaching staff had turned over since Super Bowls XLII and XLVI. The ghosts of those losses still loomed large in New England. Add in the fact that New York appeared to be getting hot at the right time and was playing solid defense—just like 2007 and 2011—and you can understand why New York would be a discomforting opponent.

But Patriots fans were saved from Patriots-Giants III, thanks in large part to Aaron Rodgers. For a while, it looked like it might have been New England and Green Bay, as a pair of absolutely transcendent performances from Rodgers (against the Giants and Cowboys) set up a Green Bay–Atlanta NFC title game. But by this point, the Packers quarterback was holding the whole thing together with bubble gum and baling wire. By the time the Packers got to Atlanta, they had run out of gas. The Falcons rolled over Green Bay in the NFC title game, allowing Atlanta to advance to just its second Super Bowl in franchise history.

The Falcons, a team that finished the year 11-5, didn't offer a ton of story lines, in regard to any sort of potential rivalry with the Patriots or otherwise. A solid team that was enjoying one of the great offensive seasons in NFL history, they were led by quarterback Matt Ryan, a former Boston College star. There was a pair of dynamic running backs in Devonta Freeman and Tevin

Coleman, an otherworldly talent at wide receiver in Julio Jones, and an excellent complementary receiver in Mohamed Sanu. But in a group of potential Super Bowl opponents that started with some really intriguing possibilities (Dallas, Green Bay, New York, Seattle), the Falcons were perhaps the least compelling of the group, at least as far as New England was concerned.

In the moments after the AFC title game, Belichick was asked for his thoughts on the Falcons, and said he had no idea about the outcome of the NFC title game before the Patriots went out and took down the Steelers.

"Obviously they're a great team or they wouldn't be playing in this game," Belichick said of Atlanta after he found out who won. "They've had a great year."

For many of the Patriots, Super Bowl week and the sideshow that went with it were pretty much old hat. The core of the New England roster had gone through the hoopla in early 2015, a pressurized stretch that was magnified because the start of Deflate-gate was barely in the rearview mirror. That go-round served to callus up any new faces that were unfamiliar with the Super Bowl hype machine. (The barrage of questions—specifically, *What did the quarterback know and when did he know it?*—came in a steady stream over the course of those two weeks.)

As a result, the great majority of the roster knew what to anticipate this time around. And those who hadn't already gone through the experience of Super Bowl week were smart enough to make sure they stuck to the company line.

But the breakout star of the week was Martellus Bennett. The quotable tight end was at his best on the national stage. Local reporters had heard him all season long, and he had taken notes so he was ready for his time in the international spotlight. In many ways, it was like a comic honing his craft with late-night sets at the Comedy Cellar before taping an HBO special. Over the course of the year, speaking with local reporters, he work-shopped his material. Now, he was ready for center stage.

On Opening Night, roaming the floor of Minute Maid Park free from a podium, he free-associated, hitting on topics as wide and varied as Lady Gaga, how he managed to fit his occasionally outsized personality in the New England locker room, the chance to win a Super Bowl in his hometown, the upcoming *Lego Movie*, and whether or not he was going to visit the White House if the Patriots won the Super Bowl.

He kept up the patter all week, including an exchange with a reporter who asked if the 2016 Patriots were a movie, what kind of movie would it be? And who would direct the film?

"I wouldn't say it's a drama," Bennett said. "We've had some dramatic instances over the years. I think it would just be like a Wes Anderson film. Very, very good. It's beautiful. But there are little things going on here and there to keep you in it. And the color palette . . . Wes Anderson uses the same color palette in all his films. Very interesting. I love Wes Anderson. I think it would be a Wes Anderson film."

Bennett, who said the season-ending injury to Gronk would be a "plot twist," was quick to add that it wouldn't be a horror film.

"If this was a scary movie, I probably would have gotten killed in the first scene. Because there are rules to scary movies," he said.

"Most scary movies, if you want to be in a scary movie as a black guy, you have to have other black people," explained Bennett. "You have to recruit other black people, because the black cast members are all killed off first. Your best bet is to have multiple black people in the film. Then, your chances of survival go up.

"If you're the only black guy with white friends and then one of them says, 'Hey, there's some a noise in the basement. Go check it out.' I'd be like, 'Man, I don't think we should do that.' They'd be like: 'We should really check it out dude.' I think that would be a bad idea. They go check it out, and you get killed on the couch and say, 'I should have gone down there with them.'"

Bennett's cinematic tastes aside, by and large, the theme of the week was family. It was something that started out semi-organically at Opening Night when Brady teared up when talking about his father and what he meant to him. When the news that his mother was able to make the game broke, Brady broke the news himself on Instagram, sparking more conversation. Over the course of the week, several players made a note of talking about just how important their family was in helping them reach the cusp of a Super Bowl title, including Edelman, Bennett, Hightower, Blount, and Scarnecchia, who had his two grandchildren with him that week.

"I think that Super Bowl moments sort of transcend the entire family," said the veteran offensive line coach. "My wife and I are both from Southern California. We obviously have a lot of family there. Not so much me, a lot more of her now. At these events, we've had people come from California, Minnesota, friends and family, and we have always said this is a special time that everyone should share. Now, our two grandkids get to be here. They were at the last Super Bowl we were at in Indianapolis. I think all that is part of it. I think it should be shared. It should be embraced. It's a lot of fun."

That feeling went from the top of the roster to the bottom. It went for the likes of Hightower—who was a two-time national champion in college and already had one Super Bowl ring on his résumé—to backup tight end Matt Lengel, who started his college football odyssey at Northeastern, spent time on the Bengals' practice squad earlier in the year, and was now backing up Bennett in the Super Bowl for the Patriots.

"It's wild," said Lengel. "It almost hasn't hit me yet. To look back on it all and to think about it, from that day when I first got to Northeastern . . . all you want to do is do well in school and do well in football. To predict in any way I would be here right now, it really blows my mind. It hasn't sunk in yet. Looking forward to the time when it does. I'm just glad, with everything that happened, that when it comes to Northeastern football, this is just a little piece to keep the memory alive a little longer."

Truth be told, the week in Houston was a Massachusetts takeover. There were more Patriots fans than Falcons fans wandering around the city that week. And *Barstool Sports* garnered a ton of traction when it was denied credentials to the Super Bowl events, but still found a way to poke Goodell in the eye by taping its Comedy Central show from Houston all week. (In his annual Super Bowl press conference, Goodell was asked about Barstool's presence, and the fact they weren't credentialed. The commissioner pleaded ignorance about that, saying credentials weren't his department.)

Of course, there was the usual cavalcade of anti-Patriots sentiment, something that had been building over the course of the season. It hadn't approached the fever pitch of "They Hate Us 'Cause They Ain't Us" of two years before, but it wasn't too far removed.

Among the critics were Keyshawn Johnson, who said New England's wideouts probably wouldn't even make another fifty-three-man roster.

"When you see guys that fail and play for other teams at the receiver position, they can go to New England and excel and everybody goes, 'Oh my God, oh my God, these receivers are top of the game.' Well, they couldn't excel with other teams because of the system," Johnson told 92.9 WZGC-FM in Atlanta. "If they were on other teams right now, they probably wouldn't be on the fifty-three-man roster."

At a media availability session during the week, Edelman was asked about Johnson's comments.

"What did you say? Who?" Edelman replied.

Keyshawn. Keyshawn Johnson.

"Oh, Keyshawn," Edelman said. "Isn't he the disgruntled neighbor that, like, was waving down Bieber or something? Oh. That's cool."

Edelman added a small wink to punctuate the exchange. But the point had been made. (Edelman's father wasn't so kind in his retort. *Sports Illustrated* asked him what he thought of Johnson, and he replied, "Keyshawn Johnson is an idiot. He could never play on my team. And I'm certain he squats when he urinates.")

Then there was old friend Marshall Faulk, who remained convinced that the Patriots had taped the St. Louis walkthrough in the days leading to Super Bowl XXXVI, a charge that has been rejected by pretty much everyone.

"[The practice] before the Super Bowl. The guy who worked for the Patriots. If you remember, that was someone mysteriously living in Hawaii, who made his way back to the States and delivered the tapes," said Faulk when asked to clarify his past statements. "[Roger] Goodell then watched those tapes and said there wasn't enough there to deem anything being done.

"Now, I didn't see what was on the tapes, because we didn't get to see that. The only thing I could say is that they taped our practice. That was wrong."

But compared with previous trips to the Super Bowl, there was no real drama over the course of the week for New England. On and off the record, the players indicated that it was a good week of practice. It sounds simple, but the Patriots had been bedeviled by practice issues during Super Bowl week before; in 2008, trying to finish the perfect season, several players on that team would later indicate that week was one of the worst weeks of practice they had that year, as distractions would pave the way for that crushing loss to the Giants.

But this time around, there were no such problems. On the final injury report of the week, the Patriots had seven players listed as questionable, including Bennett (knee), Branch (toe), and Hightower (shoulder), but all were expected to play. By Friday afternoon, Belichick indicated that the hay was in the barn, a favorite old coaching euphemism meaning they were ready to play.

"We're ready to go," he told the pool reporter on Friday. "We've covered everything. With a little more than forty-eight hours to kickoff, we'll finish off our meetings and stuff. But we're done on the field."

There was some fine-tuning that took place on Friday and Saturday, but no major overhauls were needed. And so, by the time kickoff arrived on Sunday, the Patriots were an emotional bunch, with the Brady family at the heart of it all. Among the team, there was a feeling of wanting to win for themselves and their families, and to secure a legacy as a champion. At the same time, there was a palpable sense of what this moment would mean for Brady; not just professionally, but personally. To see Brady and his family and his teammates and their families over the course of the week was to understand New England's Super Bowl quest was not just about a vengeful attempt to right a perceived wrong from the corner office at 345 Park Avenue. It was a chance to deliver something special, not just for themselves and their franchise, but for their quarterback.

Conversely, Brady desperately wanted to repay the players and coaches for their loyalty throughout the most trying two-year stretch of his career with an extraordinary performance. Brady engendered loyalty among his teammates, and while there was always a tight bond between him and the rest of the locker room, since 2014 there had been a renewed emphasis on wanting to win *for* Brady as a way to repay him for all he had done. His teammates had been extremely defensive about the quarterback's legacy; after the "On To Cincinnati" victory over the Bengals that season, Gronkowski spoke emotionally about wanting to deliver for the quarterback when it mattered most. That continued into 2015 and 2016, as Brady's critics continued to hammer him about Deflategate. The quarterback wanted to help pay them back with a big performance on the biggest stage. He wasn't playing to silence his critics. He wasn't playing for revenge. He was playing for his family and for his teammates.

"I'm motivated for my teammates. They're all the motivation that I need," Brady said in the days leading up to the Super Bowl. "Nothing in the past is going to help us win this game.

"I don't get caught in negativity and bashing other people. I'm very blessed. I get to do something I love to do; show up to work every day, play football in the National Football League and play for the Patriots.

"I grew up watching Joe Montana and Steve Young in the Bay Area at a great time. I've got support from my family and some great support from my friends. I love playing for this team. I'm very blessed."

As the morning of the game dawned, it was hard to wrap your head around the enormity of what the Patriots had accomplished over the last dozen-plus years. "The Patriots are in their fourth Super Bowl in ten years, with seven AFC title game appearances in that time. The Falcons are the eighth different NFC team in the same span to reach the Super Bowl. And the Patriots won three Super Bowls from 2001–04, as you may know. The Patriots get a lot of notice for this run of dominance, and still they don't get enough. There is nothing like it in the sport's history. Never forget to savor it, even as it lives on and on," wrote Chad Finn in *The Boston Globe*.

On Super Bowl Sunday, once you get inside the stadium, it's always tough to try and read on the crowd. It's not like any other group of fans on the planet. First of all, regardless of the venue, there are more neutral high-roller types in attendance, which means it's not always as consistently loud as some regular-season games. Second, there are other big moments where it gets louder than many regular-season games, just because of the scope of what's going on. In seismic situations, there's an epic feel to these sorts of events, which causes the noise level to spike.

As both teams warmed up that afternoon at NRG Stadium, there was a greater buzz around the Patriots than the Falcons.

And when Brady, Garoppolo, and Brissett ran onto the field, there were big cheers. Brady ran the length of the field, and pumped his fist at the fans in the far end zone. After an anthem from Luke Bryan, it was time for some football.

Atlanta won the toss, and decided to defer, and the Patriots went three-and-out. In an odd happenstance, they have never scored in the first quarter of a Super Bowl contest, and that held true this time around, as New England moved the ball, but couldn't put it in the end zone. The offense was a little sluggish in the early going, and the quickness of the Atlanta pass rush seemed to catch the Patriots' offensive line off guard. One of the things the Falcons preached all week was doing whatever it took to get to Brady in the early going. Atlanta defensive line coach (and former Brady teammate in 2001) Bryan Cox had studied the blueprint of the Giants in Super Bowls XLII and XLVI—get to Brady, be physical and knock him around. And in the first half, his players were doing a good job following that game plan. The Patriots were getting their yards, but the Falcons were also getting to the quarterback as well.

For the New England defense, things started badly, as Freeman picked up 37 yards on a blast around left end on the first play from scrimmage that got the Falcons to midfield. But a Trey Flowers sack on third down knocked them back 10 yards to force a punt. They couldn't get any closer to the end zone for the rest of the first quarter.

Meanwhile, the best the Patriots' offense did was a brief cameo at the Atlanta 40, when Brady completed an 11-yard pass to James White just past the midway point of the first quarter. But an incomplete pass and a pair of sacks forced New England to punt it away. The teams exchanged the ball again before the end of the quarter, and remarkably, a Super Bowl between two of the best and most complete offensive teams in the league was scoreless after the first fifteen minutes.

While the first quarter was occasionally sluggish for the Patriots' offense, all things considered, it was better than the second. Following a 27-yard pass to Edelman that got the Patriots to the Atlanta 33-yard line—the best field position of the day for the New England offense to that point—on the Patriots' second play from scrimmage, the usually sure-handed Blount had the ball ripped from his hands by Atlanta linebacker Deion Jones. That sparked the Falcons' offense, as Ryan found Julio Jones on back-to-back plays, one going for 19 yards and the other for 23. The electric Jones, who was "held" to 4 catches on 4 targets for 87 yards on the day, helped steer the Falcons deep into New England territory for the first time all game.

(Given the dramatic nature of Super Bowl LI, it was inevitable that certain story lines and events would be forgotten in the wake of the game. But the fact that Jones had just 4 catches remains remarkable. The other thing that was really impressive? Just how *awesome* those 4 catches turned out to be. When the ball was thrown his way, he showcased all of his skills in coming down with it. The speed, strength, and mental toughness he displayed while battling Logan Ryan and the New England secondary is a tribute to his ability. And conversely, the work that the Patriots' defensive backs did on him in an attempt to slow him down and get him off his game was equally impressive. Other receivers may have had better totals against New England in 2016, but it was hard to find another pass catcher who not only played so well, but made the Patriots' secondary raise its collective game like Jones.)

The 2 catches from Jones helped set up Atlanta, and the running game finished off the drive. Freeman got the ball three straight plays, with the last carry putting the capper on the drive from 5 yards out. He plunged into the end zone, giving the Falcons the lead.

"Points off turnovers," lamented analyst Scott Zolak up in the booth. "That'll kill ya."

The Patriots, now forced to play from behind for the first time since late November, failed to answer, going three-and-out for the second time that game. Ryan and the Falcons flipped the switch, going 62 yards on 5 plays to make it 14–0 halfway through the second quarter. *This* was the quick-strike Atlanta offense everyone had come to know over the course of the 2016 season. The highlight of the drive for Atlanta was another ridiculous grab by Jones, where he tiptoed along the sideline while laying out for a catch from Ryan.

The darkest moment of the afternoon came on the following series for New England. The Patriots put together a really nice sequence of plays, as Brady engineered a drive into Atlanta territory that included three straight third-down conversions, with passes to Bennett and carries from Dion Lewis mixed in as needed. With just under three minutes left in the half, New England was at the Atlanta 23-yard line. A touchdown would make it 14–7, and erase some of the bad taste of the last quarter. But a quick pass to the left was picked off by Robert Alford, and he took it all the way back for a score to make it 21–0.

While the New England sideline was trying to keep its head up, it was getting tougher and tougher. These were uncharted waters for the Patriots, who rarely had to play from behind at all, much less try and wipe out a 21-point deficit. Following the

Alford touchdown, NFL Films caught sound of someone the New England sideline saying, "It's all right."

"We ain't all right," replied Hightower. "We're *not* all right."

Hightower was right. These sorts of deficits were almost impossible to overcome. Multiple teams had come back from 10 points down, including the Patriots in Super Bowl XLIX, the Saints in Super Bowl XLIV, and the Redskins in Super Bowl XXII. But 21 points was a whole different conversation.

"We've got to get one," Edelman told his teammates. "We've got to get a touchdown here, boys."

There was no luxury anymore; the New England offense was well aware of the situation. And while it wasn't a perfect drive, the Patriots finally broke through just before the end of the half when Brady got them to the Atlanta 20 with 5 seconds left. As stagehands waited in the wings to start setting up for Lady Gaga, Gostkowski booted a 41-yarder for New England's first points of the day, making it 21–3 going into halftime.

Maybe the best thing to come out of the first two quarters for the Patriots was the fact that of the six first-half drives put together by their offense, three of them went for nine plays or more. They had 42 first-half plays in all, a ridiculously high count by any measure. If this was a boxing match, you could argue the New England offense did a good job softening its opponent. (Of course, if you were a glass-is-half-empty type, you could also argue that the Patriots' offense was moving the ball, but also simply ineffectual against a really fast and really aggressive young defense. That worked, too.)

Down 18 at the half, they'd have to stage the greatest comeback in Super Bowl history if they wanted a shot at pulling off the victory. *Strange* things would have to happen. Like Duron Harmon yelling at his teammates.

Harmon was not one to speak up on a consistent basis. Quiet and steady, he was known more as the type who would lead by example instead of being a vocal presence. But when you're down by 18 at halftime of the Super Bowl, desperate times call for desperate measures. That's why he was channeling "Bluto" Blutarsky from *Animal House* as soon as they got into the locker room.

Over? Did you say over? Nothing is over until we decide it is!

"We're going to have the greatest comeback in Super Bowl history," he said, walking around the locker room and exhorting his teammates.

There were similar pockets of faith among New England fans all around Houston. Robert and Jonathan Kraft spoke about it. Tom Brady Sr. would later say that he still believed. And those hard-core fans from Bangor to Bridgeport still held out hope that Brady was capable of engineering the biggest comeback in Super Bowl history.

Harmon wasn't the only one in the locker room who had faith. There were others in the locker room who were preaching about miracles. That included Edelman, who was telling people they were about to write the greatest comeback in Super Bowl history.

"It's going to be one hell of a story," he told his teammates.

But even at that stage of the season, there were a few veterans who were a bit dubious, including Long. This was *18 points*. Three times, teams had overcome a 10-point deficit in the Super Bowl, a group that included the 2014 Patriots against Seattle. But that was the sort of stuff that happened once in a generation. The last time New England overcame anything akin to that sort of deficit *at any time* was a memorable November 2013 game against the Broncos, when Denver blasted to a 24–0 first-half lead but New England came roaring back and won 34–31 in overtime. Only that game was played in Foxboro, and the Patriots had to have a whole host of things go right in that one, including a muffed punt return by former New Englander Wes Welker on the way to the win.

Eighteen points? I mean, even if they could hit the 30-point mark—which they had done with regularity over the last few seasons—the margin for error was slim to none at that point.

"I was thinking, 'Let's just get a stop,'" said Long of Harmon's exhortations. "It was pretty gutsy of him. He said it would happen. And it did."

"I wouldn't really say it was a pep talk," Harmon recalled of the moment a month later. "It was just me just talking out loud, just kind of how I felt about this team. It was just me basically saying that I knew we had a great team and we were capable of doing great things, and I really believed that we were going to make the greatest comeback in Super Bowl history.

"It was just . . . you could feel it. People believed it and it was like everybody was getting it and giving positive energy. I really believe that it just started going throughout the team, and I think that it's one thing that just helped us get going just a little bit."

Of course, Harmon knew he had some other things in his corner. There was Brady, who he later called "the Michael Jordan of football." There was the fact that the Falcons defense, which had been on the field for the bulk of the first half, had slowly but surely been ground down, and was nearing a breaking point. And he might have known that when it came to these two teams, while the Falcons were a work in progress, the Patriots were a work of art.

Where to start? The first series of the third quarter was a positive beginning for New England, as it forced the Falcons into a three-and-out, with a tackle for loss from Hightower as the highlight. But the Patriots' efforts were fruitless on their first series of the second half, actually losing yardage (Brady had misfires to Hogan and Edelman on pass attempts) before punting away the football.

If the Alford pick-six and the 21–0 deficit were the low points of the first half for New England, the inability to get anything going on offense combined with the lackluster defensive effort on the next series represented a bottoming-out in the second half. The Falcons went 8 plays and covered 85 yards, with Tevin Coleman walking untouched into the end zone on a 6-yard pass play with 8:36 left in the third quarter. The extra point made it 28–3.

And just when you thought it couldn't get any worse, it did. While the Patriots made up some ground after receiving the kick, with roughly six minutes left in the third quarter and trailing by 25 points, they still faced a fourth and 3 at their own 46-yard line. Now, there was no margin for error. This was it. They had to be perfect for the final twenty-one minutes of regulation, and whatever it took in a potential overtime scenario. They couldn't afford any more three-and-outs, turnovers, or mental breakdowns. On offense, they would be in four-down territory the rest of the evening. On defense, they had to corral Ryan, Jones, and the rest of the Atlanta offense. According to fivethirtyeight.com, this moment represented the low point of the entire evening for New England. They calculated that, at that point, the Patriots had a 0.4 percent chance of winning the ball game.

One in 250.

Over the last dozen years, Brady had become more of a spiritual individual. Part of it was rooted in him growing older. Part of it had to do with his Catholic upbringing. And some of it was because of a natural curiosity. In that vein, he discovered *The Four Agreements: A Practical Guide to Personal Freedom* by Don Miguel Ruiz in 2006, and had come away affected by the book, so much so that he later described the four points laid out by the author as his "mantra":

1. Be impeccable with your word.
2. Don't take anything personally.
3. Don't make assumptions.
4. Always do your best.

In the book, Ruiz writes: "Every human is an artist. The dream of your life is to make beautiful art."

For Brady, that twenty-plus-minute stretch of Super Bowl LI was football as art. He and the Patriots would go from the cusp of the most disappointing professional night of his life to the most epic comeback in a long history of comebacks. There were so many things that paved the way for the greatest comeback in Super Bowl history, but for the Patriots, it all started with that fourth and 3.

The quarterback started the long climb back with a throw to Amendola, one of the steadiest and most dependable big-moment receivers he'd ever had. He hauled in the pass and spun away from the defender, picking up some extra yards before being knocked out of bounds for a 17-yard gain at the Atlanta 37. Leaning on the make-you-miss guys, Brady (who scrambled for 15 yards on one play) and the Patriots kept the chains moving, working all the way down to the Atlanta 7-yard line.

For New England, one of the things that really sparked the comeback was the same thing that helped them beat the Seahawks two years before. The weakness of the Falcons defense—just like the Dan Quinn–led Seahawks in Super Bowl XLIX—was an inability to slow running backs in the passing game. That's what allowed Shane Vereen to set a new Super Bowl record for catches by a running back against Seattle with 11. This time around, it was White who was the difference maker. Sure, the rest of the offensive skill position players made big catches and moved the chains consistently throughout the second half, but it was White who changed the game.

And so, with the Patriots on the 7-yard line, it was White who was the target. The running back collected the pass from Brady, spun on the defender and landed in the end zone for the first touchdown of the day for New England. The extra point hit the right upright, but the Patriots had cut the lead to 28–9 with just over two minutes left in the third quarter.

Following a Gostkowski field goal that made it 28–12 with just under ten minutes remaining, the defense buckled down with a pair of big plays.

The first came with 8:31 left in regulation. That was when Hightower strip-sacked Ryan, a play made possible when Freeman whiffed on a block. Hightower came screaming off the edge to get to Ryan just in time to hit the quarterback's arm. The ball was knocked away, and recovered by Alan Branch. Five plays later, the Patriots scored to make it a 28–20 game when Brady found Amendola for a 6-yard touchdown reception, and White tacked on the 2-point conversion with a direct snap and score. (The successful 2-point conversion stirred memories of another bold call from long ago—late in Super Bowl XXXVIII, also in Houston, the Patriots utilized a direct snap to Kevin Faulk to successfully convert a 2-point attempt. Somewhere, Charlie Weis was smiling.) For New England fans, the buzz was back. *So you're telling me there's a chance?*

Asked about the play afterward, Hightower offered a typically Hightowerian response:

"I'd seen Matt Ryan with the ball in his hands and I wanted it. So I hit him and took it from him."

OK, then.

With the play, Hightower cemented his status as the Last Man Standing. Collins was in Cleveland. Chandler Jones was in Arizona. Vince Wilfork and Jerod Mayo were gone. This was *his* team. This was *his* defense. And the sack of Ryan? That was another signature play, the second consecutive Super Bowl where Hightower was responsible for a seismic, game-changing event. Turns out, the team knew what it was doing when he was given The Locker. He earned it.

The second big play came with just under four minutes remaining and the Falcons holding a 28–20 lead. Atlanta was sitting on a second and 11 at the New England 23-yard line when Ryan dropped back to pass. That's when Flowers busted up the middle and dropped the Atlanta quarterback for a 12-yard loss. A hold by tackle Jake Matthews on the ensuing play knocked the Falcons back another 10 yards, forcing them to punt the ball back to the Patriots. If Atlanta had simply run the ball and settled for a field goal, it would have been a 31–20 lead with less than four minutes remaining, an almost insurmountable edge under any circumstances. Instead, the Patriots had the ball, and it was a one-score game with 3:30 left in regulation.

For the Patriots, it took all fifty-three players to win the Super Bowl. Sure, there was the brilliance of the likes of Brady, Hightower, Flowers, White, and the other stars. But there were also the special teamers—namely, Gostkowski. In many ways, the Super Bowl was a perfectly encapsulated look at his season: He connected on 2 important field goals (41 and 33 yards), missed an extra point, but would later redeem himself with multiple clutch kickoffs that helped in the field-position game. The Patriots don't win without his handiwork.

But in a game that was chock full of amazing individual plays, the greatest moment of all was The Catch.

No one is shedding any tears for the postseason struggles of the Patriots, but the fact remained that in their two Super Bowl losses, they had been done in by a pair of the most ridiculous receptions in the history of the game. David Tyree sunk them in Super Bowl XLII and Mario Manningham did them in in Super Bowl XLVI. (Jermaine Kearse almost completed the trifecta in Super Bowl XLIX.)

But this time around, with the game in the balance, it was the Patriots who came through with the ridiculous reception. With New England trailing 28–20 and the ball at the Patriots' 36-yard line, Brady fired a missile into heavy coverage. The ball was batted in the air by Alford, and as it floated through the air, Edelman dove into a pile of Atlanta defenders—between the legs of one of them—and cradled the ball just before it landed on the turf.

"I don't know how the hell he caught it," Brady confessed later.

"It's the single greatest catch I've ever seen," Hightower said after the game.

Like the Tyree and Manningham receptions, when something like that happens at that point in a ball game, it's like a thunderbolt of a realization: There are far greater forces controlling the outcome of this game. That's why it was no surprise that a few plays later, the Patriots were able to punch it in to tie it.

"Don't ever count Tom Brady out," TV analyst Troy Aikman told the Fox audience.

Of course, the Falcons' defense was absolutely gassed at this point. You could make a case that the Patriots performed a Muhammad Ali–style rope-a-dope on Atlanta. But in truth, it was simply a case of the Falcons' defense being on the field far too long. The New England offense ran 93 snaps on the night, more than double Atlanta's total (46). It was the first time in NFL history a team ran 90 or more plays against an opponent that ran fewer than 50. The Patriots' offense? To borrow a long-ago line from their quarterback, they were fresh as lettuce. They had spent all season long preparing for this. And now, that *fucking hill,* the one they had cursed out a million times over the course of the summer but had used to build the sort of cardio needed for moments like this, was proving to be the difference.

"Let's go score and win this thing," Edelman told Brady at the end of regulation. "For your mom. For your mom, bro."

In overtime, the only drama involved the coin toss: when Slater called heads and the coin came up in New England's favor, it was pretty much done at that point. Brady and the Patriots assembled an 8-play, 75-yard drive that had just one negative play.

After a couple of missed shots at the end zone on pass plays to Bennett (including one play that came within inches of being picked off—*what are they doing, passing on the goal line?*), the final play of the season from scrimmage pretty much tells you everything you need to know about the 2016 Patriots' offense.

The crowning moment didn't involve a majestic, floating bomb of a pass from Brady to Gronkowski or Hogan. It wasn't a bull run up the middle from Blount, or a quarterback sneak from Brady. Instead, it was a toss play to White, a running back who was fundamentally an afterthought when it came to the ground game to that point in his career. And twelve-plus months after he was undressed by Von Miller in the 2015 AFC title game, Marcus Cannon delivered the last block of the season, knocking linebacker Deion Jones out of the way just enough to allow White to sneak into the end zone, going the last yard with safety Ricardo Allen on his back.

Two guys who were offensive afterthoughts the previous off-season, at the center of the play that gave the Patriots a title. For all the talk of the greatness of the rest of the roster, the final play of a championship season involved two guys who were forgotten elements at the start of the year.

"It was a toss play; the offensive line did a great job blocking," White would say later. "The receivers did a great job blocking. I had to run through one guy and get the ball in the end zone. Game is on the line—just have to find a way in.

"Got to get in," he added. "That's what I said."

"James White is like my oldest son. He just does everything right and you can never get mad at him," Brady would say the next day. "I'm so proud of him."

There was some question initially as to whether or not he got in—NFL Films captured great footage of Edelman racing around the field telling everyone the game wasn't over yet, trying to shoo people off the field before Belichick came over to assure him that it was done. But he did. And the game was done.

After White got over the goal line, Hogan and Mitchell took off like they had been shot out of a cannon, racing to the other end of the field while screaming at the top of their lungs. Blount came flying off the sidelines at full speed, straight for White, and launched himself into the undersized back. Normally one of the more reserved guys on the team, Hightower gleefully scampered onto the field before being tackled by teammate Shea McClellin. Edelman eventually found Brady, and jumped into his arms. All as red, white, and blue confetti gently fell around them.

"They got balls," said Zolak as the celebration started. "And when you've got balls on the biggest stage, you win championship football games."

After things had calmed and Brady had stopped crying, the quarterback and the commissioner found themselves next to each other. It was difficult to discern specifics when it came to the conversation, but amateur lip-readers made out a simple exchange between the two.

"Congratulations," Goodell said. "Good game."

"Thank you," replied Brady, while the commissioner appeared to reply, "That was awesome."

Jim Gray, who hosted Brady's weekly appearances on Westwood One and was standing nearby, would later describe the postgame meeting between the quarterback and commissioner as cordial.

"It wasn't contentious, but it wasn't warm," Gray told the *Los Angeles Times*. "I think Tom was caught off guard, probably expecting to see him on the podium. Then the commissioner said, 'You played great,' and all Tom did was say, 'Thank you,' nodded his head. Then, Roger walked away.

"No embrace, no smiles. Just kind of matter-of-fact. Tom was classy and dignified and Roger was gracious."

The trophy celebration was massive. Willie McGinest was the ex-player chosen by the league to carry the trophy part of the way to the podium, and during the procession, several reached out to touch it. (Patricia, Gronkowski, Long, Ninkovich, and

Hightower were among those who planted greasy, sweaty kisses on the trophy in the early going, something that continued the closer that McGinest got to the podium.) He handed it to Michael Strahan, who delivered it the rest of the way to Goodell at the podium set up near the end zone.

And then, the sweet sound that Patriots fans had waited all year for. When Goodell started to speak, it sounded like someone had let loose a swarm of angry bees inside NRG Stadium.

BOOOOOOO!!!!!!

The league year started with Goodell being booed viciously at the draft in Chicago. It had ended with him being booed viciously at the Super Bowl. The more things change . . .

"What a wonderful football game here tonight," he said with a game smile, trying his best to speak over the wave after wave of boos. "That's what NFL football is all about."

Goodell paused and turned to Kraft.

BOOOOOO!!!!!

"Robert, you know how hard these are to get," he said, brandishing the trophy. "And this is the fifth under your leadership, coach Belichick, and Tom Brady. What an unbelievable achievement for your organization. Congratulations to your organization, to your fans and your community. We're so proud of you. Take your Super Bowl trophy home to New England."

With that, Goodell handed over the trophy and slipped into the background. Kraft took it and raised it over his head with his left hand. The boos quickly turned to cheers.

"Two years ago, we won our fourth Super Bowl down in Arizona, and I told our fans that was the sweetest one of all," Kraft told Terry Bradshaw, who was on the podium as part of the Fox broadcast. "But a lot has transpired during the last two years . . ."

Big cheers erupted as Kraft waited a beat, and started on a revised version of the same speech he had given in the wake of the win over the Rams in Super Bowl XXXVI.

"And I don't think that needs any explanation. But I want to say to our fans, our brilliant coaching staff, our amazing players— who are so spectacular—this is unequivocally the sweetest. And I'm proud to say, for the fifth time, we are all Patriots. And to-night, for the fifth time, the Patriots are world champions."

Bradshaw then turned to Belichick, and called him the great-est coach of all time.

"Thank you, Terry, but it's all about these players. We've got great players. They're tough, and they compete," Belichick said.

"They just keep competing. We've got great players. They just compete for sixty minutes—or longer."

The quarterback then got his hands on the prize. The quarter-back raised it above his head and screamed, "Let's go!" Bradshaw then turned to Brady, and asked him about the variety of game-changing plays that took place.

"Coach talks about 'You never know which play it's going to be in the Super Bowl.' There were probably thirty of them tonight. If any one of those had been different, the outcome would have been different," he said with a weary smile on his face. "But I'm so proud of our guys, our coaches, the team. It was unbelievable. What we've accomplished all season; I'm just proud to be a part of a great group.

"Thank you to all our fans. Everyone back in Boston, New England, we love you. You've been with us all year," he said, waving the trophy as confetti fell gently around him. "We're bringing this sucker home!"

The contrasting image of Brady after the game that night in

Houston and the sight of him on the stage after Super Bowl XXXVI was really something else. In February 2002, he was a fresh-faced twenty-four-year-old, marveling at what had just happened; the shot of him clutching his head in giddy disbelief over the outcome while confetti swirled around him was the NFL Films money shot. It perfectly captured the absurdity of what he and the Patriots had just accomplished. It looked like even *he* couldn't believe what had just happened.

Now, at thirty-nine—in what Sinatra might call the "autumn of the year"—his reaction was distinctly different. A mixture of satisfaction, elation, and relief was etched on his face. The one thing that held true over the fifteen-year span was the need to celebrate with the family. In 2002, he looked for his sisters. And that night in Houston, Brady then slipped off the stage into an embrace with his mother and wife.

Meanwhile, there was an odd and slightly surreal postgame scene in the interview area that was designated for the winning coach and MVP. Atlanta owner Arthur Blank wandered in with his friends and family, and sat down. Blank, who appeared downcast and a little disoriented, sat with his party for a few moments, while folks went up to him and his family to offer condolences while pictures of the Patriots' celebration played on TV screens just above his head. Then, someone hustled them out of there before Brady and Belichick showed up for their postgame press conferences.

"This is why he plays," Slater said of Brady. "At this point, what is he playing for? We talk about legacy, and we get caught up in that in the modern society we live in. You want to talk about a man's legacy? He's the best quarterback in the history of the NFL. He's the best."

In the locker room after the game, Kraft was handing out Padron cigars and talking about the legacy of the franchise. Players were popping some bottles and whooping it up. Brissett was showing off his "Wolfpack" T-shirt—with pictures of Brady, Garoppolo, and himself instead of Alan, Stu, Phil, and Doug—to media members. Long snapper Joe Cardona and punter Ryan Allen were holding the trophy, waiting for Gostkowski to come over so the three specialists could get a picture together with the hardware. After enjoying an embrace with his dad Jackie—a former Pro Bowler—on the field after the game, Slater was walking around the locker room with the trophy over his head, proclaiming this to be the fruit of all their hard work. Sheard, Solder, and Cannon were among those who took their turn posing for pictures and enjoying the hardware.

The only downer after the game came when Brady's jersey went missing. He had apparently intended to give to his mother, but it had disappeared. "Someone fucking took it," he shouted in the midst of the locker room. (The missing jersey sparked a massive investigation, one that ended in late March when it was reportedly discovered "on foreign soil," swiped by an international journalist who apparently also had Brady's jersey from Super Bowl XLIX and a Von Miller helmet from Super Bowl 50.) But that night, it was a minor distraction as the players and their families partied on the floor of NRG Stadium, and then moved on to the team party next door at the NRG Center.

Before Super Bowl LI, teams leading by 25 or more points at any time in any NFL game were 2,545-4-2 in the regular season and 102-2 in the postseason, according to the Elias Sports Bureau. In all, only six times in 2,655 games had a team come back from a 25-point deficit to win a game. That night in Houston, the Patriots made it seven.

"I really do think I just played on the toughest team of all time," Long marveled to *Pardon My Take* a few days later.

That night marked the end of the road for one of the most memorable teams in franchise history. It was a group that had been forged by fire, having survived a gauntlet of challenges both on and off the field to win the fifth Super Bowl title in franchise history. In six months, the '16 Patriots had gone from working together to scale Mount Belichick to the summit of the football world. The Drive for Five was complete.

EPILOGUE: "NO DAYS OFF"

As of today—and as great as today feels and as great as today is—in all honesty we're five weeks behind on the 2017 season compared to most teams in the league. Fortunately, we have a great personnel staff. . . . Look, in a couple weeks, we're going to be looking at the combine. Obviously the draft, all-star games have already occurred. And in a month, we're into free agency, not to mention all the internal Patriots players [whose] contracts are up. We're going to have to work with in some form or fashion like every team in the league does.

—BELICHICK, THE DAY AFTER SUPER BOWL LI

I am kind of shortsighted here, so I'm good certainly good here this year, good for a while. I like what I am doing. I enjoy all parts of the game—the team building, training camp, game days, the excitement of Sunday. . . . It really is . . . it beats working.

—BELICHICK ON HIS FUTURE WHILE SPEAKING
IN AN INTERVIEW WITH CNBC TWO MONTHS
AFTER THE SUPER BOWL

Speaking of Tom Brady, they had the whole jersey fiasco, it blew my mind. They went to Mexico to get the jersey, and we still don't know who killed Tupac and Notorious B.I.G., but they found that jersey. Y'all, find out who killed Tupac today.

—SEATTLE DEFENSIVE LINEMAN MICHAEL BENNETT
TO FOX SPORTS ON THE SEARCH FOR BRADY'S
MISSING SUPER BOWL JERSEY

THIS WAS GOING TO BE the day.

For Patriots fans, the day after the Super Bowl was going to be the day when Goodell finally had to stand on the stage next to Brady, shoulder to shoulder, and endure the sure awkwardness that would come with him handing over the Super Bowl MVP honor to the guy he had gone to battle with many times in the last two years. This time, instead of facing each other in a courtroom and Goodell falling back on the CBA to ensure victory, he'd had to acknowledge that Brady and the Patriots had gotten the better of him.

But the press conference the day after the Super Bowl turned out to be a relatively subdued affair for a few reasons, not the least of which was the fact that it took place first thing Monday morning, hours after the game, and most people in the audience and those onstage were a little fried from the short night. (Brady himself confessed to still being a little "wired.") In the end, there was no WWE-style chair to the head of the commissioner. There was no victory lap. And there was no mention of You Know What or the ensuing fallout. Instead, Goodell, Belichick, and Brady couldn't have been nicer to each other. After the commissioner talked up the city officials from Minneapolis (the home of Super Bowl LII) who were present, he got down to the business at hand.

"We just had an extraordinary week in Houston, capped by maybe one of the greatest games of all time. The two gentlemen we have here have set new bars across the league," Goodell said, motioning to Brady and Belichick, sitting just off stage.

"Five Super Bowl championships and four MVPs for Tom Brady, cementing his legacy as not just the great Super Bowl performer, but maybe one of the greatest players of all time. And this duo; coach Belichick with his success and five Super Bowls, cementing his legacy as perhaps the best coach of all time. It's a great honor for us, me personally, to have both of these guys here this morning."

Goodell posed with the them separately—Belichick with the Lombardi Trophy and Brady with the MVP award—as part of a staged photo op. Lip-readers tried to see if there was any surreptitious chatter between the quarterback and the commissioner or the coach and commissioner, but there was nothing.

"It's an honor to be here and have the commissioner present us with the trophy," Brady said when he got his turn at the podium. "It certainly means a lot, and my kids will be happy to see that trophy. They always ask about it, and I get to bring them one home."

Brady, who ended up giving away the truck he got as Super Bowl XLIX MVP to Malcolm Butler, reiterated his thought that White should have gotten the MVP.

"I think James White deserves it. It would be nice for him," Brady said of the running back, who had 3 touchdowns. "But it was a full team effort."

He added: "I'm so proud to be a part of this team. We faced a lot of adversities over the course of the year, and overcame with a lot of mental toughness.

"It was a great way to really culminate the season."

Brady was asked about his missing jersey.

"I put it in my bag and then I came out and it wasn't there any-more," Brady said. "It's unfortunate, because that's a nice piece of memorabilia, so if it shows up on eBay somewhere, someone let me know. [We'll] try to track that down."

The only time things got remotely awkward came when Belichick was asked about Brady's preparation and focus for this season, and whether or not it was impacted by the off-field events of the previous year-plus. Revenge? Not hardly.

"With all due respect, I think it's really inappropriate to suggest that Tom's career, he's been anything other than a great team-mate," Belichick said. "A great worker and has given us every single ounce of effort of blood, sweat, and tears that he has in him. To insinuate that this year is somehow different, that this year, he has somehow competed harder or did anything to a higher degree than he ever has in the past I think is insulting to the tremendous effort and leadership and competitiveness that he's shown.

"For the seventeen years that I've coached him, it's been like that every year, every week, every day, every practice. I don't care if it's in May, August, or January. Tom Brady gives us his best every time he steps out on the field."

The coach then reminded everyone of the reality of the situation by going Full Belichick: he noted that yes, this was all awesome, but time was wasting.

"As of today—and as great as today feels and as great as today is—in all honesty we're five weeks behind on the 2017 season compared to most teams in the league. Fortunately, we have a great personnel staff," Belichick said.

He continued, sounding moderately exasperated.

"Look, in a couple weeks, we're going to be looking at the combine. Obviously the draft, all-star games have already occurred. And in a month, we're into free agency, not to mention all the internal Patriots players [whose] contracts are up," he explained. "We're going to have to work with in some form or fashion like every team in the league does."

The Patriots got on a plane and flew back to Boston. The good manners at the press conference the next day didn't stop some the Patriots from taking a few shots at Goodell. Getting off the plane in Boston, Matt Patricia was seen wearing a T-shirt with the picture of the commissioner with a red nose, looking like a clown. Soon, an updated version of Brady's previous Shields MRI commercial featured him wearing five rings, and Brady saying "Roger that" when he was told he'd need a larger locker for his jewelry. And at a rally in Providence, Gronkowski and others took the stage with the five Lombardi Trophies. Gronkowski managed to hold four at once—and it looked like someone was about to hand him a fifth—before almost dropping all of them. The tight end asked the crowd, "What do we think of Roger Goodell?" That was followed predictably by a wave of boos.

Two days after the win, most of the team gathered for the last time as a group to take part in the parade. (A handful of players skipped out, including Hightower. Hightower stressed that there was no great reason for opting out of the parade, but if there was one guy who had gotten a little used to these sorts of championship celebrations, it was probably him. The twenty-six-year-old had already won two national championships with Alabama and a pair of Super Bowls. When someone asked if he was going to go to the White House, he said simply, "Been there. Done that.")

That day, a steady snow fell as the team rode duck boats through the city as thousands turned out to cheer them on. A shirtless

Gronkowski chugged beers next to his brothers, making like "Stone Cold" Steve Austin while waving to the crowd. While riding with the rest of the quarterbacks, Brady tossed a football back and forth with a media member. (Brissett ditched his "Wolfpack" T-shirt for a Brady No. 12 jersey.) And general mayhem ensued all day as all five Super Bowl trophies were shown off for the fan base.

The team disembarked at Government Center, where they had a rally. Belichick chanted "NO DAYS OFF!" at the crowd. (The irony of the coach chanting "NO DAYS OFF!" at a crowd of thousands of people taking the day off to go to a championship parade was not lost on people.)

Meanwhile, McCourty and Gronkowski whipped everyone into a frenzy, with Gronkowski drawing big cheers when he said, "When we get [number] six, your boy right here is going to be part of six."

But the longest and loudest cheers were for Brady.

"I told you we were going to bring this sucker home, and we brought it home," he said, waving the latest Lombardi Trophy over his head. "Thank you, guys."

And then, it was over.

The team dispersed, and the breakup of the roster began fairly quickly. Within a couple of weeks, Long, who was heading into free agency, posted to Instagram that he was planning on going elsewhere; he soon signed a free-agent deal with the Eagles. Other players moved on, as the team-building process for 2017 began in earnest. Bennett (who signed with Green Bay) bid farewell, saying he was "going to miss you Mass-Holes" with a picture of him dancing with the cheerleaders at the end of the AFC title game and a statement that read in part: "T'was Fun. Thank you for the good times. To infinity and beyond . . . We'll always dance together. Mahhhtyyy out." And cornerback Logan Ryan was rewarded for a strong 2015 and '16 with an impressive free-agent deal with the Titans.

While Bennett got some grief on the way out the door on social media, it was hard to hold his one-and-done appearance in New England against him, as he did all he could to leave on the best terms possible. A gregarious presence who was matched maybe only by Gronkowski when it came to balancing football and fun, his departure was in marked contrast to that of the last notable one-and-done star in Darrelle Revis, who stormed out the door with his nose out of joint following his lone season in New England. (It's worth noting that Revis followed his subpar 2016 with a release from the Jets.)

After an appearance at the parade, Gronkowski popped up here and there, including a trip to Europe (*Eurogronk!*). And he caused a few heart-stopping moments when he showed up at WrestleMania. In an appearance in support of his friend Mojo Rawley, he got in the ring with wrestler Jinder Mahal and delivered a crushing shoulder shot that put his buddy over the top in the quest for the Battle Royal title. *I guess the back is OK.*

He indicated that he believed he'd be OK for the 2017 season.

"I'm feeling great. I'm good to go," said Gronkowski after his WrestleMania appearance. "It's been about four months now [since surgery]. Just been back with the team a lot during the week, doing my rehab with the trainers there. I'm feeling good. I'll be ready to roll when [the] off-season program starts. Super excited to get back on the field."

The five-week head start the rest of the league had on the Patriots? It was made up a few days into free agency. In a series of moves that were faintly reminiscent of the extreme makeover he performed on the Patriots between the 2006 and 2007 seasons— when New England acquired Moss and Welker—Belichick wasn't acting like someone who had just won his fifth Super Bowl, but a coach in search of his first one. Among the highlights? The team traded for tight end Dwayne Allen (Indy) and electric receiver Brandin Cooks (New Orleans), who Kraft quickly compared to Moss.

You can argue the Cooks move was the most impactful addition, but they made more news when it came to adding on the defensive side of the ball. First, they re-signed Hightower, but only after he made the rounds as a free agent, a tour that included a stop with the Jets (where they offered up cupcakes because it was his birthday) and the Steelers. The scenario was plenty reminiscent of the way the Patriots handled the McCourty negotiations after the 2014 season. They did not franchise him, but instead let him test the market—if the player got an offer, they'd get a chance to make a competitive counteroffer. Ultimately, McCourty returned. And two years later, Hightower did the same, agreeing to a deal worth $43.5 million over four years with $19 million guaranteed.

Second, their biggest free-agent move came when they swooped in and added free-agent cornerback Stephon Gilmore to a five-year, $65 million deal. The former Bills cornerback was given one of the biggest free-agent deals in New England franchise history. It was a radical departure for a franchise that hardly ever went all-in on a defensive free agent.

For their part, those who were acquired sounded an awful lot like the players did a decade ago: When they were given the opportunity to join the Patriots, they jumped at the chance.

"It's an honor to play under Coach Belichick," said Gilmore when he was introduced. "Coming in, watching from afar, obviously I've played against them a lot. They find a way to win, so that's one thing you've got to respect about them.

"But it starts over every year, so I'm just looking forward to going in and meeting my teammates, learning from the coaches, and learning from the players and being the best team that we can be."

"They have a great owner, Mr. Kraft, and a great coach in Bill Belichick," defensive lineman Lawrence Guy said in his introductory phone call with the media, shortly after he signed as a free agent in March. "It's one of those opportunities that got put in front of me—you can't really pass up an opportunity to play for the Patriots."

According to online gambling site Bovada, the Patriots opened as 5-1 favorites to go back-to-back right after Super Bowl LI, but moved to 4-1 after the first week of free agency. The odds continued to get better for New England, as the initial indications for 2017 showed the Patriots had the easiest schedule in the league, according to *Football Outsiders*. "If you're sick of seeing the Patriots at the top of the AFC year after year, I have some bad news for you: New England has a top-five projection in all three phases of the game," wrote FO's Aaron Schatz in April. "On top of that, we also project the Patriots with the easiest schedule in the NFL for 2017. We're forecasting decline for many of their out-of-division opponents, including Atlanta, Denver and Kansas City."

New England did suffer some off-season losses, including Bennett, Ryan, and Sheard. But the biggest loss came via the sidelines, as tight end coach and presumed-offensive-coordinator-in-waiting Brian Daboll left Foxboro to become the offensive co-ordinator at Alabama. Despite the calls for Daboll to be replaced by Chip Kelly, which would would have certainly added some drama to things in Foxboro, the Patriots went with Nick Caley, a fairly predictable move considering his background (he was a John Carroll grad) and New England's penchant for staying in-house when it came to promotion (he came of age with the team as a coaching assistant). While it remains to be seen what sort of impact it'll have on the tight end position, it could have even greater ram-ifications down the road, as many believed that Daboll would have been a no-brainer to replace McDaniels if he had ever left for a head coaching job.

Meanwhile, Brady's life continued. In the days after the Super Bowl, the quarterback reached out to his friend, Celtics guard Isaiah Thomas; he texted the NBA All-Star, "It's your turn next." (Earlier in the season, Thomas had asked Brady for an autographed jersey, and the quarterback obliged with the message "Keep ballin." That, despite the fact that Thomas, a native of Washington State, grew up as a Seahawks fan.)

The quarterback kept mostly silent in the late winter, other than an interview with Peter King and the occasional random Facebook post. He got his stolen jerseys back, and showed up at Red Sox opening day, along with Gronkowski, White, and Lewis, to throw out the first pitch. (Gronkowski stole Brady's jersey, and the quarterback chased him into the outfield.)

A few weeks after that came the much-discussed White House trip. The guys who said they weren't going to go—a group that included McCourty, Bennett, Long, Blount, and Branch—didn't go. The biggest shock came when Brady bowed out, citing "recent developments," specifically, "personal family matters." He issued a statement regarding his decision:

> I am so happy and excited that our team is being honored at the White House today. Our team has accomplished something very special that we are all proud of and will be for years to come. Thank you to the President for hosting this honorary celebration and for supporting our team as long as I can remember. In light of some recent developments, I am unable to attend today's ceremony, as I am attending to some personal family matters. Hopefully, if we accomplish the goal of winning a championship in the future years, we will be back on the South Lawn again soon. Have a great day!

As for the day itself, it was fairly uneventful. Gronkowski surprised Sean Spicer—a big Patriots fan—by popping unannounced into the briefing room. The team gathered on the lawn for a picture, and at first glance it appeared the crowd that attended the 2017 gathering was far smaller than the one that went after the Super Bowl XLIX win. However, it was later revealed that the number of *players* (thirty-four, according to team spokesman Stacey James) was similar to the total who attended the White House after Super Bowls XXXVIII and XXXIX. For the record, James added that more than forty-five players went to the ceremony at the White House after Super Bowl XXXVI, and roughly fifty were there after XLIX.

The only awkward moment came when the president went to

single out Amendola, only to find that the wide receiver wasn't there. (He was apparently attending a funeral.)

"Whether you're trying to win a Super Bowl or rebuild our country, as Coach Belichick would say, 'There are no days off,'" joked Trump.

"This Super Bowl win was a complete team effort," he added. "That's the beauty in what they do—they win as a team."

But while the team continued to be celebrated, for the most part, Brady was the focus. Even when he *wasn't* the story, he was connected in some form or fashion to just about everything the Patriots were doing or debating, including what the franchise should be doing when it came to Garoppolo's rapidly expanding rookie deal.

Of course, you couldn't solve that conundrum without first answering the question: How long could Brady keep going? Given the fact that his fortieth birthday was looming, it was a reasonable question to ask. Brady told King he'd "like to play until my mid-forties. Then I'll make a decision. If I'm still feeling like I'm feeling today, who knows? Now, those things can always change. You do need long-term goals, too. I know next year is not going to be my last year."

In late March, the owner speculated about Brady's future.

"As recently as two or three days ago, he assured me he'd be willing to play six to seven more years and at the level he performed," Kraft told reporters. "There's no one that would be happier than I, and our fan base."

He added: "I think Tommy's sustained excellence is just unbelievable. It's a lifestyle. He's in training now; it's not like he's stopped.

"He's really dedicated. The thing that's amazing about him, to this day he hasn't changed as a human being in how he relates to people, but also how he works out. The only thing that's probably changed is how he eats and his diet. I'm not sure avocado ice cream is right for me, but if I could look like him and perform half as well, I guess I'd do it."

Six or seven more years? That would take Brady until the age of forty-six. The only guy who played to anywhere near that age was George Blanda, but he started his last game at quarterback at the age of forty-one in 1968. (He occasionally lined up under center between the ages of forty-one and forty-eight, eventually going 1-for-3 for the Raiders at the age of forty-eight in 1975.) That's a lot of avocado ice cream between now and then. But if anyone is able to break the mold, it's Brady. He's already secured a legacy as the greatest thirtysomething quarterback of all time. What's to stop him—at the very least—from breaking Peyton Manning's mark as the oldest quarterback to win a Super Bowl? Manning was 39 years and 320 days when the Broncos won Super Bowl 50. If Brady can stay healthy and carry the Patriots to Super Bowl LII, he'd get that chance.

Ultimately, the key to Brady playing another six or seven years isn't necessarily tied to avocado ice cream or magic pajamas. Instead, it's making sure that the Patriots continue to surround him with difference-makers on offense and field a defense that's capable of playing competitive and sound complementary football. Even at the age of forty, Brady's work ethic, attitude, and dedication to his craft remain without peer. As long as New England continues to invest heavily in elements like the offensive line, as well as the skill positions, there's no reason to think he can't continue to play at a relatively high level.

Two more things that are remarkable about Brady and what he could still accomplish:

First, let's say the quarterback finds a way to play another four or five years, or 2021 or 2022. Although he became the first quarterback to win a title with one team, and then cycle through a completely different set of teammates and win another one, if he could continue to play until the 2020s, that would allow him to suit up alongside a *completely different generation* than when he first entered the league. There are already scores of players who have arrived in the NFL since Brady was drafted in 2000 and have since retired. But the fact that we are discussing the possibility of him having teammates or opponents who weren't born (or were in diapers) when he won his first Super Bowl is a remarkable possibility that exists if he is able to push back time and continue to stick around. Given the fact that he already has some ex-teammates who have sons who play in high school or college, the possibility exists Brady could to throw passes to or become teammates with the son of someone he had played with at the start of his pro career. For what it's worth, he's already facing the sons of players who were in the league when he was a youngster—in Super Bowl LI, Brady and the Patriots faced Atlanta tackle Jake Matthews, the son of Bruce Matthews, a legendary offensive lineman who retired after the 2001 season.

Second, given the nature of the game and the fact that careers are getting shorter every year, the idea that we're talking about someone other than a kicker or punter being able to stay healthy enough to win six Super Bowl championships is unfathomable. The Super Bowl LI win was his fifth, which ties him with defensive lineman Charles Haley for the most rings. (Brady is the only player to win all five with the same team; Haley won his with the

Cowboys and Niners.) If he wins a sixth, he'd be the only individual to win six as a player.

But those are questions for down the road. Now, the 2017 draft and free agency are done. The new team is in place. And the season is just around the corner. For the Patriots, there will be the usual trappings that go with being a defending champion, including figuring out where to put the newest banner. There will be more games to play, more stories to tell, and more memories to make. But the business of 2016 is done. It's on to 2017. Time to get back to The Hill. Time to start the work of a new season.

"No one cares about 2016 anymore," Belichick said in an April interview with CNBC. "You can't look back. We don't talk about last year. We don't talk about next week. We talk about today, and we talk about the next game. That's all we can really control."

AFTERWORD: THE BOND OF BROTHERHOOD

February 5, 2017, will be remembered as one of the most thrilling Super Bowls played in the history of our great game. For many, it will be remembered as a signature win for a franchise that has been a model of consistency and success. Others will remember it as a crowning victory for a coach and a quarterback who have established themselves as two of the greatest individuals to ever take up their craft. Some will simply remember the thrilling moments of the greatest comeback in Super Bowl history. All of these are things to appreciate and relish. We have all been able to witness history.

I have been extremely blessed to have had the opportunity to experience nine seasons as a part of what I believe to be one of the best organizations in the history of sport. We have been able to experience nearly unparalleled success. There are certainly a number of reasons for that. Each season a different story unfolds. For me the story of the 2016 New England Patriots cannot simply be summed up by wins and losses, legacies, records, or individual milestones. We will certainly be recognized as champions, but I'll remember this group for the bond that was formed over a ten-month period. I will recollect the brotherhood.

To be able to unite a group of men from different parts of the world, of different ages, races, socioeconomic backgrounds, and many other uncontrollable factors is at times impossible to do. Sports—and football in particular—provide a unique platform for this to occur. The concept of a sports "team" is one of the most powerful examples of unity and togetherness that we have in our world culture. Developing a team is one thing, but to acquire the mind-set of a family is something quite different.

Each of the men who were a part of this journey were asked to give a lot of themselves—mentally, physically, and emotionally. The demands were high. But somewhere along the way, this particular group of men found it within themselves to give even more. We began to play for the man next to us. We took a vested interest in one another's lives off the field. The relationships we forged became bigger than the game of football. This is not something you can coach, talk about, or do anything else to synthetically produce. Every team I have been on has either had "it" or hasn't. It first dawned on me how special the bond this particular group had when we took the field Week One of the season against the Arizona Cardinals. The best player in the history of our franchise had been sidelined for four weeks, and the young man playing in his place had never started an NFL regular season contest. Who knew what was going to happen? What we soon saw was a group of men who rallied around that young man and around one another. We played with passion and competed with a childlike joy. We played for each other. The feeling experienced in the locker room postgame was unlike any I had ever experienced during the regular season. There was a sense of confidence and belief that grew from that day. Our bond began to be forged. Over the course of the season, that bond grew through the highs and lows of our very unique season.

The journey finally led itself to our final stop in Houston. We entered the game with a great deal of confidence, much of which was rooted in the belief and love we had in and for one another. One last cord to be weaved into our unbreakable bond. When we found ourselves down 25 points in the third quarter, it was not panic or doubt that rose to the surface. It was not fear or defeat that we saw on one another's faces. What I saw when I looked into the eyes of every teammate I saw was resiliency, confidence, and the will to keep fighting. Everyone refused to quit because no one wanted to let down the man next to him. In hindsight, I can honestly say I felt as peaceful as I ever have being in that sort of situation. And to think, in a game of that magnitude we all remained calm. It was the crowning moment in a season that had been defined by the respect and love we had for one another and the investment we had made in each other.

I am very thankful to have been a member of such a special group of men. I will remember the laughs, the difficult times, and everything in between. I will remember the journey we shared together. I will remember the friendships forged with each individual. I will remember being around the most selfless group of men I have ever been around as a professional. What an honor to be a part of the 2016 New England Patriots.

—MATTHEW SLATER

BONUS CONTENT

Super Bowl LI included the Patriots and Falcons either tying or setting 31 new Super Bowl records. Via Elias Sports Bureau, here's a complete rundown of the list.

RECORDS SET
Most Games: 7, Tom Brady
Most Games, Head Coach: 7, Bill Belichick
Most Games Won, Head Coach: 5, Bill Belichick
Most Points, Game: 20, James White
Most Passes, Career: 309, Tom Brady
Most Passes, Game: 62, Tom Brady
Most Completions, Career: 207, Tom Brady
Most Completions, Game: 43, Tom Brady
Most Passing Yards, Career: 2,071, Tom Brady
Most Passing Yards, Game: 466, Tom Brady
Most Touchdown Passes, Career: 15, Tom Brady

Most Receptions, Game: 14, James White

Most Games, Team: 9, New England

Largest Deficit Overcome, Winning Team: 25 points, New
England

Most Points, Overtime Period, Team: 6, New England

Most First Downs, Game, Team: 37, New England

Most First Downs, Game, Both Teams: 54, New England vs.
Atlanta

Most First Downs Passing, Game, Team: 26, New England

Most First Downs Passing, Game, Both Teams: 39, New
England vs. Atlanta

Most Offensive Plays, Game, Team: 93, New England

Most Passes, Game, Team: 63, New England

Most Completions, Game, Team: 43, New England

Most Passing Yards, Game, Team: 442, New England

Most Passing Yards, Game, Both Teams: 682, New England vs.
Atlanta

RECORDS TIED

Most Games Won: 5, Tom Brady

Most Touchdowns, Game: 3, James White

Most Two-Point Conversions, Game: 1, James White; Danny
Amendola

Most Sacks, Game (since 1982): 3, Grady Jarrett

Most Two-Point Conversions, Game, Team: 2, New England

Most Two-Point Conversions, Game, Both Teams: 2, New
England vs. Atlanta

Most First Downs By Penalty, Game, Team: 4, New England

HONORS AND AWARDS

PUNTER RYAN ALLEN

AFC Special Teams Player of the Week (Week Three vs. Houston)

RUNNING BACK LEGARRETTE BLOUNT

AFC Offensive Player of the Month (September)

QUARTERBACK TOM BRADY

NFL Pro Bowl (12th selection)

Associated Press All-Pro: Second Team

Sporting News Offensive Player of the Year

Sporting News All-Pro: First Team

AFC Offensive Player of the Week (Week Five at Cleveland and
   Week 11 at San Francisco)

AFC Offensive Player of the Month (October)

PFWA All-AFC Team

CORNERBACK MALCOLM BUTLER
Associated Press All-Pro: Second Team

OFFENSIVE LINEMAN MARCUS CANNON
Associated Press All-Pro: Second Team

DEFENSIVE BACK NATE EBNER
Associated Press All-Pro: Second Team

WIDE RECEIVER JULIAN EDELMAN
AFC Offensive Player of the Week (Week Seventeen at Miami)

KICKER STEPHEN GOSTKOWSKI
AFC Special Teams Player of the Week (Week One at Arizona
   and Week Thirteen vs. Los Angeles)

LINEBACKER DONT'A HIGHTOWER
NFL Pro Bowl (1st selection)
Associated Press All-Pro: Second Team
AFC Defensive Player of the Week (Week Six vs. Cincinnati)
PFWA All-AFC Team

SAFETY DEVIN McCOURTY
NFL Pro Bowl (3rd selection)
Associated Press All-Pro: Second Team
PFWA All-AFC Team

SPECIAL TEAMER MATTHEW SLATER
NFL Pro Bowl (6th selection)
Associated Press All-Pro: First Team

2017 Bart Starr Award Winner
PFWA All-NFL Team
PFWA All-AFC Team

GUARD JOE THUNEY

PFWA All-Rookie Team

The 2016 Patriots achieved a pair of honors that few teams in the history of the NFL were able to accomplish. First, they were only one of a handful of teams that won eight regular-season road games in a year, and the second New England team to do it (2007). They joined the Niners (1984, 1989, 1990), Rams (2001), and Cowboys (2014). And they became just the third team to go 8-0 on the road in the regular season and win a Super Bowl. What follows is a complete list of all the teams prior to the '16 Patriots to go unbeaten away from home in the regular season and how they did in the playoffs.

In the context of this conversation, however, it's worth mentioning two points of clarification. First, the 1982 Redskins were technically unbeaten away from home, but because it was a strike-shortened season, they only had to play five road games that year. They won all five, and finished the regular season with an 8-1 record on the way to a win in Super Bowl XVII. And second, the 1972 Dolphins played a fourteen-game schedule—the league would expand the regular-season to sixteen games in 1978—and so they ended up 7-0 on the road that season.

It's also worth noting that the Patriots' two-year stretch that includes the 2015 and 2016 seasons included thirty wins, including the playoffs. (They had a mark of 30-7.) They were the tenth team since the 1970 merger to win at least thirty games in a two-year span, and how they ended up (ranked by total victories). Here's a look at how each of those teams did and where they ended up.

2003–04 Patriots: 34–4 (won Super Bowl XXXVIII and XXXIX)

1972–73 Dolphins: 32–2 (won Super Bowl VII and VIII)

1985–86 Bears: 32–4 (won Super Bowl XX)

1989–90 Niners: 32–5 (won Super Bowl XXIV)

1997–98 Broncos: 32–6 (won Super Bowl XXXII and XXXIII)

2006–07 Patriots: 32–6

1992–93 Cowboys: 31–7 (won Super Bowl XXVII and XXVIII)

2004–05 Steelers: 31–7 (won Super Bowl XL)

2005–06 Colts: 30–7 (won Super Bowl XLI)

The 1972–73 Miami teams deserve a significant tip of the cap for a few reasons, not the least of which is the fact that they're the only group on this list that did it in a fourteen-game season.

With twelve regular-season wins in 2016, the Patriots have now had seven straight seasons of 12-plus victories, which is tied with the Colts (2003–09) for most sustained regular-season excellence over a seven-year span. In all, New England has had eleven 12-plus win seasons since the 1970 merger, tied for third behind San Francisco (13) and Dallas (12). Denver also has eleven 12-plus win seasons in that same time period.

A TIMELINE OF MARTELLUS BENNETT'S 15 BEST QUOTES OF 2016

March 17, 2016: "Just like any other thing in life, you just prepare to make sure you flow where the wind goes. Try to be a dandelion."—on his reaction to the trade from Chicago to New England

June 8, 2016: "Dr. Seuss said, 'No one can be you-er than you.' Oscar Wilde said, 'Be yourself, because everyone else is taken.' I can only be one person. I just try and continue to be who I am and don't change that. I'm a little chameleon. I just try and fit in wherever I am. When you're authentic, people appreciate that."—on whether or not he'd mesh with the Patriots' culture

July 29, 2016: "I've dated two girls at the same time before."—on building chemistry at the same time with two quarterbacks he's never worked with

Aug. 3, 2016: "Gronk? Gronk is really fucking good."—on his pairing with Rob Gronkowski

Aug. 3, 2016: "I feel like I'm the Kanye of the NFL."—speaking with ESPN

Sept. 28, 2016: "I fly around every day. You can't land this jet, you know what I'm saying? It's like having a private plane, wherever I want to go, I just go. I don't have to worry about no jet fuel. I would say Gatorade but they don't sponsor me so I'll just go get me some good ole something to drink, and Gatorade can have the plug."—on whether he was "flying around" on the field

Oct. 6, 2016: "That's just who we are as human beings. You can't play this game without a chip on your shoulder. Whether it's guys that got cut, guys that got traded, guys that feel like they got passed by other teams—to play this game, you've got to have a chip. And everybody's chip is a little bit different. Like Lay's, I guess. You might be a barbecue guy, you might be a sour cream and onion guy, but as long as you have your chip, that's what gets you through the game. [Roger] Goodell looks like a Pringle guy. I don't consider those chips."—on playing the game with a "chip" on your shoulder

Nov. 27, 2016: "Because we work fucking hard every fucking day. We work at the shit. Those moments, we work in those moments. They get paid millions of dollars to stop us, and we get paid millions of dollars to make plays. And we're going to make them."—on why the Patriots expect success

Dec. 1, 2016: "Only thing I can control is what's going on with my body—cut my grass before I cut someone else's. I use that analogy because a lot of people tend to other people's gardens and never worry about the weeds in their own garden. Therefore your garden gets overflowed with weeds and your flowers die."—on focusing on your own work and not the work of someone else

Dec. 13, 2016: "I had it. I had it. Sometimes there's one slice of pizza left and there's two hands that reach into the box. I'm always going to get the last slice. Unless it's my wife's hand. Then I'll let her get it."—on wrestling away a touchdown catch from a Baltimore defender during a win over the Ravens

Dec. 18. 2016: "When I see Julian Edelman, I just see Julian Edelman. A lot of times when you see a small white guy, you want to call him Wes Welker or something like that. But that's Julian being Julian. So, he's making a name for himself. So, the next small white guy comes in he's going to be called the 'Julian Edelman' of the NFL."—on Edelman's contributions

Dec. 29, 2016: "No one likes Canadian bacon. It's like a different form of ham. I prefer crispy bacon. American bacon. Good, good American bacon. The grease. The kind that crunches when you chew it. You don't even chew it, you just bite it. Crunchy bacon. Bacon's delicious. I haven't met too many who don't [like bacon]. My wife don't even like pork, and she eats bacon. Bacon doesn't even count. It's like in its own food category. Bacon is bacon. There's everything else, and then bacon's over here. I like bacon."—on his favorite breakfast food

Jan. 5, 2017: "I mean, shit, I don't know. I like cake a lot, and every time I get a new slice, I'm just as happy."—on why Patriots fans have been able to maintain their passion after so many trips to the postseason over the last dozen years

Feb. 1, 2017: "I wouldn't say it's a drama. We have had some dramatic instances over the years. I think it would just be like a Wes Anderson film. Very, very good. It's beautiful. But there are little things going on here and there to keep you in it. And the color palette . . . Wes Anderson uses the same color palette in all his films. Very interesting. I love Wes Anderson. I think it would be a Wes Anderson film."—on what it might be like if the Patriots' season was made into a movie

March 8, 2017: "I'm going to miss you Mass-Holes. T'was Fun. Thank you for the good times. To infinity and beyond . . ."—via Twitter, announcing that he was leaving New England as a free agent

THE 2016 PATRIOTS BY THE NUMBERS

1: The number of first-round draft picks who were on the field for the Patriots' offense for the last play from scrimmage in overtime. (Left tackle Nate Solder)

3: The Patriots won a title in a year where they did not have a first-round pick, but that's not all that rare, at least these days. Three of the last five Super Bowl champions have won it all in a year when they did not have a first-round pick. The group includes the 2012 Ravens and 2013 Seahawks.

3: The 2016 team was the first since the 1987 Redskins to win a title with three different quarterbacks to throw for at least 400 yards in the regular season in the year they won it all.

5: The Super Bowl LI victory was the fifth Super Bowl win for

New England. The Patriots are tied for second with San Francisco and Dallas. Pittsburgh is tops with six.

5: No other team in the league had more than five pass catchers finish the season with 500-plus receiving yards. The 2016 Patriots were Belichick's first team in New England to have five different receivers finish the year with 500 or more yards receiving: Edelman (1,106 yards in the regular season), Bennett (701), Hogan (680), White (551), and Gronkowski (540).

10: Belichick coached in his NFL-leading tenth Super Bowl (seven as a head coach), and his five Super Bowl wins are the most in NFL history. He is one of four NFL head coaches to win at least five championships since the league began postseason play in 1933, joining George Halas (6), Curly Lambeau (6), and Vince Lombardi (5).

14: Brady threw 28 touchdowns and just 2 interceptions in the regular season for a TD-to-INT ratio of 14-to-1, the best in a single season in the history of the league. In addition. Brady's 2 interceptions in 432 pass attempts resulted in an interception percentage of 0.46, the fourth-lowest total in NFL history.

14: The Patriots went 14-1 when they scored 23 or more points, including the postseason. Overall, including the playoffs, New England is 179-15 when scoring 23 or more points under Belichick.

18: The number of rushing touchdowns LeGarrette Blount had in the 2016 regular season, most in the league and a career-high for the veteran running back. Blount also had career numbers when it came to regular-season carries (299) and yards (1,161).

237: With a September win over the Texans, Belichick picked up the 226th win of his career as a head coach, moving him past former Green Bay coach Curly Lambeau and into fourth place on the list of most career wins for an NFL head coach. Belichick ended the season with 237 career head coaching wins. Don Shula (328 wins), Halas (318), and Tom Landry (250) make up the top three.

250: The total points allowed by the New England defense over the course of the regular season. It was the third-lowest number of points allowed in a single season by a Patriots defense since Belichick took over in 2000. (New England allowed 237 points in the 2006 regular season and 238 in the 2003 regular season.)

500: The Patriots became the first team that originated in the American Football League to reach 500 franchise wins—including the postseason—with a Week Twelve win over the Jets.

1.000: Since he arrived prior to the start of the 2016 season, the Patriots' winning percentage with Dion Lewis in the lineup is perfect. New England is 17-0 with Lewis in the lineup, which included a 10-0 run in 2016.

ACKNOWLEDGMENTS

This is always the most fun aspect of writing any book: thanking the people who made it all possible along the way.

If my three other books were a marathon, this was more of a flat-out sprint, writing from just after the Super Bowl until April. The bottom line is that given the nature of the subject, this book needed to come together superfast. Honestly, it wouldn't have happened without the hard work of several people. This topic was kicked around an awful lot over the course of the season, especially in the weeks around the election when Gillette Stadium was the nexus of American politics and sports. But an email chain with super-agent Alec Shane in the early-morning hours after Super Bowl LI got the ball rolling in earnest. Alec is good people, and he's a great agent for several reasons, including the fact that he willingly embraced the idea of taking me on as a client.

Getting players Matthew Slater and Devin McCourty to sign on shortly after that was huge. Their hard work and mindfulness when it came to hitting their deadlines was a big help, and their writing and insight lent a sizable amount of gravitas to the product. Revisiting old notes and asking colleagues for some memorable moments also helped move things along nicely. But the hard work and dedication of everyone in a relatively short period of time helped this see the light of day.

In many ways, this book is the spiritual sequel to *The Blueprint,* my 2007 book that detailed the rise of the Patriots under Bill Belichick and Tom Brady. Ten years later, revisiting some of the same territory with many of the same people was a pleasure, particularly when it came to working with Pete Wolverton, Joe Rinaldi, and Jennifer Donovan at St. Martin's. Any time you want to write a book about the greatness of the Patriots, I'd suggest giving them a phone call.

If Vince Wilfork was describing Rob Bradford, he'd say he's the best boss you'd ever want to work with—point-blank. Ryan Hannable, Mike Petraglia, DJ Bean, John Tomase, Alex Speier, Ben Rohrbach, Paul Flannery, Jerry Spar, and Pete Neudel are the best dotcominators a guy could hope to go to digital battle with. I want to thank the more than half-dozen guys I've worked with on the air the last few years, including Greg Dickerson, Steve DeOssie, Gary Tanguay, Pete Sheppard, and Jerry Thornton. Whether it was staying warm in the studio, freezing in a lousy shed on Route One, or broadcasting from a faraway remote studio somewhere, it was a lot of fun for a long time. And Matt Loper and Pat O'Day are the best producers in the business. *Pointblank.*

I thanked many of these same people when *The Blueprint* came out a decade ago, but what the hell: the colleagues on the beat the last dozen-plus years have all been great, including Jeff Howe,

Shalise Manza-Young, Jim McBride, Ron Borges, Steve Buckley, Mike Whitmer, Ben Volin, Karen Guregian, Adam Kurkjian, Tom E. Curran, Phil Perry, Mary Paoletti, Mark Farinella, Glen Farley, Mike Lowe, Rich Garven, Kevin Duffy, Jen McCaffrey, Mark Daniels, Dave Brown, Doug Kyed, Zack Cox, Chad Finn, Dan Hatman, Fred Kirsch, Paul Perillo, Andy Hart, Erik Scalavino, Mike Parente, Henry McKenna, and Erik Frenz.

A special shout-out to Mike Reiss, who is one of the best people you will ever come across in any business. Spend five minutes with him and you'll know why. I'm not sure I've ever seen anyone maintain such a high level of excellence when it comes to his professional career and a similarly high level of enthusiasm for his job over an extended period of time.

Broadcast buds include Matt Chatham, Mike Giardi, Kevin Walsh, Dan Roche, Butch Stearns, Tom Leyden, Chad Amaral, Bob Halloran, Josh Brogadir, Bob Socci, Scott Zolak, Marc Cappello, Alan Segal, Kevin Collins, John Rooke, Alex Corddry, Nick Coit, Ed Berliner, Michele Steele, and Levan Reid. (Can't forget camera guys like Glenn Gleason, Joe Giza, Scott Sullivan, Walt McGraw, Greg Glass, Barry Alley, and Bill Messina.) There are plenty of national reporters and analysts who I've come to call friends, including Greg A. Bedard, Kevin Armstrong, Albert Breer, Field Yates, Ian Rapoport, Judy Battista, Brian Baldinger, Eric Edholm, Kevin Fishbain, Will Carroll, Doug Farrar, and Kevin Clark. A special shout-out to my podcast partner Don Banks. And I'd be lost without my guys Aaron Schatz, Scott Kacsmar, and Mike Tanier. (If you're standing and reading this in a bookstore, put this down and go buy a *Football Outsiders Almanac*. Then come back and pick this up again.) And there's always a place at the sports media table for my buddy Miguel "Pats Cap"

Benzan and the rest of the crew at Patsfans.com, including Ian Logue.

I'd also like to acknowledge Stacey James and his PR staff, who have always been really accommodating. When the *Boston Metro* first opened its doors in May 2001, Stacey and the Patriots were the first outlet to credential us. That meant a lot; it gave us some legitimacy, and opened some doors with other teams around Boston.

My friends and family are the best. I thanked many of these good people the first time around, but they all deserve another shout-out: Dan Brem, Greg Petronzio, Mike Biglin, Jon Tapper, Dan Tapper, Gerry Brown, Paul Howard, Steven Kaye, Greg Levy, Darren Levy, David Guarino, Jason Lefferts, Ian Lefferts, Mike Merriam, Ed MacLean, Andy Mahoney, Kim Allen, Julie Cornell, Jen Lefferts, Amy Cantin-Kaye, Heidi Guarino, Heidi Witt, Anne Kathleen Guy, Jo Evans, Rachel Resnik, and Sandra Torres. The crew at Starbucks on Central Street in Wellesley is awesome for many reasons, not the least of which is the fact that they don't skimp on the espresso shots; it's also a great place to get work done. Our community friends: the Ferrara, Meister, Kundu, McMahon, Boecher, McCarthy, and Picher families, as well as Trish Weston and the rest of our Linden Street neighbors. Special acknowledgement goes out to Mo Jones, Kenn Craig, and Moe Henzel, who are simply as good as it gets. *Point-blank.*

I want to thank the readers who have hung around, especially the veterans who followed me on Twitter from way back in 2009 and the people who just joined this year. Basically, anyone who has read my stuff along the way or listened to something I said or watched me talk on TV, just know it's meant the world to me. It's been a blast. It's been an interesting road for me since last November. For those of you who had my back, just know that I really appreciated all the good thoughts. For those of you who didn't? Well, it's your loss.

I started covering the team in 2001 on a total lark. I was sports editor at the *Boston Metro,* and because the Patriots had availability during the day, I figured I could go to Foxboro during the day, get quotes and find a story, and then come back to the office and write and lay the pages out at night. That summer, there was very little buzz around the team. "I'll just go down to Foxboro, like, once a week," I told my girlfriend at the time—who would later become my wife. "It's not going to be a big thing. They're probably not going to be all that good. It'll be something different and fun." And yeah, my first game was the one where Tom Brady came in in relief for Drew Bledsoe.

Flash forward fifteen-plus years, and my work as a football writer has come to define my professional life. I've written two books on the Patriots, won awards for my work, and gone places and met people I would have only dreamed of meeting if I had never gotten on this roller coaster. My life has been enriched, both literally and figuratively, because I cover the team. Three books and roughly half-a-billion stories later, it's been remarkable.

Ultimately, the people who really allowed this to come together are my family. None of this happens without them. Molly, Marc, Mina, Kelly, Jas, Mom and Dad, as well as Kari, Paul, and Caroline—you all have my love and appreciation. And finally, Kate and Noah (and Stretch) provide the greatest home-field advantage any sportswriter could ever hope for. I'm the luckiest guy on the planet because they're in my corner.

P.S. The Whalers book is on the way. Seriously. Sooner rather than later.

INDEX